UPWARD BOUND

Nine

Original

Accounts

of How

Business

Leaders

Reached

Their

Summits

Michael Useem | Jerry Useem | Paul Asel

CROWN
BUSINESS
NEW YORK

Published by Crown Business, New York, New York.
Member of the Crown Publishing Group, a division of Random House, Inc.
www.randomhouse.com

CROWN BUSINESS is a trademark and the Rising Sun colophon is a
registered trademark of Random House, Inc.

Printed in the United States of America

Design by Karen Minster

Library of Congress Cataloging-in-Publication Data
Upward bound : nine original accounts of how business leaders
reached their summits / [compilers] Michael Useem, Jerry Useem,
and Paul Asel.—1st ed.
1. Success in business.   2. Mountaineering.
I. Useem, Michael.   II. Useem, Jerry.
III. Asel, Paul.   IV. Title.
HF5386.U54 2003
658.4'092—dc21   2003008239

ISBN 1-4000-5048-0

10 9 8 7 6 5 4 3 2 1

First Edition

ACKNOWLEDGMENTS

Michael Useem, Jerry Useem, and Paul Asel extend special thanks to several individuals for their outstanding support of the book: John Mahaney and Shana Wingert Drehs of Crown Business and Howard Means for their editorial direction and work, Raphael Sagalyn of the Sagalyn Literary Agency for his backing and guidance, and Susan Useem for inspiring and informing the enterprise.

Paul Asel:
To my wife, Mary, and my parents, David and Virginia.

Rodrigo Jordan:
To Christian Buracchio (1964–2002), who by practicing excellence in extreme climbing taught us all an important lesson for life: Pursuing excellence is the ultimate expression of human aesthetics.

Al Read:
To Glenn Exum, whose trust, guidance, and friendship enabled me to pursue a life of adventure.

Royal Robbins:
To my best friend, coach, and beloved life companion, Liz. Your belief in me has crowded out any self-doubt.

Chris Warner:
To the staff and friends of Earth Treks: Rest up, for tomorrow we're climbing even higher.

CONTENTS

FOREWORD

WE KNEW WE WERE IN TROUBLE WHEN THE PREGNANT woman passed us.

It was a clear, warm day, and a dozen mostly inexperienced mountaineers were clinging, for all they were worth, to the cable that marks the way (and gives its name) to the Via Ferrata—a high-exposure trek through the Dolomites of northern Italy. We were mostly New York businessmen and -women, brought together by Outward Bound for a five-day exploration of ourselves. For the vast majority of us, high altitude—even with the safety of being clipped in—was new, exciting, and scary.

But we were eager on this, our first day. The path was narrow, barely wide enough for two goats to pass each other. At over 9,000 feet, the views were breathtaking, but the sheer drops demanded serious respect. All of us worried, in varying degrees, about the very real possibility of losing our footing and dangling off some precipice, or worse. Still, we thought we were moving well, given the size of our party and the occasional knocking knees—until the pregnant lady passed us. I think she was German, and I know she viewed us, at best, with disdain.

Our goal that evening was a climbing hut, complete with hot meals and warm beds. To give our group a greater challenge, we chose to bypass a closer hut. As it turned out, the more distant lodging was almost our "bridge too far."

At 4 P.M., we ran out of water. In an attempt to build up speed, we shifted weight from some of the struggling members to those who were moving more assuredly.

By 8:30 P.M., we ran out of daylight, too, and were still far from our destination—a dispirited pack of tired and increasingly terrified climbers. We knew we had signed on for something more than a walk in the park, but none of us, our three Outward Bound instructors included, had expected that we might actually find ourselves in peril.

As darkness descended, we broke into two groups to ensure better control and communication. Those few of us who had headlamps donned them, but the light wasn't enough and the progress of our lead group ground to a halt. Then that big, beautiful Italian moon rose over the horizon, illuminating our path, and we began to move again.

While the going was slow and demanded total concentration, we had a new, dogged focus. Sometime deep into that memorable evening, I found myself sitting on a ledge with Bob Smith, an investment banker and fellow member of the board of the New York City Outward Bound Center. Bathed in the lunar light glinting off the snowfields around us, our legs dangling into nothingness, we were waiting for the other members of our worn-out group to carefully descend an iron ladder bolted into the rock face. And in that moment of almost idyllic peacefulness, we started to laugh.

It wasn't nervous laughter or even exhausted laughter. It was a release that marked the moment of realization that we were going to be okay: the primal exhilaration of survival. We still didn't have a clue when we would reach the hut—that didn't happen until around 2 A.M., after nineteen hours of climbing and hiking—but we knew we had taken care of each other and ourselves.

Hours later, over bowls of steaming minestrone with a roof over our heads at last, we learned that the second group, off in the darkness some distance behind us, had heard our laughter and used it to renew their own fortitude and determination to continue their climb. Unwittingly, we had stumbled upon one of the great lessons Outward Bound teaches: You affirm and strengthen your own situation by helping others.

Meanwhile, back at the ranch, The New York Times Company was going through a decision-making process as difficult as any I'd been involved in since having been named chairman three years earlier. This was the very height of the dot-com bubble, and we were grappling with whether and how to spin off our Internet division in a new public offering.

The debate had been arduous, even occasionally rancorous. Some thought we were giving away our future; others of us were convinced that it was the only way to grow what we had carefully built in *The New York Times on the Web* and Boston.com. More than one discussion ended with references to Solomon and splitting the baby.

When I got on the plane for Italy, I was unsure whether I should leave New York while this battle raged. Ultimately, I concluded that since I was the host of the Dolomites trip, I had a responsibility to actually be there. And as one of the few experienced climbers in the group, I am grateful that I was able to honor my obligation.

But I didn't realize how important my night on the rocks was until I returned to New York. Suddenly, the business decisions we faced were put into much sharper perspective. Yes, it was important to make the best call we could and give as many people as possible ownership of that important decision. But at the end of the day, it wasn't life or death; no one's fate was truly hanging in the balance. The New York Times Company, which had been around for almost a century and a half, would flourish under either scenario.

(For the history books, our decision to launch a tracking stock of what we now call New York Times Digital was made moot as the Internet market imploded. When the value of similar businesses plummeted faster than a climber falling off a Dolomite ledge, it became readily apparent that it is better to be lucky than smart.)

The book you are holding is filled with stories that relate much more risk, courage, and determination than the one you just read—even though we felt pretty good about ourselves once we left the Via Ferrata. It has been written by men and a woman whose books I've enjoyed, whose climbs I've marveled over, and, in the case of Royal Robbins, whose T-shirts I wear.

I'm grateful that Mike Useem, Jerry Useem, and Paul Asel asked me to write this introduction. I'm a rank amateur adventurist—my idea of a rugged outing includes a cold martini at the end of the day—but I've had my share of adventures in business. And it's clear to me that there is much any businessperson can learn from high-mountain leadership.

At extreme altitude and raw exposure, the room for error decreases, while the need for excellence in planning, communications, and execution grows almost exponentially. Sloppiness kills. So does hubris.

At *The Times*, all our leadership, training, skill, and planning were put to the ultimate test during the horrors of 9/11. Even as we grappled with covering the biggest story of our lifetime, we had to comfort colleagues who had lost loved ones in the tragedy and deal with a succession of anthrax hoaxes, all in the middle of the biggest drop in advertising since the Great Depression. Our success during those trying weeks and months was constructed on a carefully built foundation of talent, purpose, and commitment.

We were again tested during the spring of 2003 when we discovered that one of our reporters had fabricated stories, thereby violating our most sacred promise to our readers: that what appears in our pages is as reliable and trustworthy as humanly possible. In the painful weeks that followed, our two senior editors resigned for the good of an institution they loved. And as with climbing expeditions that have undergone tragedy, we set as our goal understanding and fixing what went wrong while recommitting to our mission—in the case of *The New York Times*, producing the finest news report possible.

Dramas that may take months or years to play out in business can come to fruition in days or hours, even minutes, when you take on the planet's greatest climbing challenges. It's in this very compactness of that time that essential leadership lessons most easily can be seen, dissected, debated, and understood by those of us who may never see the view from the top of K2, or even from its base.

Most of us acquire wisdom the hard way—through trial and error. "We learn geology the morning after the earthquake" was how Ralph Waldo Emerson put it. This book offers an alternative route: a chance to become wiser by learning from the successes and mistakes of others. Indeed, it's full of such teachings. I am confident that you can both enjoy and profit from them. I certainly have.

ARTHUR SULZBERGER JR.

Why We Climb

JERRY USEEM

The first question which you will ask and which I must try to answer is this, "What is the use of climbing Mt. Everest?" and my answer must at once be, "It is no use." There is not the slightest prospect of any gain whatsoever. . . . So, if you cannot understand that there is something in man which responds to the challenge of this mountain and goes out to meet it, that the struggle is the struggle of life itself upward and forever upward, then you won't see why we go.

—GEORGE LEIGH MALLORY

•   •   •

Onward and upward.

—ANDREW CARNEGIE

THERE WAS A TIME FOR JIM COLLINS, LONG BEFORE HE GREW obsessed with the stock charts of Gillette and Walgreens, when regular encounters with death were a way of life. Most of these occurred high on the walls of Eldorado Canyon outside Boulder, Colorado, where Collins would engage in ritual battles with gravity and fear. Once, clinging 400 feet up on a vertical crag of granite known to climbers as T-2, his rope unaccountably came untied from his harness, leaving him just a toehold or two away from eternity. He was in the tenth grade at the time.

"The audacity of it!" Collins was marveling years later. "The sheer adventure." He could have been reliving the exploits that landed him on the cover of *Mountain* magazine in 1980. But Collins was talking about Boeing and its airplanes. "They were always thinking in terms of triple redundancy," he continued. "If A failed, then system B was there to back it up. If B failed, then C would be there to back it up." Always an extra rope.

Collins was back in Eldorado Canyon, and as we passed the forbidding wall of T-2, he paused to gaze up at its crevices, white with chalk from other climbers. Though he still spent hours clutching Spiderman-like holds inside his garage-turned-rock-climbing-gym (the sole visible extravagance at his Boulder home), Collins was now better known as a business researcher and thinker—arguably the most influential one of his day, given the runaway sales of his books *Built to Last* and *Good to Great* and the who's who of CEOs that came seeking counsel at his "management lab." I was there to profile Collins for my employer, *Fortune* magazine, and had made the mistake of suggesting that I interview him while we hiked Eldorado Canyon—a route, I soon learned, that Collins *ran* almost daily. My lungs were grateful when his springy frame finally came to rest at a vista point.

"I get most of my ideas sitting here on this rock," Collins said, "watching the sun go down on the high country covered in snow." Though most of those ideas revolved around great companies and what separated them from lousy ones, a climbing reference was never far from reach. Typical was his distinction between real entrepreneurs and the sort of opportunists—*opportuneurs,* I offered—who proliferated during the dot-com boom. "It's kind of like people who go and climb Everest without oxygen, alpine-style," he said. "That's climbing. And there are people who are carried down by the Sherpas when they get in trouble. That's not climbing. You're going to have to be someone who can be up there on your own, know that you can't screw up, and if you do, you die." That's what made climbing so refreshing, he said. "Markets can become distorted, but gravity never lies."

Gravity, defiance, luck, risk, opportunity, death. To Collins, mountains weren't merely a scenic backdrop to his work. They were a range running right through it.

MOUNTAINS AND BUSINESS, AT FIRST BLUSH, would seem an unlikely pairing. Mountains are the dominion of a select few; business the vocation of the many. Mountains rise and fall over millennia; markets over hours and minutes. Most of all, mountains hover at an otherworldly remove—planets with a vocabulary all their own: *crevasse, crampon, couloir,* and the best-sounding of them all, *bivouac*—while commerce is worldliness defined. You might get away with a touchdown metaphor at the office, but it's doubtful you'd say *bivouac.*

Yet mountains not only possess a singular power to inspire, they hold a surprising power to instruct. Long regarded, as Edwin Bernbaum writes in *Sacred Mountains of the World,* as "symbols of supreme efforts by men and women to overcome their limitations and attain transcendent goals," mountains can also be regarded as high-altitude laboratories. In these unforgiving places, where the margin for error is as thin as the air, where our heads thicken along with our blood, even the smallest lapse in execution—the lost mitten, the unfastened carabiner—can undo the soundest strategy, error cascading into mistake, mistake compounding into mishap, mishap kicking loose disaster until . . . well, there's one swing of the ice axe left between you and the 5,000-foot plunge.

It's a reminder that placing someone atop a summit is, above all, a triumph of organization—which is why mountaineering is no mere metaphor for management. It is management itself.

Upward Bound represents a first expedition of sorts into this terrain. It does not pretend to offer a new corporate way of life. No one has discovered the Shangri-la of management techniques, nor will the Sherpa Way be unveiled as the future of the factory floor. It offers, rather, what mountaineers relish most: an unclimbed route. Because there is no established path to follow, we have chosen to strike out along many different routes, setting loose some of the world's elite climbers and leading business thinkers—and in several cases, people with feet in both camps—to chart their own courses toward the summit.

The approaches they follow in the coming chapters take us, variously, to avalanches on the "savage mountain" of K2, the boardroom of Royal Robbins, Inc., the "impossible" Genesis route in Eldorado Canyon, the business of Earth Treks, and the "death zone" of Mount Everest. Each in turn maps a different set of contours along our unclimbed route. For starters, Jim Collins explains his distinction between "failure" and "fallure" and why he set his calendar a decade ahead to conquer a sheer sheet of granite, while Paul Asel describes what "ridge walking" between deadly avalanches and the lure of Mount McKinley's summit taught him about nurturing risky start-ups in Silicon Valley and Russia. Wharton School professor Michael Useem (always something of a father figure to this writer—partly, I suppose, because he's my father) combines a longtime study of organizations with a lifelong love of mountaineering to extract some guiding principles for making fast and accurate decisions. And entrepreneur and legendary rock climber Royal Robbins tells the story of his ten-day, first solo ascent of Yosemite's massive El Capitan as his awakening to the power of perseverance.

In the truly harrowing department, entrepreneur Chris Warner describes his ascent of India's Shivling peak and its influences on the development of his climbing business, Earth Treks, while fellow businessman Rodrigo Jordan talks about the essential ingredients of a peak performance team, as thrown into sharp relief on the slopes of Everest and K2. Stacy Allison, the first American woman to summit Mount Everest, reveals what happened when a leader abdicated responsibility on the same mountain. Meanwhile, *Sacred Mountains* author Edwin Bernbaum takes us to Mount Fuji and Mount Sinai, exploring why more accessible peaks can exert a pull every bit as powerful as Mount Everest's. Finally, businessman and famed explorer Al Read shows us how tenacity can help catapult a climbing passion into a lifelong career.

The collective goal of these individual forays—every expedition, after all, needs a goal—is to bring the lessons of the world's high places down to earth—lessons that apply equally at sea level and five miles up. But they address another question in the process. It's the timeless question posed of all mountaineers, and one that applies to everyone who's ever wondered why they push themselves so hard. For we are all, to one extent or another, upward bound.

Why do we climb?

The original riposte—George Leigh Mallory's gnomic "Because it is there"—set the standard for all time, helped no doubt by the fact that *he* is there, too, having never descended from Everest's northern slopes in 1924. But Mallory's gibe (to an irritating reporter during a U.S. lecture tour) has stuck mostly because we enjoy its impish suggestion that motivation comes from without, when obviously it comes from within. From exactly *where* within is, of course, the Himalayan-sized question. It's undeniable that climbing can involve elements of selfishness: We want to make the peak *ours*, to bag the trophy, to be king of the mountain—risks and loved ones be damned. In the 1930s, Nazi Germany announced its intention to conquer Kashmir's Nanga Parbat by dubbing it *Unserberg*: "our mountain."

Yet reducing mountaineering to a "selfish hobby"—as a Japanese newspaper did when Junko Tabei became the first woman to stand atop Everest in 1975—is more than a gross oversimplification. Because in climbing there is also aspiration for something higher than the self: communion with the eternal; humility before forces larger than mankind; even the sort of extranormal connectedness Maurice Herzog experienced as he approached the summit of Annapurna in 1950. "I felt as though I were plunging into something new and quite abnormal," he wrote in his account of the expedition, *Annapurna*. "This was a different universe—withered, desert, lifeless; a fantastic universe where the presence of man was not foreseen, perhaps not desired. We were braving an interdict, overstepping a boundary, and yet we had no fear as we continued upward. Something clutched at my heart."

"Upward," as it happens, was a central motif in business's formative years. A century before Americans were speed-reading man-versus-nature-and-man-loses tales, they were devouring Horatio Alger books like *Struggling Upward, Bound to Rise,* and *Strive and Succeed,* which depicted upward mobility as something both noble and attainable. The most upwardly mobile man of his era, Andrew Carnegie, preached that it was the upward struggle itself—not the millions attained from it—that elevated mankind. He rid himself of the by-product by founding libraries "to lead the people gently upward" and advised an 1885 audience of young men: "Say each to yourself, 'My place is at the top.' . . . Your foot, in such a case, is upon the ladder; the amount of climbing done depends entirely upon yourself."

Today, we're less sure how to feel about upward ambition. In broad swaths of society, living standards have risen to the point where basic needs—shelter, safety, food on the table—can be fulfilled without extreme economic exertion. Yet the march of commerce has not borne out *Time* magazine's 1956 prediction that "not far distant is the time when Americans need spend comparatively little time earning a living," freeing them to "unleash their considerable powers for cultural, ethical and spiritual accomplishments." Instead, many of us work longer and harder than ever, sacrificing precious family time, leisure pursuits, and even health to move another rung up the ladder. We look up from our work late one night, having skipped dinner at home, and wonder: What keeps us climbing so hard? Is it a laudable capacity for self-denial? Or a modern form of self-indulgence? Even George Mallory once noted that "we do not live to eat and make money. We eat and make money to be able to enjoy life."

Yet just as climbing can't be reduced to a "selfish hobby," neither can work be reduced to a mindless race for money or status. Some people view their jobs—even humbler ones—less as careers than as vocations with a higher calling. Patagonia founder Yvon Chouinard created his line of environmentally sound outdoorwear and gear as a means of helping his fellow climbers in Yosemite: "It is the style of the climb, not the attainment of the summit, which is the measure of personal success," Choirard and his business partner wrote in a 1974 manifesto. "Climb clean." Others describe "peak experiences" that come from deep feelings of mastery at work. That sounds a lot like Rodrigo Jordan's description, atop Everest, of "the calm happiness that floods the spirit when we know we have done things well."

Climbing, of both the alpine and career variety, thus can't be boiled down to a single motivation. (Though maybe mine can: It's about the gear. I like explaining *crampon* to airport security personnel—"It's a shoe, see, with twelve knives sticking out of it"—and enjoy owning my own ice axe.) The messy truth is that conflicting motives often exist in the same person. Beck Weathers, the Texan left for dead during the 1996 Mount Everest tragedy that killed eight climbers, on the one hand described "the moments of genuine pleasure, satisfaction and bonhomie out in the wilds with my fellow climbers." Yet he also wrote in his personal account, *Left for Dead,* that the sport "became my hollow obsession," leaving him impervious to his wife's warnings that "this cold passion of mine was destroying the center of my life." So when someone asks, Why does the mountaineer climb? we'd do well to ask the same of ourselves. Is it for the upward journey itself? For the glory? For the scenery along the way? For the people we support? Or is it simply because Citigroup is there?

The choice of a bank here is not random. At many business schools each year, students read a classic *Harvard Business Review* article entitled "The Parable of the Sadhu," written by Bowen McCoy, then a managing director at Morgan Stanley. There's a short movie that goes with it. It begins with McCoy contemplating the view out his office window.

As the skyscrapers of Manhattan (themselves expressions of business's loftier aspirations) fade into the peaks of the Himalayas, his story unfolds. On a rare sabbatical from work, McCoy and his friend Stephen were halfway through a sixty-day, "once in a lifetime" trek across Nepal and approaching the trek's exhilarating high point: the crossing of a treacherous, 18,000-foot pass. The day of the crossing, however, they encountered something for which they were wholly unprepared: a half-conscious, half-naked, hypothermic holy man, or sadhu. *What on earth was he doing up there?* Probably returning from a pilgrimage site on the far side of the pass, though why he hadn't taken a lower route was anybody's guess. McCoy took the sadhu's pulse while Stephen and four Swiss climbers clothed him from head to foot. But further delay would come at a cost: The rising sun would soon melt the ice steps leading up to the pass, meaning McCoy would have to abandon his dream of crossing it. Distraught at the notion, and worried about the onset of altitude sickness, he told Stephen he was continuing up.

It wasn't until Stephen caught up with him on the far side that McCoy's exultation gave way to a sudden crush of guilt. "How do you feel," Stephen asked, "about contributing to the death of a fellow man?" McCoy asked if the sadhu was dead. "No," Stephen replied, "but he surely will be!"

The holy man's actual fate was never determined—he was last seen listlessly throwing stones at a dog, after Sherpas had carried him down to a sunny rock and a Japanese group had given him food and water. But McCoy's story invariably sets off a firestorm of reactions among students. Some take up McCoy's initial defense: "Look, we all cared. We all stopped and gave aid and comfort. Everyone did his bit." Others support Stephen's position: "No one person was willing to assume ultimate responsibility for the sadhu" by assuring his safe descent to the nearest village. It was "a good example of the breakdown between the individual ethic and the corporate ethic."

Deeply shaken by the episode, McCoy searched for answers. The problem, he concluded, was that the group had lacked a "sense of purpose or plan," leaving it to react "instinctively as individuals." The lesson, he wrote, was that "organizations that do not have a heritage of mutually accepted, shared values tend to become unhinged during stress."

MCCOY HAD, IN EFFECT, rediscovered the original meaning of the word *corporate*. Before it became coterminous with big business, corporate meant "united or combined into one," as the Random House dictionary defines it. Though McCoy thought he had left the corporate world behind, he had merely stepped into a corporate world of a different sort—one in which people depended upon each other for their lives, not just their livelihoods.

That McCoy came to this insight only belatedly isn't surprising, given our penchant for celebrating individual goals over collective ones. We fixate on celebrity CEOs as if they were Edmund Hillary and Tenzing Norgay, the heroes who finally conquered Everest in 1953. Yet even that famous example hides a more complex truth. Many people are surprised to learn that the man who led that historic expedition was neither Hillary nor Norgay, but an unsung Briton named John Hunt. The former military man directed a classic "siege" ascent, a mountaineering style in which a large team of climbers methodically shuttles supplies between ever-higher camps so that a few team members—usually those who have been climbing strongest and happen to be in high camp on the right day—can have a shot at the summit. When Hillary and Norgay stood atop Everest for the first time, in other words, they were also standing atop a pyramid of people.

McCoy's analysis and Jim Collins's research point in the same direction: It's organizations that stress their *corporateness* that tend to thrive over the long haul. Indeed, the company that now stands on the roof of the corporate world—Wal-Mart Stores, whose $246 billion in annual sales is to business what 29,035 feet is to climbing—could serve as a case study. Why don't we know the name of its CEO? Because Lee Scott understands he didn't create the system that powered Wal-Mart up the mountain; the system picked him to be its man on top.

If there's a main principle to be derived from McCoy's story, though, it's the importance of principles themselves—of establishing them before crisis hits, and of sticking to them when it does. Many people, for instance, know the story of Johnson & Johnson CEO James Burke and his decisive move to pull Tylenol off store shelves during the cyanide-poisoning crisis of 1982. Yet Burke's defining moment arguably occurred three years earlier, when he led a searching overhaul of J&J's core principles. A stark contrast is Enron, whose messy unraveling contains one shining moment of stupidity: its board of directors' decision to suspend the company's code of ethics.

The strongest allure for suspending such principles is often the summit, whether that's a lofty stock price or a literal peak. As the leader of the first all-woman attempt on one of the world's fourteen 8,000-meter peaks in 1978, Arlene Blum hadn't laid down clear decision-making principles until the group was high on the slopes of Annapurna—slopes that were being raked by constant, unpredictable avalanches. As chronicled in her book *Annapurna: A Woman's Place,* when Blum voiced misgivings about continuing—"I feel as if something is telling us we should give up before one of us dies," she told her team—another team member cut her off. "I don't feel like talking about it," said the team member. "I just want to climb this mountain." It was the same dynamic described in a 2003 *Harvard Business Review* article entitled "Why Bad Projects Are So Hard to Kill": Managers who argued for giving up on endangered projects, author Isabelle Royer found, were often met with denial and accusations of defeatism. "We didn't dare wonder whether we should stop or not," one manager told her. "It was too hard."

Blum thus faced a classic leadership dilemma: Attaining the summit can require the sort of optimism that is classically associated with onward-and-upward types. In the words of a National Outdoor Leadership School (NOLS) handbook: "Leaders think in terms of 'dos' rather than 'don'ts'. . . . They are cheerleaders and lighthouses. . . . Knowing where they are going is more important than how they are going to get there. . . . They have become 'TOUGH-MINDED' by overcoming obstacles, setbacks, negative thinkers and disappointments. They don't stay down." Yet negative thinkers, it turns out, are statistically more realistic in the presence of real danger, recommending the slogan of Intel chairman Andy Grove: "Only the paranoid survive."

In the end, two of Blum's climbers did not survive, falling a thousand feet after Blum failed to dissuade them from attempting an unclimbed secondary summit. Most tragic of all, the deaths occurred after the group's mission had already been accomplished: A day earlier, two women had summited Annapurna.

Herein, then, a final point: The summit is not the finish line. In both mountaineering and business, statistics show that decision making becomes poorer—and danger therefore greater—after the mountaintop has been reached. A dramatic business case was Cisco Systems, which had enjoyed forty straight quarters of growth before it suffered a $400 billion tumble in 2001. The problem wasn't its much-vaunted forecasting system, which by all accounts was state-of-the-art, but the assumptions its managers had plugged into it: They never bothered to model what would happen if growth stopped or reversed. So even when storm clouds began massing on the horizon—competitors started to stumble, suppliers warned of a drop-off ahead—the company's sunny outlook persisted. "I have never been more optimistic about the future of our industry as a whole or of Cisco," CEO John Chambers declared shortly before disaster hit.

What was Chambers thinking? Perhaps something akin to what Everest guide Rob Hall was thinking on the afternoon of May 10, 1996. Though the stakes were far different—life and death versus profit and loss—Hall, too, had enjoyed an uninterrupted run of success, at one point remarking that he could put almost any client on the summit. (Mountaineering, let's not forget, is also a for-profit business.) He, too, had elaborate systems that were supposed to prevent catastrophe. And he, too, had been the beneficiary of good luck: Year after year, an associate noted, Hall had enjoyed brilliant weather on summit day.

Mountain gales, of course, are no more subject to human control than the economy's "perennial gale of creative destruction." But success can create a heightened sense of control, an illusion that shatters quickly once the storm finally hits. When it did hit, Hall and a client paid the steepest price, joining Mallory on the mountain.

WHEN MALLORY'S FROZEN CORPSE was finally discovered on Everest in 1999, there was the brief, tantalizing hope of finding the Kodak Vest Pocket camera he'd carried with him on that day in 1924.

Perhaps its film held the answer to one of mountaineering's great mysteries: Was he on his way up when he perished? Or on his way down?

The camera was never found. But the familiar brand name invoked another mystery: Why does a company like Eastman Kodak, after so many decades of dominance, eventually peak and head downhill? Jim Collins has stewed over such questions for years. But as we sat in a Boulder coffee shop following our brisk "hike" through Eldorado Canyon, he was discussing the opposite phenomenon: how mediocre companies (and perhaps mediocre climbers like me) can overcome vertical limits. The companies that had made the leap from good to great, as he put it, were those that had defined success not as a single summit but as a principle to push toward as they attempted successive summits. Then Collins noticed something out the window. "Look," he said, pointing to a silhouetted mountain ridge. "Good to great."

Say what?

Finally my eyes got it. The ridgeline swept horizontally from left to right, like the stock chart of a mediocre company, before starting a steep, jagged rise. Good to great. Collins grinned. His mountains, as usual, knew the answer.

1

Hitting the Wall:
Learning that Vertical Limits Aren't

JIM COLLINS

IN 1999, NICK SAGAR REACHED THE END OF HIS ROPE. HE
had a dream: to climb The Crew, a route at the upper end of the rock-
climbing difficulty scale in Rifle State Park, Colorado. In his twenties,
Sagar had given his life over to the monomaniacal dedication required
to climb 5.14 routes (the highest rating possible on the Yosemite Decimal System), living off a few dollars of sponsorship money with his
wife, Heather, munching donated energy bars and living out of a truck
parked at the crags for months at a time.

Then Sagar saw the dream crumble before his eyes. During a rest
day while preparing for his next attempt, he got the bad news: His
sponsorship from a climbing gear company—money he desperately
needed to survive while working on the route—failed to come
through. Out of money, he had no choice but to abandon his quest for
The Crew and head home, seeking work. Sagar knew that he would
likely never again be fit enough to ascend the route; never again would
he have an entire year to do nothing but live in Rifle Park and train all
day every day, like an Olympic decathlete in the year before the games.
The loss of sponsorship virtually guaranteed that he would never reach
his goal. Sagar removed the gear he'd fixed on the route months earlier. Tears streaming down his face, he packed up his equipment and
walked back to camp. He and Heather said good-bye to their friends
and drove toward the exit, defeated.

But then a lone figure stepped into the middle of the road, holding
something in his hand.

"That's Herman," said Nick. "What the heck is he doing?"

Herman Gollner, a dedicated climber in his mid-fifties, had watched Sagar's quest with quiet admiration. When he heard about Sagar's situation, he drove back to his home in Aspen, visited his bank, and made a withdrawal. Now, here stood Herman, with a handful of cash, flagging down Sagar's truck.

"Here, take this," he said, thrusting the cash at Nick. "You must finish The Crew."

"No . . . I couldn't possibly . . . no," Nick stammered.

"You must take it," asserted Herman, in his Austrian accent. "You are so close. You may never have a chance again. I am older now—never again to climb at the top—but you . . . maybe I can help you. Please, take it."

The Sagars reluctantly accepted the cash, and Nick returned to the route for another attempt. This was his Olympic Gold Medal attempt, his shot to come through. He launched into the upper section of the wall, feeling strong, knowing he could do it. But just before the top, he heard a sickening sound—a little crackle under his foot and the skitter of his climbing shoe against stone. He had broken a key foothold!

Like one of those movie scenes in which the hero grasps for something in a dream, only to watch it disappear from his outstretched fingertips as he wakes, Sagar watched the top of the route suddenly fly up out of his grasp as gravity pulled his body off the rock and into midair. The rope snapped tight, and he knew he'd just expended his best effort ever. And now, without the key foothold, the route would be even more difficult.

"I almost wanted to quit," he said. "But Herman and all my friends believed in me. I couldn't let them down." Foothold or not, Sagar was determined to do the route, working on it through the autumn months and into early winter. Finally, on the last possible day of the season, with snow falling all about, Sagar made a final attempt. The overhanging rock shielded his hand holds from snow, but that was the only relief from the weather. Despite subfreezing temperatures and fingers so numb that he could barely feel the smaller edges, Sagar pulled through to the top and fulfilled the dream.

"I learned so much from The Crew," reflected Sagar three years later, "but very little of the learning was about climbing. I learned that the highest individual achievements are never solo events, that you only reach your best with the help of other people, and their belief in you. It's a lesson I will never forget, no matter what I do with the rest of my life."

The adventure of The Crew became not just a climb, but a classroom for life. It was not reaching the top that mattered most, but the lessons—the struggle and the adventure—learned along the way. Says Sagar: "I'm a better person for the experience, not the success."

I've been a rock climber for more than thirty years now, and while I'll probably never break through to climb 5.14 like Nick Sagar, my whole approach to life and career has been inextricably linked with my development as a climber. I began in my early teenage years, when my stepfather signed me up for a climbing course against my will. ("I'd rather study," I whined.) At the end of the first day, however, I knew I'd discovered one of the burning passions of my life. Growing up in Boulder, Colorado, I had one of the great climbing centers of the world as my backyard, and some of the greatest climbers in the world as my mentors. When I applied to Stanford University as an undergraduate, I noted in my application that one of the main attractions of Stanford was its sandstone buildings and wonderful weather that would enable me to train year-round by climbing on the walls between classes. (Climbing on the walls had long been a tradition with the Stanford Alpine Club, which had even published a small guide to routes on campus.) One day while trying an unclimbed route on the side of the philosophy building in the main Quadrangle, I heard a shuffle of feet behind me and then the voice of emeritus philosophy professor John Goheen: "Really, Mr. Collins. Do you think this is the ultimate solution to the existential dilemma?" I named the climb Kant Be Done.

Rock climbing for me has been the ultimate classroom, with lessons applicable to all aspects of life, including business, management, leadership, and scientific study. It is a sport from which you do not always get a second chance to learn from your mistakes—death tends to stop the learning process—but I've been fortunate to survive my own blunders. In this chapter, I offer five of my favorite lessons from climbing as a classroom, and how they apply to life and work outside of climbing:

1. Climb to fallure, not failure: How to succeed without reaching the top
2. Climb in the future, today: How to succeed by changing your frame of mind
3. Separate probability from consequence: How to succeed— and stay alive—by understanding the true risks
4. Form the Partner's Pact: How to succeed by practicing the discipline of First Who, Then What
5. Don't confuse luck and competence: How to not let success kill you

LESSON 1. CLIMB TO FALLURE, NOT FAILURE: HOW TO SUCCEED WITHOUT REACHING THE TOP

Matt and I walked around the bend in the trail and I stopped dead in my tracks, looking at an absolutely beautiful sheet of rock—smooth and slightly overhanging, with a thin fingertip-sized seam splitting right up the middle of the gray-and-silver granite wall in the Colorado Rockies' Front Range. "You can see why I named the route Crystal Ball," Matt said, pointing to a baseball-sized quartzite handhold fifty feet up the climb.

We roped up and I set off up the route, shooting for an on-sight ascent. An *on-sight* means that on your first try you lead the climb without any prior information about the moves (other than what you can determine looking from the ground) and without any artificial aid. Other climbers may have climbed the route before you, but they have not given you any information on how to climb the difficult sections, nor have you watched anyone else attempt the route. *For you,* in other words, the route is an entirely blank page, no matter how many other climbers have ascended the route. You get one chance for an on-sight. Once you start to climb, if you blow it (and thereby fall onto the rope), you've forever lost the chance.

Ten feet below the crystal, my feet began to skitter about, slipping off slick pebbles, and I curled my thumb around a little edge, thinking to myself, "If I can just get a little weight off my fingers . . ." The adrenaline of the on-sight attempt made me overgrip every hold, clamping down as hard as I could—like an overanxious runner who goes out too fast in the first 800 meters, only to pay the price for the indiscretion with lactic acid and gasping breaths.

If you've ever taken a pull-up test, you can get a sense for the feel of a hard sport climb. With the first pull-up, you feel really strong—like you

Jim Collins scopes out the moves on Sonic Youth from the ground, Clear Creek Canyon, Colorado

can do this forever. But when you get close to your limit, the movement that earlier felt so easy becomes impossibly hard. If you could just let go of the bar and rest for a minute, you could do two or three more pulls-ups, easy. But when you try to do all of your pull-ups in one hang, you hit a wall; drawing on all your will, you just can't get over the bar again. End of session.

A hard sport climb is similar to a pull-up session: It's a race to the top before you run out of power. The moves that would be so easy if they were moves one, two, and three become much harder when placed higher on the route, at, say, moves twenty-five, twenty-six, and twenty-seven. (A move is simply a hand movement. If you move your right hand from one hold to the next, it counts as a single move.) As we say in the realm of steep routes, "the clock is ticking" as soon as you leave the ground. You only have so many minutes and seconds before you will reach a point where your arms and fingers unwrap and uncurl, and you go plummeting down until (hopefully) the rope catches you.

"Breath, Jim. Relax." Matt's voice soothed me for a moment.

I gathered a bit of composure while hooking my thumb and resting my fingers, trying to get my breathing to settle down. But to little avail. My mind chattered away: "Should I go right hand or left hand to the sideways edge above? . . . If I get it wrong, there's no way I can reverse . . . and even if I get it right, I'm not sure I'll have enough power to pull up to the crystal ball. . . . And if I can't get to the crystal ball, there's no way I'll be able to get the rope clipped into the next point of protection. . . . How far would I fall? . . . Matt's a good belayer. . . . I hope I checked my knot. . . . God, my fingers hurt . . . but this is the on-sight . . . don't blow it. . . . You only get one chance to on-sight the route. . . . But what if I go for it and I can't clip? I'll take a huge fall. . . . But I won't hit anything . . . I'll just fly off into space. . . . It's only scary, but not unsafe. . . . Just do it. . . . Just punch for it. . . . What have you got to lose? . . . I wonder if I can go right left right. . . . But I don't like to take big falls . . ."

Tick, tick, tick—the clock ran on while I hesitated.

"Okay, Matt, here I go."

Right hand to the side pull. Left foot to the edge.

"Uh-oh." Wrong call. I should have gone to the edge with my left hand! I rolled my body to the left, groping for an edge, a pebble, a wrinkle—something, anything—that would allow me to pop my right hand up and move my left onto the side edge. I smooshed my right fingers into a little edge that pointed down and sideways—the wrong direction for a good pull. I now had a less than 20 percent chance of success. If I tried to make the move up, I'd almost certainly fall, a drop of twenty feet. Even if I did manage to surge upward, the higher I went without making the next bolt clip, the bigger the eventual fall. (On most modern routes, like Crystal Ball, the first person ever to climb the route affixes permanent protection bolts in the rock, to clip the rope through. These bolts exist only to catch you if you fall; they do not help you actually climb up the rock. If you fall when leading, you descend about 2.5 times as far as the distance to your last successful clip.)

"Off!" I called down to Matt.

"No," he yelled back. "You're only three moves from the crystal. You can recover there."

"OFF!" I repeated, with angry emphasis.

And I let go, dropping onto the rope in a nicely controlled fall.

I hung on the rope for about ten minutes, recovering, and then swung toward the rock on the end of the rope, pulled myself back onto the holds, and climbed to the top, just as if I'd rested below the pull-up bar. But, of course, it didn't count. I hadn't done a clean on-sight. And even though later in the day I managed to ascend the route from bottom to top in one shot—a success by most measures—I had nonetheless failed. Not failed on the climb, but failed in my mind. When confronted with the moment of commitment, the moment of decision, the moment of go-for-it on the on-sight . . . well, I let go. I went to failure, not fallure.

Failure and fallure. The difference is subtle, but it is all the difference in the world. In fallure, you still fail to get up the route but you *never let go*. Going to fallure means a full 100 percent commitment to go up, despite the odds against you. You'll only find your true limit when you go to fallure, not failure. Sure, I had less than a 20 percent chance of pulling through to the crystal ball, but because I let go, I'll never know for sure. Perhaps I would have had an extra reserve; perhaps I would have surprised myself and had an extra bit of power to hang on for one more move. Or perhaps—and this turned out to be true—the very next hold is better than it looks. And that's the rub. On the on-sight, you don't know what the next holds feel like. It's the ambiguity—about the holds, the moves, the ability to clip the rope— that makes 100 percent commitment on the on-sight so difficult.

Jim Collins tackles the overhanging roof section of
Sonic Youth

One of my mentors in life, design guru Sara Little Turnbull, gave
me a wall hanging with a quote from her speech at the 1992 Corporate
Design Foundation Conference: "If you don't stretch, you don't know
where the edge is."

Turnbull, director of the Stanford University Process of Change
Laboratory, built a distinguished career as a design consultant to major
corporations such as Corning and 3M. The Corporate Design Foundation described Turnbull as "CEOs' secret weapon in product design development." Turnbull once told me that some of her best designs came
when she was on the brink of a failed concept but didn't let go. Of
course, many—indeed, most—of her brink-of-failure designs ended up
being failures. But every once in a while, by not letting go, she would
push herself to a completely different level, and something extraordinary would come about. "And of course, that's when breakthroughs
happen," she told me. "You have to be on the brink of failure and then
surprise yourself. You just go to a different level." Fallure, not failure.

In my research on enduring great companies, I've noticed how the best executives intuitively understood this idea. Darwin Smith made a failure-versus-failure decision in vaulting his company to greatness. For 100 years, Kimberly-Clark languished in mediocrity, with most of its business in traditional coated-paper mills. Smith realized that the company's best shot at greatness lay in the paper-based consumer goods arena, where it had a side business called Kleenex—a brand that had become synonymous with the category, like Coke or Xerox. But how to get the company to fully commit to making the consumer business great, when the bulk of the company's history and revenues lay in the traditional industrial paper mills? Like the general who burned the boats upon landing, leaving no retreat for his soldiers, Smith decided to sell the mills. He would sell even the mill in Kimberly, Wisconsin, and throw all the proceeds into the consumer business, going head-to-head with rivals Scott Paper and Procter & Gamble. Wall Street derided him, the business media called the move stupid, and the analysts wrote merciless commentary. After all, how on earth could such a mediocre paper company take on the giants of the business? But in the end, Smith's decision paid off. Kimberly-Clark became the number one paper-based consumer products company in the world, eventually beating Procter & Gamble in six of eight product categories.

In climbing jargon, Smith removed the ability to "take" (to tell your belayer to pull the rope tight and catch you in a controlled fall, as I did with Matt when I failed on Crystal Ball). Of course, there was no guarantee that Kimberly-Clark would succeed in the consumer business—it could have taken a huge leader fall—but Smith understood the only path to success lay in a full commitment to climb to failure. Anything short of this commitment and Kimberly-Clark would never have become a great company.

I now see life as a series of choices between going to failure or fallure. Like an on-sight attempt, the next holds in life remain unclear, ambiguous. And that very ambiguity holds us back from making a fully committed attempt. We fail mentally. We let go. We take a nice controlled fall, rather than risking a bigger fall. But as with most hard sport

Jim Collins climbing to failure
on Global Gorilla in
Boulder Canyon, Colorado

climbs, going to failure in life is scary, but not dangerous. Whether it be starting a business or publishing a book or trying an exciting new design, failure rarely means doom. And, most important, the only way to find your true limit is to go to fall-ure, not failure.

At age forty-four, my body does not allow me to pull as hard on holds as when I was twenty. But I've since learned that what you lose in physical strength you can gain by increasing your mental strength. And so I continue to work in the realm of overhanging rock, trying to go to failure. I've even redefined "success" less in terms of getting to the top and more in terms of the quality of my mental effort. I keep a record on my PalmPilot of my hard on-sight attempts. A recent listing reads:

2002 HARD ON-SIGHT ATTEMPT LOG

REACH THE TOP	24
CLIMB TO FALLURE	18
FAILURE (LET GO/QUIT)	16
TOTAL ATTEMPTS	58
% SUCCESS RATE (TOP + FALLURE)	72

Note that I calculate the "success rate" not just as the percentage of times to the top, but the percentage of times to the top *plus* the percentage of times to fallure. Just the other day during a climbing session, I did not make it to the top of a single route. Not one. Still, it was one of my most successful days of climbing ever, because I went to failure on every single attempt. I felt good on the way home because my mind felt strong that day, compared to the weak feeling on most days. For in the end, climbing is not about conquering the rock; it is about conquering yourself. And this is what fallure is all about.

The ability to change your frame of mind—to increase your odds of success not by increasing sheer physical capability but by changing your way of thinking—is a key dimension of climbing as a classroom. But the failure-fallure distinction isn't the only mental leap to make. Sometimes it means vaulting yourself into the future.

LESSON 2. CLIMB IN THE FUTURE, TODAY: HOW TO SUCCEED BY CHANGING YOUR FRAME OF MIND

In 1978, I became obsessed with a climb called Genesis, a smooth, slightly overhanging hundred-foot slab of red rock in Eldorado Canyon, near Boulder. The route had never been free climbed, and most people doubted it would ever fall that way. (To *free climb* a route means that you climb with ropes, but only as a safety device. The whole point of a "free" ascent is that you move up the rock entirely under your own power and via your hands and feet gripped on the rock, without pulling directly on any gear or the rope. The rope and the protection devices are there to catch you if you fall, not to help you ascend the rock.)

Then one day I watched John Bragg, a six-foot-two, blond-haired giant visiting from the East Coast, attempt Genesis as a free climb. He pulled up onto a smooth overhanging section (the part everyone thought would never be climbed) and launched himself upward with a huge throw. His hand hit a little something up on the wall, and he stuck to it for just a second—a momentary pause—before his hand unlatched and he plummeted down twenty-five feet onto the rope. Bragg tried this throw ten or twenty times, and then gave up. "It's not going to go for a long time," he said.

Still, my imagination had been kindled. "If he could hang onto a little hold for even a second," I thought, "it must somehow be climbable."

And so, before returning to college for my junior year, I ventured up the cliff to give it a try. I just could not, however, find an obvious way to climb with precision to the little hold Bragg had been jumping for, so that I might be able to hang on it long enough to pull up to the next hold.

I made a mental map of the holds and, upon my return to school, found a building wall on the Stanford campus that had moves similar to what I thought Genesis would have. I created a training routine called the Genocide Traverse, as a reflection of the painful intensity of the route. Between classes I trained on the wall, carrying a needle in my shirt pocket to pop the blisters on my fingertips that arose from the regimen. Yet even with all this training, I failed to get up the climb when I returned for Christmas break. I was physically strong, but psychologically intimidated by the supposed "unclimbability" of the route. I needed to change my frame of mind.

But how to do it?

In studying climbing history, I noticed a pattern: Climbs once considered "impossible" by one generation of climbers eventually became "not that hard" for climbers two generations later. A 5.10 route seemed nearly impossible to climbers in the early 1960s, but by the late 1970s, top climbers routinely on-sighted 5.10s as warm-ups for harder projects. I read up on how records fell in other sports and noticed the same pattern. For ten years, the world record in the mile stood at 4:01, and no one seemed able to break the four-minute barrier. But once Roger Bannister broke it in 1954, the world record fell by six seconds over the next ten years. By the late 1970s, when I was trying Genesis, the mile record had fallen to under 3:50. People had not only figured out how to run a sub-four-minute mile, but they were doing so at the end of a 5,000-meter race!

So I decided to play a psychological trick on myself. I realized that I would never be the most gifted climber, or the strongest climber, or the boldest climber. But perhaps I could be the most futuristic climber. I did a little thought experiment: I tried to project out fifteen years, two generations of climbers later, and asked myself, "What will Genesis seem like to climbers in the 1990s?" The answer came back clear as a bell. In the 1990s, the top climbers in the world would routinely on-sight Genesis, viewing it as simply a warm-up for even harder routes. And less-talented athletes would view Genesis as a worthy challenge, but hardly impossible. The barrier, I realized, was primarily psychological, not physical.

I decided to pretend in my own mind that it was not 1979, but 1994. I bought a little Day-Timer calendar and changed all the year dates. I walked into the canyon and tried to picture Genesis the way a 1990s climber would look at it.

With that change in psychology, I managed to free climb the route. It caused quite a sensation and confused many of the best climbers of the day. They were still climbing in 1979, whereas I had "transported" myself psychologically to 1994. And, indeed, by the early 1990s, these same elite climbers climbed Genesis routinely, no longer thinking of it as particularly hard. I watched one elite climber visiting from out of state walk to the base, nonchalantly rope up, climb flawlessly to the top, and lower down. All he said was "Nice route"—and then he ambled off in search of stiffer stuff.

Climbing teaches that the biggest barriers are not on the rock, but in our minds. I've seen this lesson come to life with my wife's coaching of the local high school cross-country team. When she first became head coach, her varsity boys averaged 5:47 per mile over a cross-country course. Now, seven seasons later, the boys average 5:25 per mile—an improvement that made the difference between a team that didn't even qualify for the state meet and two state championship teams in a row. Does she have better athletes on the team? Not really; the primary difference is psychological. She has changed the psychological definition of fast for her varsity runners. The same kids that in a different frame of mind would have considered 5:47 to be fast now consider 5:47 to be slow. And when they go out in 5:25 or better, they don't even blink an eye. They *expect* themselves to run that fast. Same genetic talent. Different "set point" psychology. Different results. She changed their frame of mind.

Changing the frame of mind carries over to all walks of life, particularly for entrepreneurs and visionary company builders. The key is to recognize underlying patterns, often with the benefit of historical perspective, and then to project forward what those patterns will mean for future generations. When Steve Jobs visited the Xerox PARC research facilities in 1979, he saw a bunch of desktop computers using point-and-click devices and screens that displayed exactly what would be printed on the actual page, formatting and all. Today, we take this for granted. I'm typing these words while looking at a display that will print exactly what I see, and I can move around the page using a mouse. But in 1979, no commercial computers—certainly not personal computers—had these capabilities. A student of the history of technology adoption, Jobs recognized immediately that ten or twenty years down the road, these innovations would be standard fare, even for low-cost computer producers (as we see today with Dell).

Instead of waiting for the world to make this shift, however, Jobs decided to act as if the world had *already* changed. And in 1984, the Macintosh computer came forth, long before the natural forces of the market would have required such a device. It caused quite a sensation, stunning stronger and better companies such as IBM. But of course, today we think nothing of these features. Jobs had simply stepped forward in time and built his company's next-generation computers with this changed frame of mind.

Fifteen years after Genesis, I applied this same idea to a significant personal career shift. In graduate school, I'd taken career tests that gave me two contradictory answers: I should be either a professor or an entrepreneur. My first solution was to become a faculty member at the Stanford Graduate School of Business in the field of entrepreneurship.

Being genetically encoded to be irreverent, however, I chafed against the traditional academic path, refusing to subject myself to choosing a specific department and doing a traditional Ph.D. When you join a specific field, you become a member of the church of that field: You become a member of the church of leadership, the church of strategy, the church of organizational behavior, the church of finance, and so on. If you are a member of the church of strategy, your answers to questions will be framed through the lens of strategy; if you come from the church of finance, you come up with finance answers; and so forth. I wanted to be a member of the church of *questions,* and to be completely agnostic about which field the answers to the questions would fall into. If the answers fell in organization, in leadership, in finance, in strategy—or none of the above—then so be it.

Being at odds with the academic establishment (and being immature to boot), yet wanting to pursue a lifelong academic career of research and teaching, I found myself in quite a conundrum. But then I noticed a pattern: Increasing numbers of management faculty found themselves outside the traditional academic fold, becoming essentially entrepreneurs. Even so, this did not resolve my dilemma. Those who had taken the entrepreneurial path had become consultants or built big training companies—a path that did not fit with my talents or passions. I didn't want to be in business; I still wanted to be a professor.

But then I asked myself the Genesis question: What might this same challenge look like to people thirty years down the road? If this were 2025, rather than 1995, what additional options might I have?

The answer flashed clearly in my mind: I could choose to invert the phrase *professor of entrepreneurship* and, instead, become an *entrepreneurial professor.* In the previous two decades, it had become a well-trodden career path to forgo a traditional corporate structure and launch one's own company. So, I reasoned, why not apply that same idea to academics? Why do you need to be at a university to be a professor? Being a professor is not a position or a title; it is a role in the world. Thirty years into the future, I figured, there would perhaps be an entire group of people who became professors to the world, but outside the traditional academic structure.

That's when I moved back to Boulder, Colorado, set up my research laboratory in my old first-grade classroom, and became a self-employed professor. I explicitly did not set up a consulting business or a training company. Rather, I organized my calendar exactly as I did when on faculty at Stanford, allotting 50 percent of my time for research, writing, and idea development; 30 percent for various forms of teaching; and 20 percent for administrative stuff that just needs to get done. I know of few other academics who have explicitly considered this path, but perhaps in a few years many more will. Indeed, what looks like a difficult and risky path today might seem commonplace to people in two decades—a path easily followed and embraced by many.

Now, you might be wondering: How did I fund my professorship? Ah, the answer to that lies in the topic of luck. Jerry Porras and I had recently published *Built to Last,* and we were hit with the good fortune of having a bestseller. Not that we expected a bestseller—after all, who would have thought that an idea-driven book based on six years of academic research would become a bestseller? But the book came out at just the right moment (just as people tired of restructuring and craved a return to building, rather than destroying), and the zeitgeist of the times fell into our laps. Then, seven years later, my research team and I were struck again with phenomenal good luck, as the first book to come out of the research lab—*Good to Great*—landed in the market just as Enron imploded, the new economy fell out of favor, and the stock market bubble burst. We had the zeitgeist in our favor once again, and we had an even bigger bestseller. Taken together, *Built to Last* and *Good to Great* enabled me to become a fully self-employed professor, to endow my own chair and to grant myself tenure.

Of course, it could have turned out differently. Had the zeitgeist not been on our side, my career shift might have failed, dashed on the rocks of reality like so many other entrepreneurial dreams. But that brings me to the next lesson in climbing as a classroom.

LESSON 3. SEPARATE PROBABILITY FROM CONSEQUENCE: HOW TO SUCCEED—AND STAY ALIVE— BY UNDERSTANDING THE TRUE RISKS

In the summer of 1975, a young climber named David Breashears set his sights on a beautiful, unclimbed sheet of rock rising from the ground on a cliff south of Boulder, Colorado. For years, no rock climber had given serious thought to climbing this section. "Someday that wall will be climbed, but not in this generation," said many a climber looking at the smooth sheet. The challenge lay not in the apparent difficulty of the climbing, but in the absence of natural protection. Breashears saw no cracks where he might slot wired climbing nuts, and he was climbing in an era before it became acceptable to drill expansion bolts directly into the rock for protection. (Wired nuts can be attached to ropes and slotted into tapering sections of cracks, where they wedge tight and might hold a leader fall.) The wall rose dead vertical for about five stories, with little pebbles and sharp edges, then the angle kicked back to eighty-five degrees with holds that looked larger. To Breashears, it looked like the lower sections posed the main problem—where falling would only mean injury, not death.

Breashears headed up the route, trailing a rope and carrying a small selection of wired nuts that he hoped to maneuver into one of the upper pockets after the hard climbing. At the fifty-foot mark, with the angle easing off just a bit, he had a horrifying realization: The climbing above would be more difficult than the opening moves. The rock had become water polished from thousands of years of runoff from above, the sloping handholds had no sharp edges to grip, and there were still no places to slot nuts.

The rope dropped away from his waist harness to the ground in one arcing loop, clipped through . . . absolutely nothing. No gear, no placements of any type. If he fell, he would plummet sixty feet straight down onto the jumble of sofa-sized boulders strewn at the base. At thirty-two feet per second squared, he would slam into the boulder field at nearly fifty miles per hour at a force of 20 g's. *Ka-smack!* One dead climber.

Was this a risky situation?

Well, it depends on what you mean by risk.

For David Breashears, it was *not* a risky situation. Sure, the *consequences* of a fall were severe, but the *probabilities* of a fall were close to zero. David was such a gifted climber in his prime that—to him—the route formed a puzzle to solve, but not a particularly difficult one. It would be like handing a world-class crossword puzzle expert the Wednesday *New York Times* crossword puzzle (a challenging puzzle, but well within her capabilities) with these instructions: If you don't get the puzzle right, we're going to drop you off a sixty-foot cliff to your death. The consequences of failure are extreme, but the probabilities of failure are low.

Of course, if the puzzle solver allowed the consequences of failure to rattle her into a series of panicky decisions, she might slip up and be thrown off the cliff to her death. And if Breashears had allowed the sixty-foot ground-fall potential to infect his brain, he might have died. But he didn't. He was able to separate the probabilities of falling from the consequences of falling, and he climbed with focused precision to the top, establishing a new route aptly named Perilous Journey. Since that day in 1975, fewer than a dozen climbers have ascended the route on lead. Not because it is particularly difficult (it is 5.11 on a 5.14 scale), but because of the severe consequences in the event you happen to fall off.

To date, no one has died on Perilous Journey. The people who choose to climb it are those for whom the odds of falling are close to zero, yet who understand that it doesn't matter how easy or hard the climbing, how high or low the probabilities of falling: If you fall hundreds or thousands of feet, the consequences are severe. They go at Perilous Journey with a mindfulness that respects not just the climb, but the potential fall. They don't let the potential death fall rattle them, but equally, they don't climb with a cavalier attitude.

It turns out that some of the most tragic episodes in rock climbing have come when climbers mismanaged this distinction, becoming blasé on easy terrain. Take the case of Cameron Tague. On July 6, 2000, he made the approach to the Diamond Face on Longs Peak in Colorado, a thousand feet of sheer granite that begins a thousand feet above another cliff, called the Diagonal. To get to the Diamond, he decided to traverse in from the side of the Diagonal, then advance along a sloping ledge at the base of the Diamond. The sloping traverse ledge, called

Broadway, marks the point of separation between the two cliffs—the Diamond rising above for a thousand feet, and the Diagonal falling below for a thousand feet. For a climber as gifted as Tague, it would be an easy traverse to the base of the Diamond, and to save time for the difficult climbing ahead on the actual face, he didn't even bother to rope up. He remarked to his partner that it was going to be a gorgeous day on the face. Then, somehow, just as he reached the point in the traverse where the whole thousand feet of the Diagonal fell away below him, he lost his concentration, pulled on a loose piece of stone, and stumbled backward. Tague tried to recapture his balance, his hands grasping and waving about as he skittered toward the edge of the ledge, but he could not stop. He disappeared over the edge, and fell 800 feet to the talus below. The probabilities of falling were remote, but the consequences were lethal.

Separating probability from consequence applies not just to climbing, but also to work, life, and business. In 1994, when Intel Corporation first discovered the floating decimal point flaw in its Pentium microprocessor product, engineers estimated that it would cause a rounding error in division once every 9 billion times, or only once every 27,000 years for the average spreadsheet user. This astronomically small probability blinded Intel's leaders from worrying about the astronomically high consequences on the other side of the coin, given that Intel's products had become a widely used consumer brand extending far beyond its traditional customer base of technical sophisticates. When that one-in-a-billion event happened to a math professor, it ignited an explosion of Internet chat, which, in turn, caught the attention of the media. As then–Intel CEO Andy Grove described in his book *Only the Paranoid Survive* (a good title for climbers, by the way), Intel found itself hounded by CNN, pilloried in the press, and jolted by unhappy customers. On December 12, 1994, Grove awoke to read the horrific headline: IBM stops all shipments of Pentium-based computers. Ultimately, Intel took a $475 million write-off—an amount equal to half a year's R&D budget, or five years of Pentium advertising spending.

While Intel didn't die from the fall like Cameron Tague, it certainly crashed onto a ledge and shattered its leg. To Intel's credit, it learned from this experience and changed its way of doing business to account for the consequences, not just the probabilities. To date, we have not seen another problematic Pentium event from Intel.

The key lesson here is to be clear on the difference between probability and consequence, and to act accordingly—to know when it makes sense to climb to failure and when to not. On dangerous routes like Perilous Journey, or even the easy approach to the Diamond, you should avoid climbing to failure—no matter how difficult or easy the terrain. On sport routes with big solid bolts (like Crystal Ball) you can get on difficult climbs with a 5 percent chance of success and throw yourself into full failure mode. It might be scary, but it is not dangerous.

Separating probability from consequences—being able to see clearly when the consequences of failure are minimal—is the key to leading an entrepreneurial life. When I taught at the Stanford Graduate School of Business, many of my students failed to grasp this distinction, and it limited their options. One student came to my office and said, "I'd really like to start my own company, but it just seems so risky, so I'm going to take a job with IBM."

"What would happen if you gave your start-up the full try, and failed?" I asked. "What would you do?"

"I suppose I would go and get a job," she said.

"And with your background, energy, and skills—how hard would that be?"

"Not very hard."

"So, you're telling me that the worst-case scenario is that you would fail and you'd be right back where you are now: looking at getting a regular job."

For a Stanford M.B.A., trying a start-up is like going to failure on a well-bolted sport route. Sure, the odds of success are low, but the consequences of falling are minimal. The rope will catch her. She went out on her own, gave it the full effort, and managed to climb through and build a successful start-up. But she would have never known that if she hadn't separated probability from consequence, seen her M.B.A. as a big solid bolt that would catch her, and been willing to throw herself into full failure mode.

When in a game with high consequences to falling, be mindful, no matter how low the odds of falling. When in a game with minimal consequences to falling, you can take on challenges with low odds of success and throw yourself into the endeavor and climb to failure.

Of course, we have left unanswered the question of how to think about a different probability/consequence scenario: high odds of falling *combined with* severe consequences. Unless you are searching for true adventure or *kleos* (the ancient Greek notion of everlasting glory attained through the achievement of heroic deeds), I'd recommend staying away from this combination. But if you do elect this extreme brand of adventure—and accept the very real chance that you will kill or maim yourself—be sure to give yourself the best hedge against the risks: Pick the right partner. And that brings us to the next lesson in climbing as a classroom.

LESSON 4. FORM THE PARTNER'S PACT: HOW TO SUCCEED BY PRACTICING THE DISCIPLINE OF FIRST WHO, THEN WHAT

In 1978, Jim Logan set his sights on the North Face of Mount Robson, an unclimbed wall in the Canadian Rockies of British Columbia known as the Emperor Face. Logan had made two prior attempts, only to be defeated. On the third attempt, he succeeded. When asked for the key to his ultimate success, he said: "The problem lay in the fact that above the midway mark, you reach a point where it is impossible to retreat. No one's going to come get you—you either summit or die. I scoped the face from photographs, but I couldn't tell if the route I envisioned would ultimately be climbable. I realized that the most important element of my strategy lay not in the specifics of the route, but in who I picked as a partner. I needed a partner who would give the greatest chance of success, regardless of what we encountered high on the face. That's when I teamed up with Mugs Stump."

In Logan's recollection, Stump had been so deeply infected with a passion for climbing that he turned his car around on the way to a National Football League training camp and returned to Yosemite Valley, where he'd spent the summer climbing. "Mugs came from one of those steel towns in Pennsylvania, the local boy who made good as a college star defensive back and NFL draft pick. His family and friends just couldn't understand why he abandoned his promising football career to climb. But Mugs didn't care. He just wanted to climb, and he threw himself into it with a ferocious intensity. He was going to make good on his decision by getting up some of the hardest climbs in the world."

Mugs's sheer physical strength and agility, combined with his fanatical dedication to making a mark in the climbing world, made him an unbeatable partner for the Emperor Face. "I had this feeling that no matter what would happen up there, Mugs was strong enough to get us out. Of course, I learned later that he felt that I was the partner for him, as I had the intellect needed to find the most elegant path. We were sort of brains and brawn. He thought I was the strength of the team, and I thought he was the strength of the team. We had faith in each other, and it gave us the confidence to go into the summit-or-die zone."

Stump and Logan swapped leads, taking turns at tackling the difficulties of the face. More than once, each said something like "Whew, I'm glad *you* led that pitch." On the final day, Logan held responsibility for the last hard section: a snow, ice, and rock pitch all rolled into one long headwall 7,000 feet above their base camp. (A *pitch* is the amount of climbing between two sets of gear anchored in the rock, no longer than a single rope length. The lead climber moves up the pitch first, roped to his partner, who is attached to the bottom anchor. The leader puts in the next anchor at the top of the pitch and uses the rope to protect the second climber as he ascends the pitch.)

"I had to climb forty feet above a single one-inch angle piton—that's all I could get in. There just weren't any good cracks in the wall to place protection. If I didn't make it, if I fell, if I lost concentration, if I blew it in any way—not only would I die, but so would Mugs. Both our lives were in my hands, and I had to come through. I remember digging my ice axe into the very top of the wall and mantling over the top, tumbling into an exhausted heap over the top. But I have very little recollection of the rest of the pitch. I think I was on the final headwall—one hundred thirty feet of climbing—for something like eight hours, but I had no real sense of time."

A quarter of a century after their ascent, Jim Logan remains the only living climber to have ascended the middle of the Emperor Face. It has killed or defeated every climber who has attempted it in the intervening years, and, sadly, Mugs Stump died a decade later, while guiding a less-experienced group of climbers out of a storm on Mount McKinley. Everyone who knew Mugs and had the privilege to climb with him says the same thing: "I miss him. He was a great partner." In the world of adventure, there is no higher compliment.

The Emperor Face illustrates a fundamental lesson: The most important decisions we make are not about what, but about *who*. We live in a "what" culture: What are we going to do? What is our strategy? What are our tactics? What! What! What! The most important decision is not "What strategy should I use to get up the mountain?" but "*Who* should I climb with?" Hand in hand with this is the idea of the "Partner's Pact": the dedication not just to getting up the mountain, but a commitment to getting *each other* up the mountain, *and* down, safely. When you combine the principle of "First Who, Then What" with the Partner's Pact, you get a magical combination that increases the odds of success and infuses the whole ascent with deeper meaning.

The idea of First Who turns out to be a fundamental principle for other walks of life, especially building great companies. In a five-year research project, my colleagues and I studied the rare companies that managed to make the leap from being merely good performers (or worse) to truly great performers that sustained that performance over time. When David Maxwell became CEO of Fannie Mae, it was losing $1 million every business day with $56 billion of mortgage loans under water. With a negative 6 percent spread on its portfolio, and no end in sight, most analysts saw nothing but a bleak future for Fannie Mae, perhaps even extinction. When the board asked Maxwell what he would do to save the company, he responded that this was the wrong question. Not the wrong question forever, but the wrong question at the start. He would not decide where to drive the bus until he had the right people on the bus, the wrong people off the bus, and the right people in the right seats. Then, and only then, he would figure out where to drive it. Like Logan, he had a broad idea of the mountain (save Fannie Mae, and turn it into a great mortgage finance company), but no idea what exact path would get him to the top. So he picked the right partners, figuring that great people provided the best "strategy" for ultimate success.

Maxwell's approach reflects a general pattern we found in our research. The leaders who took companies from good to great did not first set strategy and then figure out how to get people to do it. Just the opposite, in fact. We also found that those on the good-to-great teams loved their work, in large part because they loved who worked with them. They tended to become and remain friends for life, still keeping in touch with each other years after retirement. They understood that getting to the top in and of itself has very little to do with a meaningful life, while who you choose to spend your time with has everything to do with the quality and meaning of your life. And for the kicker, those who found the right people in the first place had a better chance of getting to the top in the end.

Once I understood the First Who principle, I changed my own approach to climbing. Now I no longer think first in terms of what I want to climb this weekend; I think in terms of who I want to go climbing with, and *then* we'll figure out what to climb. My love of climbing and the meaning it brings to my life has increased, in large part because I so enjoy the people I choose to climb with.

I've also discovered the joys of the Partner's Pact. Jim Logan has become one of my favorite "whos" to go climbing with. When we're working on a sport climb and one of us gets up the route first, he returns to the climb as many times as needed until his partner also ascends the route. One route, Captain Crunch, required days of work to climb forty feet of overhanging rock. Being taller than Logan, I was able to get the route first because I could more easily reach a key handhold. Nonetheless, we returned five or six more times, until Logan also got up the route. The day he succeeded, I felt just as excited as when I made it to the top. The joy and meaning of the climb came not just in the individual achievement, but in getting *each other* up the route—and enjoying the minute-by-minute process of being outside in the mountains with a great friend. This is what the Partner's Pact is all about.

Of course, every climber is accompanied by another partner, silent and invisible. It's called luck. Climbing has taught me that there is no pact to be made with this partner—which is why, if you rely too heavily on it, you just might end up dead. And that brings us to our final and perhaps most important lesson in climbing as a classroom.

LESSON 5. DON'T CONFUSE LUCK AND COMPETENCE: HOW TO NOT LET SUCCESS KILL YOU

On a spring day in 1979, I learned a lesson in humility—a lesson whose tuition was nearly my life, and the life of my partner.

In the previous year, I'd been on a roll, having done some difficult climbs and surviving some close calls along the way. On one climb, I'd felt small grains of stone skittering down the rock, then heard the awful rumble of a car-sized block cracking loose and bouncing down the cliff. Somehow, it shattered into pieces, all of which bounced around me without a single hit. On another climb, I'd belayed my partner over the steep overhang looking down the north face of the Third Flatiron in Boulder, Colorado, with my feet dangling out over a 200-foot straight drop to the talus. Reaching the top, my partner looked at the anchor and went ashen. He pointed to what I'd failed to see: that I'd set the anchors behind a giant block that wasn't actually attached to the wall. Had my partner fallen on the overhang, he would have pulled me tight on the anchor and the two of us, detached block and all, would have tumbled in a tangled mass of rope and bodies in a free fall to the ground. We would have been airborne just long enough to think, "We're gonna die." Then on a third climb in Boulder, called Jules Verne, I'd climbed ten feet to the right of where I should have been, and when I realized my mistake, I was well above where the hard climbing should have ended, and thirty feet out from my last protection nut wedged in a crack. I tried a delicate traverse across the wall to get back on route, but my foot popped, and I found myself looking down at a huge arc of rope as I fell sixty feet. Somehow, I sailed right past where the wall jutted out just a bit and came tight on the rope without hitting anything. I came away scared—my partner tells me that I let out a primal yell on the way down—but unscathed. Not so much as a scratch.

Being young and male, it never really occurred to me that I was lucky. I was alive—and got up the climbs—because, in my mind, I was *good*. If other climbers died, I reasoned, they must have lacked some skill I possessed. It couldn't possibly be *luck*.

But on a cliff named Cynical Pinnacle, near Pine, Colorado, I came to see how terribly wrong I was. I would be humbled—luckily, before my hubris killed me.

I had grabbed an inexperienced partner to go with me, a fellow named Dick. I didn't even know his last name. I just recruited him to the adventure from the front of the local climbing store. "Come along," I cajoled, "it will be the adventure of a lifetime!" It didn't matter to me whether Dick had the experience required to get up the route. I felt so fit, and in such control, that all I needed—or so I thought—was a warm body to hold the belay rope. I gave him mechanical ascending devices to clamp on the rope, so that he could climb rope behind me at the end of each pitch.

We reached the ledge before the summit headwall of Cynical Pinnacle late in the afternoon. The air felt full, the way it always does before a big storm in the early spring. Looking out from my perch, I could see the snowcapped peaks of the Colorado Rockies becoming engulfed in a shoal of mist. The rock, which had only hours earlier been warm and friendly to the touch, now felt cold and unfriendly.

"Only fifty feet to go," I said, looking up at the final section of rock. "I think we should go for it."

"I don't know, Jim," said Dick. "I'm tired, and besides, there's a storm moving in. If we reach the top and the lightning starts, we'll be sitting ducks."

He was right. We would be sitting atop a giant lightning rod. But I felt strong, and I thought I could get us up and off quickly enough. I led up the final pitch, moving fast, leaving Dick wide-eyed at the belay ledge.

My euphoria upon reaching the top of the Prayer Book, the hardest route on Cynical Pinnacle, came to an abrupt end, terminated by an unusual popping sound. "Something's wrong," I thought to myself. "Something's terribly wrong." Then I noticed that it was the rope and climbing gear making the sound. I reached up to touch my head, and realized that my hair was standing on end. "Dick! The whole spire's about to be hit by lightning." I looped the rope through the anchor bolts on top, like a pulley system. "Lower me back to you."

Dick, less experienced than me, fumbled with his gear. "Now!" I yelled. "Quick!" He cinched the rope around his waist and hesitantly lowered me back to the ledge just before the lightning blasted all around us. Amazingly, it didn't carry down the rock to us.

I had the metallic taste of fear and adrenaline still in my mouth when Dick asked, "So, how are we going to get down?"

It was a good question. The side we'd come up had no established descent route. (The established route lay on the east side, as a rope descent from the top of the cliff. We were stuck about a hundred feet down from the top, on the west side, and we could not go back to the top because of the lightning.) Worse, the walls dropped off at an overhanging angle, which meant we would be hanging out in space and needed to swing on the ropes to get into the next anchor points. But since we didn't bring any food, water, or extra clothing, we couldn't wait out the storm. Dick only wore shorts, as it had been a warm seventy-five degrees when we began. But now, with the temperature in the fifties and dropping, we were facing a full early spring front. With only a few hours of daylight left, we had to do *something*.

We set up a rappel (a method of descent that involves leaning back on the rope and sliding down using a friction device, just like you see in the movies or the U.S. Army's "Be all you can be" commercials). I went first, kicking the wall with my feet, to ensure that I would be able to swing back into an anchor point. Near the end of the rope, I swung into the wall, slammed in some gear, and tied myself down into a set of anchors.

Dick rappelled down. Because he didn't kick the wall, he just dangled out in space, spinning like a wad of gum on the end of a long hair. Fortunately, I had the end of the rope with me, so I just pulled him into the wall where I had already anchored in, and tied him down.

"Okay, you pull the rope through, and I'll set the anchors for the next rappel," I instructed. We were 300 feet from the ground and had at least two rappels to go. I set to work on the anchors.

"Jim, the rope won't pull."

"What? Maybe you're just pulling the wrong end. Give me the rope."

He did, and I pulled. It didn't budge. I could tell it was really jammed. I started to get a sick feeling in my stomach.

"Did you check to make sure the knot was clear of the crack when you started down?"

"No. Was I supposed to?"

I knew then we were in serious trouble. It was likely that the knot holding the two ropes together had wedged itself in a crack. The harder we pulled on the rope, the more stuck it would get.

I spotted a crack system about twenty feet to our right. "I'm going to tie into the ropes and swing over to that other crack. Maybe that will give us enough angle on the rope to pull the knot free."

I tied in and swung out on the rope, pushing myself with my feet so I would fly over to the other crack. I reached it and clutched the edge, pulling myself onto a little ledge so that I could insert another anchor. I pulled the rope. No luck. "Dick, maybe I can climb up this crack a ways and free the rope from higher up. I'm going to give that a try."

"Before you do, could you swing your shirt over to me? I'm really starting to get cold, and my hands aren't working so well." I took off my long-sleeved rugby shirt and tied it into the ends of the rope. Dick leaned out on the anchors, to which he remained directly tied.

"Okay, Dick, here it comes." I flung the rope in his direction and it sailed out across the wall.

He missed it.

It swung back in my direction, and I leaned way out in an attempt to grab it. It was as if the whole thing happened in slow motion—frame by stomach-sickening frame—as the rope swung just short of my grasping fingers. Stunned, I just stared in disbelief as it came to rest midway between us. There we were, 300 feet above the surface of the earth. And now we didn't even have a rope.

For the first time, a terrifying thought crossed my mind: that I'd been lucky all along, and that just when I needed it most, my luck had somehow run out.

I had three options. First, I could try to climb up to the stuck knot. This option seemed highly improbable, given the steepness of the rock above. Second, we could hope that someone would notice that we'd failed to return home when expected, and wait for a rescue. That option, I concluded, meant certain death—falling temperatures, increasing rain, and exhaustion added up to hypothermia. I concluded that the best option lay in climbing down to a lower-angle crack system below me, and then to the ground. From there—presuming I didn't fall off and kill myself—I could find a phone, call one of my climbing buddies, and then climb back up to Dick and get him off the cliff.

"Are you sure that's what you should do?" asked Dick. "What if you fall?"

"I think it's our best option. We've got to do *something*, or we're going to die up here."

I promised Dick that no matter what, I would come back for him that day. Then I took a deep breath, unclipped from the anchors, and began the exposed down climb. The rock, slick with rain, had one big advantage: It had two-inch-wide cracks, just the right size to wedge my hands in and lock them tight against the sides, using my bone structure. I made sure each hand-jam was so solid that if my feet slipped, the hand would just torque even tighter into the crack, like a human camming device. After an hour or so of deliberate moves, one after another, inching down the crack, I finally stepped onto the ground.

I hadn't eaten for fifteen hours, my throat felt parched from lack of water, and my muscles were completely spent. The wall loomed above—tall, dark, and gray. And it still had my partner in its clutches. We only had a couple hours of light left.

Then I heard a strange sound. *Waka-waka-waka-waka.* I saw a helicopter coming our way. Then I looked down on to the road and saw a caravan of some twenty vehicles—jeeps, cars, vans, fire engines, and trailers. It suddenly dawned on me that a woman who'd been hiking in the area and seen our plight must have called for a rescue. "Now we're in real trouble," I thought.

Not that I doubted their good intentions. But sheriffs and firefighters generally do not know how to do severe rock rescues. I ran down the hill, looking for the person in charge.

"That's him," somebody said, pointing to a large, potbellied figure.

I ran over to him, gesticulating wildly and talking about how we had to get back up there soon, before dark—and hypothermia—set in.

"Just calm down, son. We've got everything under control."

"Look, I just need a person who can belay, a rope, and some gear. I can get to him myself."

"No, this is very serious business," he said.

"I know it's serious. If we don't act now, it's going to get a lot more serious. I'll just take a rope and go up there myself, if you won't help."

"Son! If you don't calm down, I'll put you under arrest for your own protection."

I felt the anger well up inside. Not so much at the sheriff, but at myself. It wasn't his fault we were in the mess. It was mine. And mine alone.

"Okay," I relented. "What are our options?"

"Can we get to him by horseback?" the sheriff asked.

"Not unless the horse can climb overhanging 5.10 cracks." He looked confused, revealing his lack of comprehension of the situation. He must have thought we were two lost hikers, or something. I asked to use the radio to talk to the helicopter pilot. I directed the pilot to train a spotlight on the lone figure up on the wall. Dick looked like someone who'd ventured out onto the side of a space shuttle and then had the scaffolding pulled away, leaving him perched precariously on the side.

"Roger. We have him in our sights," radioed the pilot.

There was a long pause, then: "Jesus H. Christ! How in the hell did he get up there?"

I think the sheriff then realized that horses would not work.

After wrangling over a range of options, including dropping me out of the helicopter on top of the cliff with a set of ropes, we concluded that the best option was the simplest. Get me a climbing partner and rope, and we'd climb straight up to Dick and get him off. A man on the rescue team had climbing experience and volunteered to belay me up the cliff in our attempt to reach Dick. Darkness had fallen and the sheriff had directed all the searchlights onto the spire. The Pinnacle, shrouded in mist, lit up with an eerie green tint on a backdrop of pitch black.

We found a crack system that headed in Dick's direction, and after an hour of negotiating our way up in the jagged shadows, we finally reached him.

"Don't worry, Dick. We've got you now." He didn't respond, other than to slowly nod his head. His skin felt cold—very cold—to the touch. We rigged a descent line, and with the help of the rescue part-ner, we lowered Dick to the ground. At around 3 A.M. the ordeal finally came to an end, and Dick received emergency treatment. As his body core temperature rose, I knew he would live, and come back to climb another day.

And so would I, but more sobered and with a different perspective. I'd learned perhaps the most important lesson in climbing as a class-room: When you operate with the arrogance of self-attribution—"I'm successful because, well, I'm me, and I'm really good"—that's when you run the biggest risks of all. Sustained results (and in climbing, you can only attain sustained results if you stay alive) require not just courage and will, but also a rigorous form of self-honesty called hu-mility.

Twenty years after Cynical Pinnacle, I found myself trying to under-stand the inner workings of the few executives who had managed to take good companies and turn them into great companies, in contrast with executives who had failed to lead their companies to a sustained leap from good to great. My research team and I noticed a fascinating pattern that we came to call "the Window and the Mirror." When con-fronted with the undeniable fact of their extraordinary success, the good-to-great CEOs had a great propensity to point out the window to factors other than themselves for that success, being very careful to give credit to other people and to good luck. One good-to-great CEO said that about 80 percent of the success of the company during his tenure could be attributed to the wind at their backs. I pointed out that the less-successful comparison company had the same wind and bigger sails, to which he responded: "Hmmm, then we must have been *really* lucky." But when asked about setbacks and failures along the way, the good-to-great CEOs never pointed out the window; they would stand in front of the mirror and say, "I am responsible." In contrast, we no-ticed that executives in the comparison companies would point out the window to account for failures and setbacks: unfair competition, the economy, the markets, and so forth. But when things went well, they would look in the mirror and attribute much of the success to their own personal greatness.

I look back on the late 1990s, when an entire generation of businesspeople benefited from one of the most extraordinary bull markets in history. CEOs saw the stock of their companies rise at double-digit rates, and paid themselves handsomely with stock options—as if they had somehow caused the entire upward swing. Young dot-com entrepreneurs thought of themselves as invincible; they came to believe they could defy the laws of gravity and ignore fundamentals like creating sustainable profitability. Thousands of investors fell into the trap of equating the rise in their 401ks with their investment savvy, and hundreds of venture capitalists came to see themselves as smarter than Warren Buffett. Then the market crashed, and CEO stature fell right along with it. Dot-coms imploded. And investors watched their retirement accounts decline back to more realistic levels. En masse, we'd made the mistake of confusing luck with competence.

I had a professor in graduate school named Robert Burgelman who pounded into me the idea that the single most dangerous perspective in business and life is not outright failure, but to be successful without being absolutely clear about why you were successful in the first place. Success, he pointed out, clouds judgment. Better to operate with brutal self-honesty about the role of factors other than yourself. As I look at the best executives from my research, they used this idea not as a form of weakness, but as a form of self-discipline: "Perhaps we were just lucky, so we'd better be just that much more disciplined to make ourselves just that much stronger, so that we'll still be strong if our luck ever runs out . . ."

Of course, sustained excellence isn't just about humility; it is also about will. The will to go to fallure. The will to climb in the future, today. The will to separate probability from consequence, and to act accordingly. The will to pick the right partners, and to come through for them. And at times, perhaps even the will to go for it when the odds are low and the consequences severe. But those who climb enough eventually learn that luck is a factor in life, and we cannot control all the outcomes. Those who have a long, sustained career of ascents eventually learn to acknowledge and distrust their luck, constantly honing their competence to deal with the day when their luck runs out.

Nearly a quarter of a century after Cynical Pinnacle, climbing continues to hold a prominent place in my life. Indeed, as I write these words, I am on an airplane, flying back from the East Coast. Upon landing, I plan to amble up the First Flatiron. (Start the day in Manhattan, and end the day on top of the First Flatiron—a nice combination.) And if the weather turns bad or we arrive too late, then I'll work out in my home rock-climbing gym. No matter how you slice it, I am a very lucky guy! Still, as I reflect on Cynical Pinnacle, I'm continually reminded of a line a great poet once wrote: "A man is a fool who counts too much on his luck, particularly when he's had more than his share."

2

Peak Performers:
Leading Teams in High Places

STACY ALLISON

WE WERE SO CLOSE. FROM WHERE WE SAT, CURLED IN THE dim light of our snow cave, the top of the world was only 3,500 feet away—less than two days climbing on the jagged North Face of Mount Everest.

But we weren't climbing. We were hiding. It was late in the season, and the winter winds had descended—no one knew for how long. Sitting in my sleeping bag, balancing a cup of hot coffee in my lap, I could overlook the heart-squeezing pressure of life at 25,500 feet. In the dim light of the cave, I could imagine the raging blizzard outside vanishing. I could even almost convince myself that we wouldn't have to turn around when morning came. But doing so wasn't easy.

I'd spent years dreaming of leaving my footprint on the crown of the earth, and now it was all on the line—dreams, months and months of planning, hundreds of thousands of dollars, commitment from people some of us had never even met, seven weeks of climbing, and our reputations as well. No matter what anyone says, it comes down to black or white: The expedition either touches the summit or comes home ready to explain what went wrong. We had to get to the top. We had too much invested not to.

In my heart of hearts, though, I knew even as I told myself otherwise that 25,500 feet was as close as we were going to get. We had begun this climb as a team of friends, five women and ten men, with no Sherpas to assist us. It didn't matter to us who led, who followed.

47

That kind of hierarchy was for corporate life, not mountain climbing. We were bound by higher goals: a common commitment to place the first American woman on the peak of the world. But it was leadership, finally, that failed us—the leaders we had and the ones we never bothered to make.

A TEAM WITHOUT A LEADER

Scott Fischer had procured the permit to climb Everest. Co-owner of the guide service Mountain Madness, Scott managed to get permission from the Chinese government to scale the fabled mountain's Direct North Face, one of the most difficult routes, in 1987.

Having obtained the permit, Scott assumed the role of expedition leader. He chose his team carefully, for our diverse abilities in both planning and staging the climb. Scott and his business partner, Wes Krauss, were skilled guides, as were Evelyn Lees, Rick Wyatt, Melly Rueling, and Michael Graber. Plugged in through her health food business, Liz Nichol became food director. Bond trader Q Belk and Ben Toland, the marketing director for outdoor gear manufacturer Sierra Designs, became our marketing directors. I was equipment director, qualified by virtue of running my own construction business. Orthopedic hand surgeon Dave Black agreed to take on the medical support, and Mimi Stone, just out of medical school, would serve as our backup. No expedition would be complete without its very own attorney, and we had three: Bob McConnell, Peter Goldman, and George Schunk. For extra cohesion, we were all Scott's friends.

While preparing for the climb back in Seattle, we had decided the best angle for obtaining sponsorship was the possibility of getting the first American woman to the top. Six women from other countries had made it to the summit of Everest, but none from the United States. This would be something corporations and the American public could wrap their arms around. We worked well together to raise our $250,000 budget and procure 30,000 pounds of gear and food. Preparations went smoothly.

Stacy Allison and Q Belk hole up in a snow cave at
25,500 feet on the North Face of Mount Everest

During these early, nonthreatening stages of the expedition, Scott was clearly the leader and manifestly successful at the role. He channeled our competitive natures and kept us on task. Each of us had a specific role and area of responsibility. We established detailed systems and set up open lines of communication, and Scott held everyone accountable. He was so organized that he even recruited a consultant to facilitate our team meetings, making sure we kept to our agenda and timeline.

At our last team meeting before leaving the United States, though, Scott set out to change the rules of engagement. "When we get to the mountain," he announced, "I want to stop being expedition leader. I'll still be the designated leader for official purposes on our way to base camp, but in decisions on the mountain, I wield no more authority than anyone else. We're all experienced climbers; no one needs to be led."

On one level, he was right. Most of us had known one another for years; we'd climbed together many times. If we couldn't run a well-organized, leaderless expedition, who could? That question would come back to haunt us.

During the first weeks of an expedition-style climb, the goal is to establish a route and set up intermediate camps. As we make our way up the mountain, we select the specific route and then secure safety ropes into the snow and ice with three-foot-long aluminum stakes and one-foot-long ice screws. Once the ropes are in place, we can attach ourselves onto the ropes with an ascender, a device that allows us to move up and down quickly and safely.

Our first camp was Base Camp. From Tibet, trucks drove to this initial drop-off point at 17,000 feet. We then moved most of our gear closer to our route, the North Face, and established Advanced Base Camp. Advanced Base Camp then functioned as our base of operations. From there we would establish Camps One, Two, Three, and Four perched on the side of the mountain approximately 2,000 vertical feet apart. These camps served as intermediate stops for rest and acclimatization purposes. Once a camp was established, we could begin ferrying loads of food, fuel, and equipment to the next camp. It was all part of building the pyramid of support that we would use when we finally climbed to the top.

Most expeditions have specific load agendas; the expedition leader and Base Camp manager work together to ensure that the appropriate gear gets up the mountain at the appropriate time. But we didn't have anything so formal. It was understood that carrying loads of fuel and equipment up the mountain was to be done on an ad hoc basis. In the morning, anyone who felt like climbing would eat an early breakfast and start up the mountain. Load weight and content varied according to the climber's opinion and mood. We had all climbed on big mountains before, so a "go-with-the-flow" attitude prevailed. Everyone had the same ultimate goal; we all knew what had to be done.

In that spirit, while the rest of us were ferrying loads to Advanced Base Camp, Scott and Wes climbed up to Camp One and didn't return. Knowing that lines hadn't yet been fixed to Camp Two, they headed off higher up the mountain, hammering in ice pickets to anchor about 800 feet of line onto the lower reaches of the North Face.

Down below, we weren't sure what had happened to Scott and Wes. Evelyn Lees, an experienced climbing guide with Exum Mountain Guides in Grand Teton National Park, suggested sending someone up. We were seriously thinking of doing that when our no-longer-leading leader and his partner radioed down from Camp One, just as the afternoon faded to twilight.

"We're going to spend the night up here," Scott announced.

Most expedition climbs move in small increments, like a caterpillar. You push ahead inch by inch, building a solid base of stocked camps and fixed lines as you go. Not us. Not anymore. We all knew how it should be done, yet we weren't doing it. Our freestyle plan was showing its flaws.

It was only our first week on the mountain, and already we seemed to be falling apart. Our co-organizers were gliding up the mountain so fast the rest of us had to hustle just to keep them in sight. Doing so was not only frustrating and confusing, but demoralizing; Scott and Wes had set an example of pursuing individual goals at the expense of the team. Soon, other team members were making choices that didn't serve the expedition.

Individuality became the order of the day, and as that happened, group comity vanished. I was resting at Advance Base Camp one day when Bob McConnell, our Base Camp manager, approached me in the dining tent and asked if I would carry a load of food up to Camp One.

"No," I answered, without even looking up. Bob knew where the bad blood was coming from.

A week earlier, I'd come down to Camp One expecting to find a fresh supply of food and equipment ready to go up the mountain, but instead I found an empty supply tent. Furious, I called down to Bob on the walkie-talkie.

"Where's the gear?" I shouted.

"What gear?" Bob's puzzled voice crackled over the radio.

"The stuff you're supposed to have carried up here, so we can carry it up the mountain."

"What do you need right now?" Bob asked patiently.

"We need stuff, Bob. Stuff to carry."

"Well, what exactly? Rope? Fuel? Food? We've got it all down here. Just let me know what you need."

"All that stuff!" I shouted. "We're ready to make carries, but we need stuff to carry up the mountain!"

However good individual team members are at what they do, they must have clear expectations about their interdependent roles. I couldn't do my job of ferrying supplies because Bob didn't know what he had to do to make them available. Time was wasted; energy was not utilized efficiently; efforts were duplicated. No one knew the plan for a very simple reason: We didn't have one. Without clear roles and expectations, the work went undone, and jobs that should have been binding us into a single working unit drove us apart instead.

In declaring himself a nonleader, Scott had created a leadership vacuum. Without a strong hand to direct our team, we lost confidence, trust, and respect in each other. We felt little obligation to contribute and help one another. The easiest thing was to concentrate on one's own advancement and to act out of self-interest, not in pursuit of a common agenda. The idealism of Seattle had fallen apart in the crucible of the Himalayas, and mighty Everest had yet to even test us.

As the days turned into weeks, tensions continued to rise. Each day as I climbed with different people, I was measuring my teammates' speed and skill, just as they were measuring mine. Once on the mountain, previous reputation meant nothing. We were all keeping a close watch on how everyone worked on *this* climb, under *these* circumstances, and our assessments were unforgiving. Any perceived weaknesses brought open scorn. Stay up, or stay in camp: That was our new motto.

Rick Wyatt, an avalanche forecaster for the Utah Department of Transportation, was an experienced climbing guide and exceptionally strong climber, but as we pushed higher up the North Face, diarrhea sapped his strength. Climbing one morning between Camps One and Two, Rick could manage only a slow pace. At one point, it took him more than a half hour to creep inch by inch up a forty-foot section of brittle rock and ice. As we waited, swinging our arms and legs to try to keep the blood flowing in the frigid predawn of morning, Mimi, a recent University of Washington Medical School graduate, was beside herself.

"What is his problem?" She shot a dark look at Rick. "I'm freezing. If he can't hack it up here, he oughta stay down below."

Our first serious conflict came before Camp Two had officially been established. The route to the camp was finished, and there was even a temporary supply tent, but we still hadn't dug the snow cave that would be the main residence. Our reasoning was that it would best to stock the camp before sleeping there. That way, we could build up our supplies from below without depleting food and fuel until it was necessary.

We all stuck to the arrangement for a week or so, until Michael and Mimi made a run to the second camp. Storm clouds had been brewing on the horizon since mid-morning, and when they called down to Advanced Base Camp at noon, Scott had specific instructions: "Get down before the storm hits."

"No," Michael replied. "We want to acclimate up here for the night."

Scott stared at his walkie-talkie for a moment. "That's not exactly the plan," he said, frustration growing in his voice. "And you'll be up there a hell of a lot longer then a night once the storm blows in."

"That's okay," Michael's voice crackled. "We'll take the chance."

In the end, Michael and Mimi did as they pleased, and so did the storm. Trapped by it, they stayed up on the ridge for days, consuming the food and fuel that had been meant to keep all of us going while we fixed the route higher on the mountain.

It wasn't the last such incident. Without leadership, we lacked unity of purpose; and without that, the results were predictable: un-

Stacy Allison carries a load on the North Face of Mount Everest

clear priorities, misdirected efforts, ineffective utilization of resources, and turf wars.

Was the entire team going to dissolve into a loose federation of free-lancers? Would Scott ever assume responsibility and lead? If he didn't create some sense of team responsibility, who would? How could we count on one another to get anyone to the top? These are not questions you want to be asking as you set out to ascend the highest mountain in the world.

WHO NEEDS A LEADER?

It seems obvious: Every team needs a leader. Yet, if it is so obvious, why does poor leadership continue to plague organizations worldwide, sapping employee motivation and destabilizing organizations? Our Everest expedition illuminated some of the answers.

During the preparation stage, Scott had done a tremendous job of recruiting people to support his vision of climbing Everest. He chose well—everyone was motivated to work together—but because this early stage was so easy, it became equally easy to convince ourselves that Scott's "no leader" plan would work, too. We were still in Seattle, after all. What was at risk?

"What about load-ferrying logistics? Who's going to coordinate that?" Bob McConnell asked when we were first debating mountain life without an official leader.

"We'll figure out what we need as we progress up the mountain," said Scott.

"What about climbing teams and summit teams?" asked Q Belk.

"Once we start climbing, the mountain will sort it all out," Scott replied.

And so it went. Because we cooperated so successfully when we weren't under duress, we assumed we could make decisions by consensus and lead ourselves up the mountain once the pressure was on. But it didn't work. As conflicts arose and as the stakes mounted, individual glory took priority over team success. We had trapped ourselves in the illusion that we didn't need a leader, and by the time we knew we did, reality was closing in on us.

The truth is, not everyone makes a great leader. Some people just don't have the capacity to lead; others choose not to. Scott had demonstrated the capacity but wasn't willing to assume the mantle full-time. He wanted to be climbing, which is what he loved; and he wanted to reach the top himself, which is why he organized the climb. That's all understandable, but it's not how a leader needs to think.

When you're in charge, your first priority should be to keep the team safe and move it forward. Personal agendas have to go on the back shelf. In order to function effectively as our leader, Scott needed to pay less attention to the work of climbing himself and more to the work of leading and directing from Base Camp. To do that, he would have had to compromise his chances of reaching the top himself, and that he simply was not willing to do.

Why did it take us so long to realize the fix we were in? In part because of the illusion we had all bought into, but in part also because

Scott did intermittently assert his authority. As he kept stepping into and out of his leadership role, he not only created confusion at that moment but fostered the future assumption that he would take charge when the chips were down.

Just as important, why did no one step forward to assume the leader's role once we could no longer blind ourselves to the fact that Scott wasn't going to fill it? We had plenty of ability and experience. Ben Toland and Q Belk were both Stanford M.B.A.'s, and Liz Nichol and I ran our own businesses. Scott, Wes, Rick, and Evelyn were experienced climbing guides. George Schunk, Bob McConnell, and Peter Goldman were practicing attorneys. We never would have allowed our professional lives to get so far off the track, but this was different.

Maybe we were too close, in too intense an environment, to really see what was happening. Maybe our individual desire to get to the top clouded our judgment of what we needed to get there. Or maybe the primary reason no one stepped forward is that no one felt that they would be accepted. Most team members had strong personal agendas, and granting authority to a leader would probably have threatened those agendas. In retrospect, individual autonomy was a core value of the team, and empowering a leader meant sacrificing some of that autonomy. Maybe the disintegration of the team had been predetermined by the selection of its independent members.

Overhanging everything else was the fact that Scott had known nearly all of us before the expedition, as climbing colleagues and friends. Not inclined by nature to make tough decisions concerning personnel, he was further incapacitated by his unwillingness to compromise long-time relationships.

THE ENEMY IS US

When you're climbing in the Himalayas, there is always a sense of urgency. Often, it's weather that determines whether you'll succeed or fail. At the top of the world, expeditions have only a small window of opportunity to set the route, acclimate, and summit before the jet stream descends and the winter winds pick up or the monsoons move in.

A leader's job in such an extreme setting is to balance drive with caution, but it's every climber's responsibility to recognize the true limits of survival—to know just how far you can push yourself before inviting disaster. By the beginning of our seventh week on Mount Everest, we were in danger of failing on both counts.

We had already spent a week at 25,500 feet, stranded in two snow caves. Q Belk looked like a sitting skeleton. His once-full cheeks were sunken, the taut skin stretched tight against bone. Scott had a hacking, high-altitude cough. Like everyone else, I had been sitting for so long that I couldn't find a comfortable spot anymore; every position, every move ached.

After another long day and one more freezing, endless night in the snow cave, we crawled outside only to find that the winds above us were blowing even harder. We crawled back inside the cave and sat again in silence, absorbed by our own thoughts. We had worked so long and so hard, had dreamed of Everest for so many years, and now the weather wasn't cooperating. How long could we wait? Should we go up or down? Pursue our goal regardless of the consequences or retreat altogether? No one wanted to be the first to say, "Let's go down. We'll get another shot. We'll do it again." The truth was that we might not. So we just sat there. The silence was as cold and oppressive as the weather outside.

Finally Q spoke: "If I don't go down now, I don't think I'm going to make it off this mountain."

In fact, he was voicing what we all knew—not just about himself but about the rest of us, too. We couldn't survive much longer at this altitude, and the probability of the winds letting up was slim. We had to go down. Even though I didn't have the courage to say it, when someone else did, I welcomed the decision to turn around.

Q's public admission of defeat was like the breaking of a long fever. We could let it go now, leave without summiting, admit the impossibility of our situation. Not that we didn't have hard work in front of us. Coming down from over 25,000 feet is no walk in the park, especially in our weakened conditions. But at least we would be walking toward safety, not toward greater peril. Yet even as we began packing, I think a part of each of us was in denial. It takes so much strength and courage to climb a mountain like Everest. Summoning the strength, courage, and wisdom to do the opposite, to turn around, to quit the mountain, is oftentimes harder still.

Forty-five days after we had started climbing, we finally gave it up. We had lost too much time, squandered too much of our energy and resources. The winter weather ultimately foiled us, but the weather wasn't the problem. As Pogo once so memorably said, "We have met the enemy, and he is us."

Major companies have also faced much the same consequences when dealing with the absence of a strong leadership team at the top, predominant self-interests, and lost confidence, trust, and respect. Consider what followed when Enron vice president Sherron Watkins visited Chief Executive Kenneth Lay in his Houston headquarters on August 22, 2001, and warned him that the company could "implode in a wave of accounting scandals." At that moment, Lay might have taken actions to prevent the implosion. But that would have required a top team that recognized the gravity of the moment, and Lay barely had a leadership team at all. Chief Executive Officer Jeffrey Skilling had quit the company a week before. Chief Financial Officer Andrew S. Fastow had devised the improper accounting schemes. Outside auditor Arthur Andersen had been approving the scheme's special features. The audit committee of the governing board had been inattentive. And Lay himself remained unmoved by the implications of Watkins's warning. Three months later Enron went bankrupt, the nation's largest corporate failure at the time.

After my unsuccessful experience on the North Face of Mount Everest, I spent a lot of time reflecting on what went wrong. Obviously, we needed a full-time leader with a greater sense of investment in the group's mission. But our failure was more complicated than Scott Fischer's shortcomings. The rest of us had had a hand in it, too.

As so often happens with weak leadership, followers tend to mirror the boss's example. One of my clients, a university teaching hospital, has been struggling to build viable primary care practices. Although the hierarchy is clearly defined, the hospital leadership is weak and divided on the importance of primary care medicine. Without a strong voice at the top, strategy has floundered. Middle managers don't know where to turn for direction. In the resulting leadership vacuum, doctors and academic department heads tend to pursue their own agendas in accordance with their individual visions.

Just as happened with us on the mountain, the organization has degenerated into turf wars over limited resources. The wars have led to multiple lost opportunities, ineffective implementation, loss of operational efficiency, poor staff morale, high turnover, and ultimately—and worst of all—poor patient care.

"The departments don't share information with each other," one department chair told me. "We're too concerned other departments will try to take over or use the information for their own good. Our culture has developed such that people just do the minimum to support the organization, choosing to focus on their own advancement. There's no forward momentum. We're wasting time, energy, and resources because no one is taking charge."

Amen, I felt like saying. I've been there, more than four miles above sea level, with a hurricane howling outside the ice cave.

BACK ON THE MOUNTAIN AGAIN

As glad as I had been to start down Everest, I desperately wanted to go back up again. The mountain still hadn't been climbed by an American woman. Why shouldn't that woman be me? The problem was that back in the late 1980s, getting on an Everest expedition wasn't easy. A year after quitting the mountain, I sent a letter and my résumé to Jim

Frush, the leader of the 1988 American Everest Expedition, asking for a slot on his team the following year. Three months before leaving, Jim invited me to join them. This time we would climb the South Col route from Nepal—the same route Sir Edmund Hillary and Tenzing Norgay took in 1953 when they became the first known humans to stand on top of Everest.

The South Col route is the easiest route up Everest but far from risk free. The most hazardous section looms right above Base Camp: the Khumbu Icefall, 2,000 vertical feet of ice. Raked with huge ice towers called seracs and riddled with deep crevasses, the icefall tumbles slowly down the thin throat between Everest's West Shoulder and Nuptse, the mountain immediately to the east. Like frozen river rapids, the icefall changes constantly, moving downhill at a rate of about three to four feet a day. In some places it morphs into huge towers; in others, it splits into gaping chasms. As the ice moves and breaks apart, the icefall shifts. Crevasses can widen or close by several feet in the space of a few days; towers the size of buildings can collapse without warning.

As if the tumbling ice towers and yawning, frequently hidden crevasses aren't challenges enough, sporadic avalanches plunge into the narrow funnel from the cliffs on Everest's West Shoulder.

Preparing a path through the icefall can take up to two weeks, an eternity spent zigzagging around impassable towers and seeking out natural ice bridges to cross the crevasses. What can't be avoided must be bridged, and so our expedition brought along seventy-five aluminum ladders from the United States, each of which had to be carried into the icefall and then hoisted over or across obstacles. Each ladder could span an eight-foot divide. Anything wider and we had to splice the ladders together, connecting the spans with rope and custom-built metal clamps.

Each day we spent in the icefall amounted to a game of Russian roulette. We would rise at 2 A.M., walk across the glacier, meet at our equipment depot, strap on our crampons, clip onto the rope, and follow the rope along its tangled path, moving up as quickly as possible.

Meanwhile, the icefall would be plotting its own strategy, following its own idiosyncratic logic.

The rules were self-evident: Be safe. Don't make any impulsive judgments. Always do the right thing. And yet the whole time we all knew that no matter where we were inside the icefall, we would be a thousand times safer if we were almost anywhere else outside it. Needless to say, this created a very real sense of urgency. The sooner we set the route through to the top, the better.

Although we couldn't eliminate the risks in the icefall, we were able to reduce them by establishing a strategy and sticking with it. One such strategy was to break our team into three smaller climbing groups that took turns fixing the route in the icefall. This decreased the number of people exposed in the icefall at any given time. We also climbed only at night, while the ice was still frozen. Once the sun climbed higher into the clear skies and warmed up the snow and ice on the surrounding peaks, we knew that our day's work was finished. We hurried back down to Base Camp before the melting snow could trigger an avalanche.

We also kept our own antennae on full alert. Out on the icefall, I felt like a deer during hunting season: constantly skittish, aware, ears open, eyes wide, toes feeling for the slightest vibrations, any rumble in the distance. I tried to make certain I saw everything and ignored nothing.

Each day, the climbers who were heading out in the icefall made decisions and solved problems as a group and tried to be as logical as possible. Which was the bigger threat: avalanches or crevasses? One morning, we took a moment to consider this. We were about a third of the way up the icefall, poking around for a route beneath the West Shoulder of Everest. If we set the path closer to the mountain, we could avoid a long line of crevasses. But being closer to the hill also meant being closer to the avalanches that might come roaring down the 1,500 vertical feet from the overhanging glaciers.

We opted for the shorter route, but after the fifth day of work on the path, coleader Don Goodman returned to Base Camp unconvinced and worried.

"I think it's too close to the West Shoulder," Don told us. "I think we need to move it further into the middle of the icefall."

So far, we had decided almost everything by mutual agreement. Now Don was asking the group to reconsider its decision. I can't be certain how the group I had been climbing with a year earlier would have reacted, but I think I know. By this point in that earlier expedition, common purpose had evaporated. Even our putative leader was operating more as a solo practitioner than as a managing partner.

Jim Frush had interpreted his leadership role far differently. He and Don established open communication and encouraged questioning, and that's the model we turned to now. Even though Don was the only person who wanted to move the route, we had a team meeting and discussed it for hours.

"Changing routes would mean two lost days of work," I said.

"It would set us back at least a week, time I don't think we can afford to lose," Jim Frush added. "And I don't want any of us to risk working in the icefall any more than we have to."

So much time, work, and effort had gone into setting our route, anchoring our safety ropes, and laying the ladders over the crevasses that no one wanted to back up, take our route apart, and start over.

Finally, Don assented. "Okay, I still don't feel good about it, but I'll go along with the group's decision to leave it where it is."

Climbing is not just physically exhausting. The stress of being in a life-threatening situation day after day and the pressure of making decisions like the one we had just made about our route wears you out emotionally, too. To combat this, we built rest periods into our schedule.

On one such rest day at Base Camp, while the sun was still hidden behind the mountains, I was wide awake and sipping a cup of hot tea, cozy and relaxed in my sleeping bag in my tent. Then I heard the explosion. *Kaboom.*

I had gotten so used to the sound of avalanches on the surrounding mountains—the crack of release, the roaring rumble as the snow and ice spills down the slope—that they had become little more than background music, but this one registered deep in my sternum. I vaulted

An avalanche hits the Khumbu Icefall on Mount Everest

out of my sleeping bag, pulled on my jacket, and scrambled out of the tent, just in time to see a huge white cloud billowing from the West Shoulder. The biggest avalanche I had ever seen was sliding down toward the icefall where eight of our team members had been working since well before morning, and there was nothing I or anyone else at Base Camp could do for them. We watched the avalanche together, faces slack with helplessness.

Up on the icefall, the cold wind that preceded the avalanche tore Don Goodman's hand and those of his Sherpa, Kami, off the fixed lines. The first wave of ice came in a cloud, a hail of sharp fragments that sliced skin like razor wire. The next wave of debris consumed them both, pitching Don and Kami backward with enough force to tear the fixed line away from its three-foot pickets. They were somersaulting, pitched like rag dolls down a thirty-foot ice cliff.

At our end, we kept trying to radio up to the icefall, but the silence was deafening. An eternity—ten minutes that seemed like two hours—passed before we finally got through.

It was Don: "Everyone's alive." Something in his voice, though—an uncertainty, a catch—told us everything wasn't right.

"Yeah," he said when we asked. "Looks like maybe we're gonna need some help getting down."

We were lucky this time. Don and Kami were banged and bruised and Don had broken a finger, but everyone was alive. A rescue team immediately raced to the icefall to assist our teammates in getting down.

RALLYING AROUND SOLUTIONS

As impressed as I was by Don and Kami's ability to survive the avalanche, I was more impressed by how Don handled the aftermath. As soon as his finger and cuts were bandaged and he was rested, he began to strategize on where we were going to move the route. Don could have chosen to focus on the problem and blame the fall and his injuries on the decision made by the rest of the team. Instead, he accepted responsibility for his part and focused on finding solutions that would move all of us forward.

Blame inevitably has a negative emotional impact. The team was painfully aware of what we had done wrong. We had listened to Don's advice but decided against it in favor of preserving a route that could have been the death of him and Kami. Telling us what we already knew might have served as a release for Don, but it would have left the rest of us feeling attacked and defensive.

Moving beyond the problem as rapidly as Don did not only got us past our own guilt; it demonstrated respect for the team as a whole. By continuing to keep us in the planning loop even after we had erred so badly, Don created an environment of respect and trust. What could have been a bitterly divisive moment became instead a chance to bring the team together around the solution. And without the solution, we were never going to get to the top.

I've had the chance since to apply Don's example in my construction business. John, my lead carpenter, had miscalculated the angle for the cut on an entire section of roof rafters. The next morning, as I examined the previous day's work, I could see that something wasn't right. I must have had a puzzled look on my face as I stared up at the roof, because my crew came out of the house to have a look for themselves. Immediately, everyone saw what I'd been staring at. Someone had made a big mistake.

No one said anything, but I could feel the tension mounting, so I finally remarked, in a light tone, "That's one way to build a roof." The resulting laughter broke the tension, so I followed by asking, "Does anyone have any idea how we should fix this?" We brainstormed ideas for about twenty minutes and finally decided to hang the expense and tear it off. Everyone pitched in and worked harder than ever. Later that afternoon, John approached me to say he was sorry and thanked me for not embarrassing him.

I appreciated the gesture, but I knew that I owed much of my response to Don Goodman. He had shown me on Everest to lead by example and create an environment that motivates—that shows people how to regroup, refocus, and move forward. And move forward we did.

Much the same can be seen at large companies such as IBM, where chief executive Louis Gerstner rallied his demoralized troops in the early 1990s to focus on where computer technologies were moving, rather than hand-wringing about how sales of mainframe computers, IBM's bread and butter, were declining. Similarly, Microsoft's Bill Gates mobilized his software forces in the late 1990s to catch up with the Internet and not worry about their past mistakes in letting other companies momentarily take the lead.

Thanks to the strong leadership provided by Don and Jim Frush, the South Col route proved easier than expected once we had cleared the icefall. Our team of three women and ten men, with Sherpa support, would ultimately spend a month and a half on the mountain, with three Americans and four Sherpas reaching the summit. On September 29, 1988, after twenty-nine days of climbing, I became the first American woman to summit Everest.

K2: THE TRANSITION TO LEADING

In 1993, five years after I first stood at the top of the world, I organized and led the American/Canadian K2 Expedition, a team of six men and myself bound for the Abruzzi Ridge in Pakistan. K2 is the world's second-highest mountain, but its weather patterns and technical challenges make it one of the most dangerous climbs in existence. What had I learned from my two previous experiences on Everest about leading such an assault? Plenty, as it turned out.

From the 1987 Everest expedition, I knew that a leader must set strong expectations from the beginning and remain consistent throughout, both to reduce confusion among team members and to promote commitment.

I had that premise hammered home in the early days of my construction business. One day I would be the dictator, barking out tasks and raving about mistakes; the next day, the empowerer, getting input from my employees on how we should proceed during the day. So I might have remained until one of my wisest workers took me aside for a little leading-upward session.

"Stacy," he said as kindly as he could, "you're a problem. We don't know what you want from us. You change like the weather. We all feel like we're walking on eggshells, and we're ready to walk unless you get it together!" It was like being smacked in the head with a two-by-four, but far more useful.

Chastened by both experiences, I built consensus on K2 when it was appropriate for the situation. When necessary, though, I made the decisions myself. I promised everyone before we left the States that I would let them get their say in decisions. But I promised them, too, that the buck would stop with me, and I kept my promises from day one. We had no sooner arrived at our K2 Base Camp than my teammates began talking about carrying equipment to Camp One the following day. When I got wind of their conversation, I immediately intervened.

"No," I told them. "Our number one objective is safety. For health reasons, we're staying at Base Camp for at least one day of rest and acclimatization before we begin ferrying loads up higher."

It was a small moment, but it set the leadership expectations for the climb, and it reinforced everything I had said earlier. I said no and gave my reasons, and we all remained at camp without grumbling.

PINK FLAMINGOS

I had also learned from my two Everest expeditions that a team needs binding rituals. One of the problems on my first Everest climb was that we had no event to bring us together after our departure from the United States. We arrived at Base Camp in scattershot fashion. Two of our party were trailing behind by two days. Two more, including our leader, had flown off to China to handle bureaucratic details. The work being done was all necessary, but it was also necessary to weld a group of individuals into a collaborative whole before we set out, and that never happened. Even when Liz Nichol and I proposed a short forty-five-minute walk down the glacier to the Rongbuk Monastery for a blessing ceremony, something to help refocus us, no one else seemed interested and we went by ourselves.

Jim Frush made sure that wasn't the case on my second Everest expedition, and so did our Sherpas. Before embarking on most climbs from Nepal, Sherpas customarily have a Puja, a Buddhist blessing ceremony, to ask the gods for guidance and a safe return. Our Sherpas invited us to join them.

Twelve Sherpas spent an afternoon building a six-foot stone altar on the edge of our camp and erecting a pole to serve as a central stringing point for 100 meters of prayer flags. The Buddhists believe these simple strips of inscribed cloth disperse their prayers as they flutter in the wind.

The following day, we climbed out of our sleeping bags just as the sun was bathing the tops of the surrounding peaks in pink, had a quick breakfast, and gathered at the altar for the Puja. The Sherpas were already there, chanting and burning juniper branches for good luck. We each made offerings to Buddha, arranging them on the shelf on the altar. The Sherpas laid out sampa, balls of barley flour. The American climbers offered what we had—M&M's, Fig Newtons, and coins.

The chanting went on for close to two hours, rising in wild crescendos, then falling to a murmur. Occasionally, the Sherpas would call us to throw handfuls of rice into the air, as another offering to Buddha. At the end of the ceremony, we were instructed to throw barley flour in the air and smear it on each other's faces and hair. The white streaks represented a long, happy life.

Although we may not have felt the religious significance of the ceremony as much as the Sherpas did, it was a powerful experience. Through it, our Sherpas told us about something deeply important to them. For us, it helped create an atmosphere of understanding and, thus, trust. The ceremony was a small act of celebration—we had spent twenty-one days walking 125 miles just to get there—and it gave us the chance to come together as a team, to renew our spirits and refocus our energy on the challenge ahead.

For good measure, Jim and Don also brought 125 pink plastic garden flamingos to the mountain with us. We used the birds as markers—they dotted the mountainside all the way to Camp Four at 26,200 feet. I even took mine to the summit. Because they were so out of context, these little bright pink statues nestled against the white backdrop of the mountain always brought a smile and a break in the tension.

On K2, we didn't have anything quite so formal, or giddy, but we did observe some simple Western rituals as we were starting out. The night before leaving Islamabad, my teammates and I had a nice dinner together and sat up until the wee hours in one of our hotel rooms sipping Scotch and talking. When we arrived at Base Camp, I asked our cook, Ghulam Mohammad, to prepare a special meal to celebrate our arrival. It doesn't matter what it is that you do, but you need something to bring the team together—something that says we're special, we value each other, and we're in this together.

Stacy Allison's team approaches the Abruzzi Ridge on K2

In my business, before we begin work on a new renovation project, my team and I always walk through the home and look at the magnitude of the project. We visualize and talk about the possibilities—what the home will look and feel like when we're finished. We're also careful to celebrate the stages of construction with a crew meal. If we're having a wretched day, as sometimes happens on mountains and in more mundane work, we might pull everyone off the job for a communal lunch. Doing so takes us away from the project. It gives us distance. We can return with a different perspective and a more positive and creative attitude.

One of my clients, DaVita, formerly known as Total Renal Care, makes a ritual of its in-house language. Founded in the late 1970s, the company was created by a rapid succession of acquisitions and mergers, with strategic focus on growth. As a result, acquisitions were poorly integrated, there was little common identity, and turnover was high. In 2000, Total Renal Care went through a complete leadership change and began a major restructuring under the guidance of the new CEO,

Kent Thiry. He and his new executive team understood that with the magnitude of change the company was undertaking, they would need buy-in and support from everyone to succeed. To make it even more challenging, they had 13,000 employees, who were located in 509 sites across thirty-eight states. The new leadership team focused on fundamentals: Thiry articulated a mission, and the top 600 leaders selected a new name, DaVita (loosely, Italian for "she/he gives life"), as well as seven core values that now guide decision making, performance management, and behavior at all levels. Today, DaVita is a "village," not a "company." Use of the word *village* helps to constantly remind all teammates that the goal is a mutually caring, dedicated, and team-oriented atmosphere. Citizens of a village take care of each other and the village, and, in return, a village takes care of its citizens. Is it simply words? Yes and no. Like the pink flamingos, the words themselves don't create the culture, but consistently using the same few, carefully chosen words is an important facet. The words help create meaningful understandings that lead to actions and an atmosphere in which teammates know they are valued and feel they belong to something special—and the culture emerges.

GIVING UP PERSONAL GOALS FOR THE TEAM

Maybe most critical to the success of the K2 expedition was my difficult decision to give first priority to my role as leader. Like Scott Fischer, I wanted to be out there climbing with the rest of the crew—climbing is what I love above all things on earth. But I had made a promise to fill the role of leader, and I was going to do it come hell or high winds.

The job got especially difficult as we neared the summit. Who would go up with the first team? Who would have to stay behind and hope that the weather didn't prevent a second run at the top? On every climb I had been on before, I was one of those hoping against hope that I would be picked for the lead assault on the summit, but this time things were different.

It was clear to everyone on the team that of the seven of us, Dan Culver and Phil Powers deserved the first crack. They were healthy, climbing well, and eager to go. But who for the third member? Logically, to be honest, it should have been me. That would have made the strongest threesome, and who knew if we would get a chance to send another team to the summit. But Jim Habrel and Dan were fellow Canadians. For a year, they had shared the dream of being the first of their countrymen to set foot on top of K2, and while Jim wasn't as ready to go as Dan, he seemed to me ready enough, especially given a favorable break in the weather.

"Do you and Dan still want to reach the top together?" I asked Jim.

"I would like to try," he answered, "but I'll approve of any decision you make."

That was all I needed to hear. Our collegiality had worked, but it had worked because one person had taken charge. Dan, Jim, and Phil did reach the top. The rest of us never got a chance to try. Obviously, on a personal level I was very disappointed. However, as a leader, I understood that in any endeavor, leaders should inspire members of the team with a passion for success within the framework of team effort.

LEADING ONWARD AND UPWARD

Effective leadership is essential for the success of any climb or organization. Every team—corporate, professional, athletic—needs someone ultimately responsible for creating direction and purpose. Even when individual members are experienced and talented at what they do, the group will achieve much greater success with a strong leader to focus its effort, define roles, and set expectations. Effective leaders also understand that leading requires conscious intent and constant vigilance to align organizational systems and build commitment for collective goals.

What's true as a general rule, though, requires breaking down in the particular. One leadership size does not fit all. Leaders have to adjust their styles to their own personalities and to the distinctive characters of the groups they are leading. Just as important, once they find a style that best serves the organization, leaders need to be consistent with it. A team that's always trying to guess where the boss is going next is going to exhaust its energies internally and sideways, at the cost of achieving external goals and forward movement.

New leaders need to be especially careful. Going from being a team member to a team director requires more than just stepping to the other side of the desk. New leaders must shift from successfully accomplishing tasks themselves to facilitating the success of others. I remember speaking with sales leaders of an international technology corporation. One told me that she "had a hard time letting my sales team do the work. I wanted to be out there, to be part of the sale. I had to learn to step back, let them do the work, and not do it myself." Another talked of his struggles directing his former colleagues: "I would see my friends doing something wrong and was uncomfortable saying anything. I had to realize that my responsibility to the organization was to lead." Authority roles often seem both unfair and unfriendly when you are newly empowered, yet that's an adjustment new leaders must go through. They must make peace with the fact that their individual goals are now secondary to the group's goals. They also need to set expectations of team members and hold them accountable, a task that many new leaders find difficult.

Whether the endeavor is climbing or business, leaders also must learn when to abandon an unsuccessful endeavor. This requires the ability to focus on broad, long-range goals, even when the emotional, financial, and other commitments to an immediate goal are great. And it demands that leaders read the bottom line for what it is, not what they hope it might be.

For example, in 1996, McDonald's spent more than $100 million in advertising to introduce the adult-oriented Arch Deluxe hamburger. Despite the campaign—its biggest ad splash ever behind a new product—and despite a series of highly successful market tests, the burger tanked. "The Arch Deluxe was an extraordinary miscalculation and a highly visible failure," one analyst concluded. Happily for McDonald's, the leadership recognized its failure, pulled the product, and moved on. In the marketplace, knowing when to say uncle saves money. On our first Everest expedition, we made the tough decision to turn around when the weather got worse, our resources got low, and our energy was spent. Even though we'd spent $250,000 to get to that point, not turning around would have been even more costly.

To move their organizations forward, leaders need to focus on solutions. They have to involve their teams in finding those solutions—that's how you get buy-in and commitment. And they need to understand the power of rituals, both in building a team and in celebrating its successes.

Through my experience and observations, I've learned that above all else, leadership is a service. The leader serves the people and organization by creating a clear focus, direction, and purpose. And the team rewards the leader in kind—one of the most crucial things to realize, feel, and remember is that when one team member succeeds, the entire team succeeds. After all, even though Dan, Jim, and Phil summited K2 while my own attempt was thwarted, I left K2 knowing we had all reached the summit together in spirit.

Falling Up:
Success Through Failure in the School of Hard Rocks

ROYAL ROBBINS

AS A ROCK CLIMBER, MY EDUCATION HAS CONSISTED OF learning not by *schooling*, but by *doing*, and, even more, by *failing*. (Come to think of it, that's been my path of learning in most other areas of life as well.) When I speak to groups about my adventures and the lessons learned from them, I use part of this chapter's title, the School of Hard Rocks, as my theme, in homage to the granite of Yosemite Valley and the other hard rock that has provided my tutorials. Sometimes I subtitle my talks "The University of Adversity," recognizing that Shakespeare had it exactly right when, in *As You Like It*, the character Duke Senior, exiled and living in the forest of Arden, reflects upon the sweet "uses of adversity." Adversity is sweet—if only we will recognize and capitalize on its lessons and opportunities. Difficulty is an effective teacher if we are willing learners. Not having myself experienced real hardship—life-threatening illnesses, lost limbs, blindness, or the like—I have gone out of my way, it seems, to create adversity in order to reap the benefits of dealing with it.

Growing up fatherless in Los Angeles, I was often out on the streets looking for adventure. I've always been inclined to push limits, both personal ones and those dictated by society, looking for that definitive line I could not or should not cross. Early on, I found myself on the wrong side of the line.

One year shy of being an official teenager, I began practicing a modest form of residential burglary with a young friend. We had been burgling for several months, and since one good burgle leads to another, we had come to the quaint and curious conviction that we were brilliant criminals and would never be caught.

One midsummer night, the stupidity we mistook for smarts caught up with us. Creeping furtively from behind a house where we had been plying our trade, we were caught in the headlights of a passing police car, which braked to a halt. Two cops jumped out as we dashed off, bent on escape. I was just clearing a fence when an officer shouted, "We've got your buddy. You'd better give up!"

Arrested by the voice of authority, I came back over the fence and approached the man in blue, head drooped, shoulders sagging, a study in shame. Riding in the back of the patrol car, I kept saying to myself, "No, no, this can't be happening. This must be a dream." Alas, it was real enough. The only dream had been that I could go on breaking and entering without getting caught.

At the police station, they booked and fingerprinted us, snapped mug shots, then hauled us off to Juvenile Hall for a night behind bars. The next day was dreary and never-ending. I was imprisoned in a land of concrete, steel, and glass, along with hordes of other boys who had gone wrong.

Sometime that day, we were taken to relieve ourselves—no stalls, just a dozen toilet seats in a row with everyone else looking on. The lack of privacy sent a powerful message: Unless I wanted to spend the rest of my life this way, I had to avoid veering from high jinks to crime. Freedom had never looked so precious.

By the grace of God, a judge let me out on probation. Determined to go straight and do the right thing, I soon joined the Boy Scouts. For once in my early years, I made a smart choice. Troop 127, sponsored by the L.A. Police Department, got me off the streets and into the outdoors, into the mountains, into the good stuff.

Not too sharp at drill and spit and polish, I shined outdoors. I would thumb alone into the mountains to explore camping spots our troop hadn't visited and routes we hadn't hiked. I planned our menus and did the shopping, rationing out hot dogs and cans of beans, and made arrangements (beg, borrow, or buy) for the equipment we needed. In my second year of Scouting I was selected as our troop's Top Outdoor Scout and rewarded with a ten-day trip into the High Sierra with Scouts from some three dozen other troops in Los Angeles.

I have a picture of myself receiving the award with my scoutmaster, police officer Phil Bailey, beside me. I'm beaming with delight and pride, standing erect with shoulders square—a happy contrast to the broken kid the L.A. police had booked less than two years earlier.

During that first trip to the High Sierra, we climbed a peak called Fin Dome in the Rae Lakes area. It wasn't very hard and it wasn't very big, but for a thirteen-year-old from the streets of L.A., it was *very real*. Five of us Scouts plus two adult leaders departed camp before dawn. As we neared Fin Dome, we left the trail and wandered cross-country to the foot of the peak, which is not really a dome or a fin, but something in between. We roped up, tying bowline knots carefully around our waists. One of the adults led up and we boys followed, one at a time, protected by the rope from above. We scrambled up one big block after another as if we were scaling an Egyptian pyramid, using the climbing signals that would later become second nature: "Belay on!" "Climbing!" "Slack!" "Up rope!" It was glorious—a parallel universe to big-city streets. I found myself alive in a world of adventure I never knew existed. And it all took place in the crystalline beauty of the High Sierra, with its lakes and streams, meadows and pines, slabs of granite sweeping upward, and peaks jutting into that perfectly clear blue Sierra sky. That day, I fell in love with climbing and with the mountains the Spaniards named the "Snowy Range." Of all the beautiful mountain systems in the world, the Sierra remains my favorite.

In the High Sierra, I matriculated in the school of hard rocks. Mountain climbing proved an arena big enough to swallow all of my youthful exuberance in ways that wouldn't go against the law, or even good manners. Almost overnight, my life had a central purpose, a severe and ever-challenging discipline to which I could devote my best energies. Climbing became like a father who demanded my best and rewarded me with love when I reached down inside myself and brought it forth. There was extra payback: The skills I had to learn to be a good climber proved transferable to other disciplines, such as skiing and kayaking, and eventually to the broader category of adventure called the business world.

Finding a career you love can be a good deal like climbing a sheer rock face. You climb and fall, climb and fall, climb and fall, until you find the holds that take you to the top. That, at least, is the way it has been for my wife, Liz, and me.

For four years in the early 1960s, we worked as ski instructors at Sugar Bowl, the resort at Donner Summit in California. From there we moved to Switzerland, where we directed sports and taught skiing at an overseas American high school. In 1967, we returned to Modesto, California, to take over Liz's father's paint business—or try to. Fortunately, I was hopeless at it, so we started our own business distributing French mountaineering boots and rock-climbing shoes to outdoor shops throughout the United States. That worked better. My name was recognized by our customers, plus I was savvy about what we were selling. We used our home as an office and at mealtimes removed the typewriter and files from the dining-room table.

Building the business over the years, we augmented our line of footwear with ropes, helmets, technical climbing gear, and up to 400 outdoor book titles. Along the way, we tripped a lot and picked ourselves up, learning from each fall. At first, we just wanted to make enough money to live on while continuing our outdoor adventures. Then, as the business grew, we began to see it as an adventure in itself, as well as a chance to make a positive difference in the lives of our employees and our customers, and in our community as well. To succeed we learned much that was new, but we also fell back on important lessons mountain climbing had taught us.

Three lessons stand out as particularly useful when transferred to the challenges of commercial enterprise. They are *self-confidence*—believing in yourself, trusting yourself, being self-reliant; *attitude as boundary breaker*—a good attitude toward a challenge is more useful in

Royal Robbins during a first ascent of Upper Yosemite Falls

dealing with it than skill level or "ability"; and *perseverance via proximate goals*—the way you get to the top of Everest is one step at a time, that is, by concentrating upon the steps, not the summit.

LEARNING SELF-CONFIDENCE

We all know self-doubt gets in the way of achievement, but how do we conquer it? I have found the discipline of climbing to be particularly useful in building inner confidence. Even with a top rope providing total security on a practice climb, the first hurdle every climber must face is the first step. That takes some doing, and a good deal of internal dialogue: "I've never done this before. It looks too hard. People are watching. What if I make a fool of myself? What will they think if I don't make it? Oh, well, the heck with what they think. I'm going to give it a go."

The first decision made, the next is soon upon the climber. It's gotten hard, his arms are tired, the next moves are tough, and the top is a long way up there. Maybe this is the place to give up, to admit it's too much. Yet something drives the climber upward. He realizes he can get a little higher—he really shouldn't give up this easily. And so he continues, move by move, small decision by small decision. True, he could get hurt if he falls and his belayer is asleep, or the rope fails, or the carabiners at the top come unhooked, or his knot comes untied; but he trusts his safety system, and so, checking his knot, climbs on.

Now he comes to the crux: the really hard section. He panics: "What happened to the holds?" He doesn't see how he is going to do it, but by now he has vowed to give it his best, and so he claws, grunts, and gasps, not caring anymore what those below are thinking, not caring about anything except reaching the top, until finally, with the last strength streaming out of his arms, he lunges desperately for the highest point, misses and falls, caught instantly by the belay. Although he didn't reach the top, the climb has yielded some valuable lessons.

He now realizes that although he nearly made it, the climb is still bigger than he is. But only for the moment. He will come back and try again, and maybe the next time he will make it. Change "maybe" to "probably." And in his bones he knows it's "almost certainly." He has learned that every time he decides to go on, that decision gives him power and confidence and propels him upward. He can now see that faith in himself is essential to have a shot at success. He knows that every time he decides not to give up, he extends the life of the enterprise. And he has learned from his final gutsy effort that even though he failed, he has at least pulled out everything within himself. Perhaps for the first time in his life, he has also come to realize that there is no disgrace in failure. Disgrace lies in giving up, in inflicting self-defeat through weakness.

From such insights, self-confidence grows. If the outcome can be seen as depending upon our own decisions, especially our decision about whether to give up or not, and if we see clearly that we are in charge of our decisions, that insight helps us realize that we have a greater power to influence the outcome than we ever imagined. We are strong. We are worthy. We can now step into the arena with renewed confidence, knowing that there is no failure as long as we don't throw in the towel. Success is having the grit to make the next move upward.

CONFIDENCE IN BUSINESS

We made such a move in our business in the early 1980s. By then, we had significantly moved into the outdoor clothing business to supplement the line of equipment we were importing and distributing. Our experiment in the clothing trade began in 1975, when Liz dreamed up a bright idea for hiking shorts different and better than anything on the market. The hiking shorts of choice were then made of stretchy synthetic fabric. Preferring natural fibers, Liz created shorts of durable cotton twill, cut for freedom of movement and featuring two elastic side panels for comfort. Taking the name from the song about that famous caprine rambler, we called them Billy Goat Shorts. The Billy Goats were an instant hit and were soon joined by Billy Goat Pants, and then by woven shirts, sweaters, and jackets, until we had a full line of stylish outdoor apparel.

By 1982, we realized our company was a house divided. We had a split personality. Half of our attention was focused upon importing and selling outdoor equipment (hard goods) and the other half concentrated on designing, sourcing, and marketing outdoor clothing. We were running two businesses, each requiring different skills, approaches, and experience, but we had the same reps selling hard goods and soft goods. It didn't make sense. In the highly competitive outdoor industry we couldn't afford the luxury of juggling two businesses. Something had to go.

We knew one choice was continuing the way we were, hoping for the best. Hard goods were a crutch we could lean on if we had a bad season with shorts and shirts. But we had already decided that was a recipe for disaster. Maybe we should back out of the volatile clothing trade and return to our roots—outdoor equipment. That was the safest, if less exciting, alternative. Or we could drop the hard goods and take a wild ride on the back of the tiger known as outdoor style. That was clearly the most risky option. We would succeed only if we showed enough creativity and imagination to create and market clothing that people wanted to wear, and did it again and again, year in and year out. That was dangerous. Who were we to think our inventions were good enough to challenge the smart, tough competition of that environment? But we believed in ourselves. We had pushed our limits to develop the clothing line, and its rousing success gave us the confidence to surge upward toward a more challenging summit. We would go for it! Liz seemed to have imbibed her strong self-confidence with her mother's milk. But I know where I got mine—I learned to trust myself in the school of hard rocks.

ATTITUDE AS BOUNDARY BREAKER

I was seventeen years old. We were practice climbing on a granite outcrop atop Mount Pacifico, a 7,000-foot peak in the San Gabriel Mountains north of Los Angeles. Pacifico, as we called the crag, was a favorite for climbers from the Los Angeles basin. Much of the climbing there is "bouldering"—rock play on boulders or short rock walls. A rope is not used unless the boulder is a big one or the landing is uneven and dangerous. This particular Sunday in August found six of us attempting the first ascent of Maniac's Face, a vertical sheet about 20 feet high, with holds of tiny feldspar crystals. We were using a rope, so we knew it was safe to fall. And fall we did, one after another, again and again. I thought, "Perhaps it's impossible. Perhaps . . ." But I wanted it badly. Each of us wanted it, of course. To have a first ascent, even of a boulder problem, is a feather in one's cap. It's a little feather, but one wears it proudly.

Frustrated after falling off the fifth time, I sat on a rock at the foot of the climb with my head in my hands, asking myself, "How can I do it? How can I do it?"

The answer came in an unexpected shape. My desire was so strong, my recognition that I didn't have the answer so clear, and my mind so open to receiving help, that the solution was delivered to me almost on a platter. It entered my mind—a gift. It wasn't as if I was praying, but I guess in a sense I was.

The picture that popped into my head was of the tips of my fingers. I could see them clearly: horizontal, gripping an edge. Then they lifted up and let go of the hold. That's all, but that was enough. I said to myself, "Ah, I see. Climb as high as you can, and then let go." I now realized that if I kept climbing until gravity actually tore me from the holds, I would get at least a smidgeon farther. The first order of business was to think differently. The simple thought, "I can't climb any higher," had caused me to come off. I had to think I was going to make it. I must believe I could go all the way. I needed to see myself reaching the top.

I didn't reason this out in so many words. I just instantly saw that a different attitude would yield different results. Until then, I had been waiting for results, in the form of success, to change my attitude: If I saw I could do it, I would believe I could do it. Now, in a moment of clarity, I realized it might happen if I first believed.

I had nothing to lose. Whatever I had been using in attitude or technique certainly wasn't working. I tied the nylon rope around my waist and announced to my belayer, "Climbing!" "Climb!" he responded. I reached up and gripped the initial crystals. Moving with assurance over the now-familiar rock, I quickly arrived at the halfway point. I didn't think about coming off. I *knew* I was going to make it. The edges were even tinier here, so I concentrated on fingers and toes, willing them to stick to the rock. I didn't imagine my foot slipping from the hold, not for a moment. I saw it *staying on*. A few more moves carried me upward, straining, clinging, hell-bent on making it.

I was almost there when the holds ran out. I reached and scanned with my fingers—nothing there! Just smooth rock. "There must be a way!" I thought. My gaze wandered downward, stopping on a ledge shoulder high and two feet to the right. It was perfect—except it was tilted sideways, forming a vertical edge a half-inch wide and facing away from me. Pulling with the fingers of my right hand against that edge, I raised my right foot knee high, placing it upon a small bump so obscure I hadn't considered using it. Now, by leaning to the left against my vertical fingerhold and pushing to the right on the mere smear of a toehold, I raised my body and just reached the square lip at the top. I transferred my right hand to the top edge and mantled up. I had made it.

The first ascent of Maniac's Face! A triumph—very minor, in the scheme of things, but still a triumph over my own weakness, over my tendency to give up. Not only that, but as I was mantling onto the top, pushing down with my arms and raising a leg to stand up, I realized I had something left. I could have done something harder!

What a revelation. I thought I knew what I could do. I thought I knew what my limits were. But I didn't know. I couldn't know. None of us can know until we go all out, giving it everything we have, with no thought of failure. Maybe we will fail, maybe we'll reach our limit for the moment, but so what? Who cares? We can always try again. And the realization that we have reached our limits should be cause for celebration, not dejection. To use the best that's in us is a supreme achievement every time we do it.

ATTITUDE AS BOUNDARY BREAKER IN BUSINESS

An attitude change propelled us to such an achievement in business during 1985. We had run into a period of tough sledding. The economy was sluggish, sales were slow, costs were high, and profits thin. Powerless to affect the situation, we hoped to ride it out. One morning, as I was sitting at my desk pondering our difficulties, I received a phone call from an advertising executive. We chatted awhile, and I explained I understood the importance of showing the flag when things are slow, but we couldn't spend money on advertising if the money wasn't there. "Yeah, I understand," he replied. "Look, I'll give you another ring when things get turned around." "Okay," I signed off, hanging up the phone.

I had no more cradled the receiver when an outside-the-box thought popped into my mind: "'When things get turned around'? What if *everyone* is waiting for things to get turned around? Who's going to do the turning? Maybe it's up to *us* to do the turning, or at least start it."

I realized I had been seeing our little company as the victim of things beyond our control, hoping and waiting for something to change. That very idea saps one's power, drains one's sense of personal efficacy. Nuts to that. If we were going to go down, we were going to go fighting. But we weren't going to go down. We were going to restart the economic engine, beginning right here in our own company. We were going to find ways to cut costs and cut prices, eliminating a barrier to sales. We were going to make sales in places our imaginations had kept locked out. We were going to find ways to get the word out about our wonderful company and our wonderful products that didn't require spending money. And we were going to cheerlead, encourage, and inspire our team to dig in and be inventive and to have fun working creatively together as never before because they were all part of a great adventure. We would let them know they were also part of an excellent company, and a company can't be excellent unless its people are excellent. And excellence isn't static. Our company's success depended upon the personal growth of each team member. They were, every one of them, vitally important to the company and to their fellow team members.

With a change in attitude from "Let's wait and see" to "Let's get busy and make the difference!" flowing through our organization, we soon did have the company back on track, and we returned to financial health and robust profitability ahead of the general economy. Attitude made the difference—and the good news is that when it comes to attitude, each of us is our own boss.

SETTING PROXIMATE GOALS

Besides the importance of attitude, my ascent of Maniac's Face taught me a lesson in *perseverance*. If I hadn't kept trying, I could not have succeeded. "The battle is not to the strong, nor the race to the swift," the Bible counsels, "but to he who perseveres." But how do you climb a mountain when you can't see the summit? By setting targets one can see and hit. I call these series of bull's-eyes "steps to the dream." Psychologists refer to them as "proximate goals," short-term objectives that move us toward a greater achievement. Whichever words you use, this incremental approach got me through my ten-day climb of the Muir Wall, the first solo ascent of El Capitan.

It was April 1968 when I started up the 3,000-foot hunk of stone that dominates the entrance to Yosemite Valley. I was feeling a bit cocky. After all, I had already soloed the overhanging face of the Leaning Tower, just across the valley. That climb, although only a third as tall as El Cap, offered an extra challenge: no escape by rappelling thanks to the "lean." Having climbed the Tower in four days, I wasn't expecting to be tested on El Capitan. I was wrong. Any hopes I had of breezing up the wall were dashed upon the rocks of reality as well as the alabaster granite of the Big Daddy.

Yvon Chouinard and T. M. Herbert had climbed the Muir Wall three years earlier. On that first ascent, they endured excessive heat and then rain and cold, in addition to short rations and hallucinations. They had consistently climbed at the highest standard, refusing to take the shortcut of drilling holes in the rock and placing expansion bolts to make the going easier. Aiming for that standard as well, I was shocked at the difficulties. Constantly on lead during this route, some of the hardest climbing in my life forced me again and again to search my bag of tricks and dig deep in my gut for the courage to keep going.

One advantage to climbing with a partner is that you spend half the time sitting on a ledge belaying your companion—time to recover. But when you are alone, you are going continuously for ten to twelve hours a day—in this case, for ten days in a row. It really gets to you, though perhaps not in the way you might think. It's not the physical effort so much. It's all of that *thinking*. I know three world-class climbers who have had their rope come untied while they were climbing. "If they're world-class climbers," you might think, "why don't they check their knots?" Because part of the reason they are world-class is their focus on getting to the top. And they can overlook a little item like a knot, as important as it is. Up there alone on El Capitan, there are dozens of technical niceties like that that you have to be checking and

The Muir Wall route on Yosemite's
El Capitan ascends just left of the
buttress, separating light and shadow

double-checking. It's like playing chess all day long for ten days in a row. After a while, it starts to drive you nuts.

When I was five days out, I began talking to myself. I had some brilliant conversations up there, or so they seemed. After a while, I was startled to realize I was talking out loud. By the end of the seventh day, I knew the jig was up. I still had a thousand feet to go, and I didn't have even 500 feet in me. My tank of stamina and energy was registering empty. You can put only so much steadfastness of purpose into a human frame.

Up to that point, it had been like repeatedly reaching into the rucksack of my soul for whatever it took to continue, whether courage, or energy, or stamina, or determining where the route went, or what equipment I should use at a certain point, or what technique would get me up the next bit of rock. And I would reach in and pull out and reach in and pull out, again and again, until I had gotten to the bottom of the sack. The sack felt like a hollow husk. I was all emptied out, all used up. This climb was so hard that I had pushed myself to my limit and finally worn out my reserves. I told myself that no one would blame me for giving up now. I had made a good effort, and there was no point in going any higher if I wasn't going to make it. I knew I was beaten. It was time to head down, and so I would, first thing in the morning, after a night's rest.

I had no sooner decided to wave the white flag than a questioning voice whispered in my ear: "Hey, just a minute there. What about your goal? What about reaching the top? What was it that brought you here and kept you going for seven days?" Yes, what was it? Suddenly I was nauseated by the thought of abandoning my dream. It made me sick just to think of heading down now. Even though my energy was gone, and my resolution sapped, my dream still held me in its grip. I couldn't give it up. I couldn't say good-bye to all that.

I was a man with a problem—alone on the massive flank of El Capitan, on a ledge 2,000 feet above the ground and 1,000 feet below the summit, pinned at the crucible between desire and weakness.

As I was dozing off on the ledge, these conflicting fancies knocked about in my dizzy head until finally the answer came. It wasn't very slick or glorious. It just came in sideways, a simple question: "Why don't you climb the next five feet? You can get down just as easily from five feet higher as from where you are, and you'll have a new high point and a little more honor." Yes, I guess I could. I could climb five more feet, and that would be a compromise between retreat and committing to the summit. And then we would see.

On the morning of the eighth day, I climbed that five feet and then said to myself: "Why don't you climb the next five feet? You can get down just as easily from five feet higher as from where you are. And you'll have a new high point, and a little more honor." So I climbed those five feet, and the next five feet, and the next five feet. I kept going that way for two days, until I got close enough to the top that I could *see* doing it. And then I didn't have to play the mental game anymore. I could just climb—not for the next five feet, but for the top.

That's how it is sometimes, isn't it? Our dreams, our goals, our deepest longings are so far out there that we can't see any way of achieving them. Guess what? We don't need to see *how*. All we need to do is to hold to the vision and let ourselves be drawn to it as iron to a magnet. Our inner creative spirit, animated by the pain and discomfort caused by the differences between where we are and where we want to be, will find ways to move us to the top of whatever mountain we are climbing. The paradox is that humans naturally seek comfort and peace, yet we are at our creative best when we are in a state of what psychologists call "cognitive dissonance"—when things aren't the same as the way we think they should be.

Royal Robbins reaches the top of El Capitan at the end
of his ten-day solo climb of its Muir Wall

In business, these situations often take the form of entrepreneurial challenges, much like the ones faced by Royal Robbins, Inc., in the early 1990s.

CLIMBING THE MUIR WALL OF BUSINESS

As we entered the last decade of the twentieth century, things were looking bad. The red ink was flowing, and for the first time in our business life our net worth was running downhill. Financial advisers warned us that if things kept going this way, we would lose not just the business but also our home, our car, and everything we had. A stark choice faced us: liquidate and avoid the risk of losing our personal assets, or make an all-out effort to return the company to prosperity.

Nothing concentrates the mind like serious danger, and we concentrated for all we were worth. The evidence said it was time to give up: Liz and I had allowed the company to slip into this mess, and we had never managed a turnaround. Even in the crisis of 1985, we had not reached the point of *losing money.* This was a new and frightening reality. But we reasoned that if we had gotten ourselves into this financial bog, we could get us out.

The first thing we did was bring everybody together in a company meeting. Then we laid the truth out before them, in all its terrifying details. The ship was sinking, and to keep it afloat we would have to make sacrifices, be more creative, and work together as never before. Most of all, we needed to see the challenge ahead as a joyous adventure, not as some dreadful, paralyzing black hole. We started to plot a course of short, reachable goals leading toward our ultimate objective: simple survival.

The first thing we looked at was cost-cutting. We asked for, and got, our team members to agree to a 15 percent salary cut. Liz and I led the way by announcing we would go for a year with no salary at all.

We next asked ourselves what the real problem was. As a wholesaler, the dilemma was not that our retailers didn't like us. They did, and they wanted to do business with us. The problem was that our goods were not moving fast enough off their shelves. To sell them, merchants had to take too many end-of-season markdowns. Clearly, customers, the end users, weren't snapping up our products as they once had. There was too much new competition.

Next, we asked, "What does it look like when the problem doesn't exist?" The answer: "The clothes are flying off the shelves at full margin." That became our next goal—to design the line so our product sold fast without a discount. With Liz's leadership, the Design Team got together to study the challenge. They began by analyzing their own behavior when going into a clothing store. What drew them? Lively colors, textures, and patterns. These weren't our strong points. Over the years, we had become known for the quality of our goods, for fit, for making classically fashionable clothes, even for leading our industry in the color coordination of outdoor clothing. All that was great, but the bottom line was telling us we had grown stodgy.

At that time, clothing in the outdoor industry came in subdued neutrals and tended toward earth tones of light browns and greens. Remembering that flowers also spring from the earth, we injected fresh excitement into our line by adding a riot of colors, textures, and patterns to our men's and women's short-sleeved shirts. We could push the edges of the outdoor fashion envelope with these styles without sacrificing our core strengths.

The test came with the Spring 1992 line, delivered to stores in early February of that year. Our lackluster preseason bookings, taken in the fall of 1991, were about the same as those for Spring 1991. We couldn't survive at that pace. We knew we had a much-improved product, but our retailers still placed timid preseason orders. Then, in late February, the miracle began—reorders flooded in for products to replace the ones flying off the shelves. It was unprecedented to get such a volume of reorders so early in the season. We had plenty of stock because we had ordered heavily from our suppliers, anticipating the increased sales we would have to get if we were going to survive.

It had worked. Clear, step-by-step goal setting had helped us inject more life into Royal Robbins outdoor clothing. Instead of hanging back on the shelves, our clothes stood out among the racks of khaki garments, selling themselves with color and energy.

But the story was not over. In spite of the excellent sell-through of Spring 1992, our bookings for Fall 1992 were so-so. The retailers wouldn't be convinced until we had a repeat of the spring phenomenon. By the time preseason orders were placed for Spring 1993, the retailers had become believers. Our bookings were double those of Spring 1992. We were saved.

The delay in our salvation—it had taken us two seasons to climb out of the hole—made us aware of the importance of precise, one-step-at-a-time goal setting. Our goal had been for the customers to buy lots of our stuff. We assumed that the retailers would see the new and improved product for what it was. But they were looking backward, at recent past sales, and that spooked them. I am sure that if we had set a goal of "selling" the retailers in advance that the stuff was going to fly, we could have done that, too. The retailers would then not have had to wait for their customers to alert them to the new reality of the Royal

Robbins product, and they would have placed preseason orders to match the sales to come.

A GRAND ADVENTURE

Liz and I have been through many adventures together, including raising a family. But the adventure of business building stands out as requiring the most personal growth, involving as it did many and varied challenges, ups and downs, the need to develop new skills, and the greatest challenge of all—working with people. That was, especially for me, difficult at first. Eventually, though, I got good enough to receive several awards for leadership. But the most rewarding part of the adventure of business has been the opportunity to make a positive difference in the lives of our staff and our customers, and in our community. That's the most *rewarding* part, but the *toughest* part has been to build a company strong and profitable enough to effect those positive differences.

We succeeded because we applied principles learned in mountaineering: self-confidence, a can-do attitude (yes, we have heard it before, but it works!), and eating the elephant one bite at a time. Liz and I, together with our team members, created a unique company where fun was part of the culture, where personal growth was a requirement, and where each team member had the opportunity to contribute to the community. We were a family, and a functional one at that. As mother figure, Liz played a pivotal role in leadership, in business savvy, and in design. We sailed through the '70s, stumbled during the '80s, had a terrific struggle in the early '90s, and then ended that decade with a net profit so ambitious it was hard to believe we could even set it as a goal, much less achieve it. But achieve it we did—our most profitable of thirty-two years in business. Shortly after, we sold the company, trading one adventure for another. Now we spend our time climbing, skiing, running rivers, traveling, writing, speaking in public, and teaching.

Enjoy the adventure. Climb the highest mountain. Learn from the hard rock.

Killer Applications:

An Entrepreneur's Education in the Death Zone

CHRIS WARNER

TWELVE INCHES OF SNOW HAVE FALLEN IN THE LAST TEN hours, collapsing the dining tent and bringing our assault on K2 to a standstill. I am a member of an international expedition attempting to climb not only K2, the world's second-highest mountain, but also Broad Peak, another of the world's fourteen peaks that are 8,000 meters or higher.

Nicknamed the Savage Mountain, K2 is shrouded in danger. Of the 198 people who have summited, 22 have died on the descent. Of the 5 women summiters, 3 died descending K2, and the other 2 died on later expeditions. Just showing up takes chutzpah, but even more so in 2002. A million trigger-happy troops are massed on the nearby border of Pakistan and India. Still closer, the sievelike border between Afghanistan and Pakistan is leaking al-Qaeda fighters.

As I lie in my tent, typing these words, my teammates are playing a game of chance known as Pigs. You can practice Pigs all you want, but there's no way to craft a strategy or ensure success. Mountaineering is just the opposite: a game of skill. Practice makes us better. Bad experiences teach us good judgment. Skill and technique, efficiency and fitness—mental, physical, and emotional—combine to help us manipulate the odds.

As if to make my point, an avalanche cuts loose on the face of the mountain above me. In mountaineering, we call avalanches, sudden storms, rockfalls, and similar events "objective dangers." We may or may not be able to predict them and thus avoid them, or luck might put us in the path of one or take us out of it, but more often than not, we expose ourselves to objective dangers by failing to act upon all of the data available to us. Just yesterday, to cite one example of hundreds I've experienced, three of us were climbing to Advanced Base Camp with backpacks full of gear when an avalanche started 2,500 feet above the glacier we were crossing, tearing rocks and ice from the face of the mountain. As the leading edge of the avalanche neared, a hump in the glacier redirected the main flow of the slide away from us. Hiding behind a tower of ice, we were merely dusted by the airborne snow. Except for a brief chill, we were fine, but surviving that near miss wasn't a matter of luck. Knowing that particular gully was prone to avalanches, we laid out our route to arc around the danger zone, keeping a wall of glacial ice between the most treacherous area and us. We also hustled through that section, using a little justified fear to keep us moving despite the thin air at 18,000 feet.

In the last thirty months, I have been on five other mountaineering expeditions to 8,000-meter peaks while simultaneously nurturing my company, Earth Treks. I tagged the summit of Cho Oyu, the sixth-highest peak in the world. Later, I guided clients to the summit of Everest via the difficult North Ridge. Four months after climbing Everest, I became the first American to climb solo to the top of an 8,000-meter peak, Shishapangma, the fourteenth-highest mountain in the world, in the same range as Everest. Applying all that I have learned about the mountains and myself, I swung my ice tools and kicked my cramponed boots for thirty-four straight hours, in a nonstop trip up and down the technical Southwest Face. During those months, Earth Treks grew from $860,000 to $1.3 million in annual sales. We surpassed our projections for 2001 despite a tough economy and massive geopolitical uncertainty.

Now, while I am in Pakistan's Karakoram range trying to climb *and* survive K2 and Broad Peak, my Earth Treks team is building our second indoor climbing gym, part of my dream of establishing a chain of state-of-the-art training facilities to complement our flagship mountain guide service. Clearly, I've turned my passion for climbing into a successful career, one that allows me and over sixty employees to share our love of climbing with thousands of people. While teaching on average 19,000 people to climb each year, we earn a decent wage and can take time off to pursue our own climbing dreams. In our business, where people's lives dangle on a thin rope, it is critical that we walk our talk. Our personal adventures must be leveraged into business successes.

We've built our little climbing empire from the tiniest of seeds—$562 scraped together in 1992—and in one of the most unlikely places in the United States: the suburbs of Baltimore, Maryland, one of America's oldest seaports.

How did we do it? How did we transform our hobby into a successful, growth-oriented business? How did we create a corporate culture that allows the most adventurous of us to leave the business for months at a time? How do we have enough emotional energy and physical stamina to grow a business at 28 percent annually and still have the drive and time to climb the most challenging routes on the world's tallest peaks?

Dozens of books address the objective dangers of business and offer fantastic solutions to those problems. Many of these books are useful—and I've read a ton of them—but the lessons that have been most critical to Earth Treks' success come from the peaks, not the library. It was on cutting-edge Himalayan expeditions where I learned the core values that helped launch and now sustain the fast-growing, entrepreneurial company that is Earth Treks: passion, vision, perseverance, and partnership. Beyond these four things, you also need the courage to apply them. Lack of courage in business will cause your company to fail. Lack of courage in the mountains will cause you to die.

One expedition in particular, a harrowing climb of India's Shivling peak, fueled my passion for all things climbing and demonstrated the critical importance of these core values. Seeing at a gut level how all the qualities worked together to overcome even the worst obstacles opened my eyes to the power of their benefits in every arena, including business, and allowed me to turn my passion for climbing into a career.

Chris Warner stands on the summit of Cho Oyu
with Mount Everest behind

Today, Earth Treks is fueled by our collective passion. Traveling at near warp speed, we steer the organization through our commitment to our vision, a proven and proud tradition of perseverance, and our emphasis on partnerships. I've been to the top of the world. The view from the summit of Everest is awe inspiring, but the feeling of pride at having started and nurtured Earth Treks is far greater.

PASSION

Even though I was born in New York City and raised in the Jersey suburbs, mountains were in my blood. Some kink in my genetic code led me to devour books about adventurers and choose them as my role models. Following in their footsteps, I fought imaginary wars, traveled to the sources of mighty brooks, built tree forts, and crept undetected from lawn to lawn under the cover of darkness.

I was a kid with a limitless appetite for conquering the unknown, but unlike most kids, my passion for adventure never tapered off. And I think I know why. Even as a youngster, when the going got the toughest, my mind and body slipped into what psychologists call the "flow state" and what athletes know as "the zone"—that amazing moment when we seem to escape physical limitations and become a problem-solving, hyperperforming, integrated machine. "We feel in control of our actions, masters of our own fate," Mihaly Csikszentmihalyi writes in *Flow: The Psychology of Optimal Experience*. "On the rare occasions that it happens, we feel a sense of exhilaration, a deep sense of enjoyment that is long cherished and that becomes a landmark in memory for what life should be like."

Once you've been in a flow state—won the championship game, made a perfect run down the ski slope, played a set of tennis so well it seemed as if you were living in someone else's body—you never forget it. Flow lingers. Despite the gnawing demands of adulthood, the mind-numbing effects of a daily commute, even the disintegration of our aging bodies, once we've tasted the euphoria and fulfillment of the flow state, we know what life can offer. The challenge is to be conscious of what truly satisfies us and to have the courage to create a life in which we can keep coming back to the flow state.

That's what I think passion is: the willingness to seek flow experiences. Positively passionate people make great entrepreneurs and leaders. They are willing to suffer extreme hardships while pursuing their dreams. They do not expect short-term satisfaction. They are internally motivated, driven to please themselves according to a set of self-imposed values. Passionate people are addicts, seeking that wonderful satisfaction from every part of life. They're pushers, too, dragging along every disciple who has the guts to play with them. Employees who get caught up in this enthusiasm love to work for passionate people because their work, no matter how mundane, is valued.

I found passion in climbing, first on small crags in the Mid-Atlantic states and later on taller cliff faces in Colorado and California. Eventually I drifted to the Andes of South America, searching for experiences that would push my limits.

As I began to build my résumé of extreme ascents, I came to the realization that climbing, while offering intense moments or even weeks of satisfaction, wasn't allowing me to fully develop all my talents. I dreamed of creating a cutting-edge climbing school. Nevertheless, I clung to my job as an administrator and lead instructor at Outward Bound. A coworker, in whom I had confided my dream, finally sat me down and said, "For someone who takes so many risks with your personal life, you certainly seem afraid of taking a risk with your professional life."

I realized he was right. Within a few months, I incorporated Earth Treks and set off on my own. My mission was to provide the highest-quality climbing courses and mountaineering expeditions. My strategy involved applying the lessons I learned on my Himalayan climbs to every aspect of the business.

Those lessons were highlighted on my climb of Shivling, a high-altitude showcase for the benefits of a tank full of passion combined with healthy doses of vision, perseverance, and partnership. When I was in college, at the University of Colorado in Boulder, I made fast friends with two other transplanted easterners, Dan Jenkins and Austin Weiss. We all scrambled for day work as rock-climbing guides and spent our summers as Outward Bound instructors. After a day on the rocks, we would sip beers, shovel beans onto tortillas, and daydream out loud about even bigger adventures. In 1989, we went on our first trip to the Himalayas: a 21,461-foot peak called Shivling, located in India's Garhwal region above the Gangotri glacier, notorious in climbing circles for its difficulty. Only a handful of people had climbed it, a veritable who's who of Himalayan all-stars. We chose to repeat a route pioneered by Chris Bonington, the famed British mountaineer. A knife-edged spine of rock, ice, and snow, the route sliced upward along the southeast ridge for over 6,000 vertical feet.

We set off carrying twenty-five-pound packs. Late on the afternoon of the third day, when we were 5,000 feet up the mountain, a cold front slammed into the Himalayas. Within minutes, the temperature dropped thirty degrees. As the blizzard hit, we rappelled down to the only ledge system we had passed that day. No larger than a dining-room table, and far too small for our tent, the biggest ledge was for two people only. Dan and Austin huddled together, lying on the uneven and sloped surface. I climbed just below them and slipped among some rocks that formed another narrow ledge. We anchored ourselves into place, running ropes from the cracks in the rocks through our sleeping bags to harnesses wrapped around our bodies. My left hip was pushed against the rock, but my right hung over the edge of a 2,500-foot cliff face.

The storm battered us for two nights and part of three days, during which we couldn't move. Exhaustion dragged us into periods of fitful sleep, bestowing relief for a few seconds or minutes—but never hours—from the anxiety of the situation. The storm seemed to scorn us. Blowing snow crept into our down sleeping bags and promptly melted, leaving useless, heavy masses of wet feathers. At some point, gale-force winds tumbled our single cook pot into the abyss. With it went all hope of boiling the water needed to cook our freeze-dried meals.

Chris Warner's teammates perched on a 20,000-foot campsite on Shivling after a two-day blizzard

On day five of the trip, the storm slowed, then briefly stopped. The sun peered through the occasional holes in the clouds. All around us avalanches peeled away from the faces and thundered down the mountain. We were freezing and fatigued. We hadn't eaten or had anything to drink in two days, and the odds of feeding ourselves soon were slim. How were we going to survive?

If we wanted to escape with our lives, our only option was to go up and over the top via the most technical climbing and dangerous conditions any of us had ever faced in the mountains—so bad, in fact, that we would have to abandon our chosen route and pioneer a new one. It was time to tap into passion as an energy source. If fear were to dominate, we would die. Consciously entering into the flow state and climbing carefully upward was our only ticket to survival. Against all odds, we needed a victory; but if life to that point had taught me anything, it was that I was in control of the tools of success. I knew what needed to be done to survive. We had to devise a plan.

VISION

If passion is the propellant, vision allows us to steer—and on Shivling, we wanted direction badly. Our small party had opted from the beginning for an alpine-style climb, in which climbers shoulder a thirty-pound backpack and ascend directly from Base Camp to the summit. We had no Sherpas, fixed ropes, or established camps, the infrastructure common on a typical Everest or siege-style expedition. If something went wrong, thousands of feet above Base Camp, our solution had to come from our small packs or our collective wisdom. There was no safety net below us. We had the overwhelming confidence of youth on our side, though, and we liked the greater-risk, greater-reward formula—the logistical simplicity of alpine-style climbs increases the risk, while the deeper commitment and more intense demands placed upon the climber yield far greater feelings of pride and accomplishment. (Alpine-style climbs are the Himalayan equivalent of bootstrapping: telling the greedy venture capitalists to take a hike while you struggle your way to financial success and industry acclaim. Your chances of success may be less, and your comfort level infinitely reduced, but in the end you still own 100 percent of the business.) Now cowering in our sodden sleeping bags, high on Shivling, those long, slow supply lines of a siege-style expedition would have been mighty comforting. Dan, Austin, and I had to pull together and see our way out of a situation that had been severely altered by the storm, the lost pot, and the avalanches.

As mountain climbers, we rely heavily on visualization techniques, just as a good golfer visualizes sinking the putt before ever stroking the ball. Like a golfer, though, we have to read the lie right for the vision to work. Many an Everest climber has visualized himself standing on the summit but failed to accompany that with a well-detailed plan of attack. Typically, plans fail because the people who made them misjudged themselves or processed the data—snow conditions, time of day, amount of food, and so on—and came up with the wrong conclusion. That's why whenever I create a vision of the whole, I'm quick to break it into the tiniest parts, examining the peak and searching for a route that is both climbable and safe. And that's exactly what we did on Shivling.

Critical to our success was rehydrating our bodies and fueling them with some kind of food. Among all our gear, we had nine Twix bars— our only non-freeze-dried food. We used the stove's foil windscreen to form a tiny, makeshift pot, taking nearly forty minutes to melt a soda can's worth of water. For the next three days, we treated ourselves to one daily meal of a single Twix bar and half a cup of boiled snow water. We climbed to a symphony of stomach growls, groans, and grumbles.

The snowstorm had greatly altered the route we hoped to climb. Snow was piled on the ledges, avalanches swept the faces, wind tore past the ridges, and the cracks were filled with ice. Our route was now far too dangerous. A gap in the clouds showed us a possible escape route—from our ledge, back up the ridge, and then out across acres of snow-covered, just-less-than-vertical granite slabs to a notch in the summit ridge. Breaking it into parts, we could see an almost continuous line of weaknesses to capitalize on, but the route was far from direct. We would have to climb up, down, and over, zigzagging across the face, all the while searching for crack systems to which we could anchor ourselves. I figured the distance to be over 3,000 feet, meaning a minimum of eighteen rope lengths. At more than an hour of climbing per rope length, this day would never end. But would it work? Would we be able to escape a slow death trapped on our tiny ledges? We didn't know for sure, but with passion and vision on our side, and the storm finally in abeyance, the odds of escape were looking far better.

Business challenges are no different: Vision is critical to surmounting them. In 1995, I returned to the cliffs above Boulder for the first time since the late 1980s. In the old days, I had been working for one of the region's larger guide services; now I was guiding my own clients. But that wasn't all that had changed. Every guide service I used to work beside, or for, had gone out of business. When I asked around, my old guiding friends told me that the local rock gym, with its greater financial and marketing resources, had gobbled up all the trade.

I owned Earth Treks, an outdoor rock-climbing school in the Washington, D.C., suburbs that I thought had a fine future, but now I could see the writing on the wall. The D.C. area had two local climbing gyms that could gobble up my business just as the Boulder one had done to other, similar outfits. It was time to open a climbing gym of my own.

I flew on from Boulder to Mount McKinley in Alaska, where I was guiding Kevin Maloney, a successful New York City real estate developer. Kevin is a chronic entrepreneur as well as a dedicated climber, which made him just the right person to hone my vision with. Every night we would lie in the tent and refine the idea. By the time we wrapped up our climb, Kevin had helped me develop a plan of attack. A few months later, with the steps needed to accomplish the vision clearly laid out and the financial projections in order, he agreed to loan me $400,000 in start-up capital.

PERSEVERANCE

Propelled by passion, with a new vision steering us, it was time to climb toward safety. Like the start-up phase of a business, cutting-edge mountaineering seems to be made up of equal doses of suffering and risk taking. In such a setting, perseverance, the ability to keep putting one foot in front of the other, is often the most important tool for success.

Chris Warner on the summit of
Mount Everest via the North Ridge

On the world's biggest peaks, the extreme physical and emotional fatigue and lack of oxygen cause some people to simply give up. Summiting Everest via the North Ridge, you step over, or around, seven bodies. Each of these people stopped moving toward safety. At forty below zero, the unconscious body freezes solid in six hours. There is nothing sexy about taking one more step, but it can mean the difference between being a landmark for mountaineers—"Step over the man with the green boots. . . . Make a left at the waving man"—or living to climb another day.

On Shivling, our motivation for moving upward was simple: to stay alive. Had we remained on the exposed ledges, we would have died a slow death of starvation and hypothermia. Had we tried to escape by descending, an avalanche would have torn us from the mountainside, twisting and crushing our bodies, then burying us alive.

On the fifth morning of the Shivling climb, we packed our gear as fast as we could, shouldered our packs, and climbed upward. We started by ascending the ropes we had placed on day three and reached our high point in less than an hour. Then we climbed into the unknown.

On a technical peak like Shivling, the only system for making vertical progress is to have one person lead out. He hammers pitons into the cracks and clips the rope to the piton with a carabiner, thus protecting himself from a long fall. If he places his first piece of protection ten feet up, climbs ten feet above that, and then falls, he'll fly twenty feet through the air before being caught by the rope. As it turned out, though, we weren't going to have the luxury of such short increments.

We were organizing the climbing gear at the edge of unknown terrain when clouds began to choke the peak and fresh snow started to fall. Suddenly, speed became our greatest concern. We quickly decided to accept even more risk by tying our two ropes together into a single 330-foot rope. The lead climber was now looking at taking falls in excess of 300 feet. With the likelihood of a long fall so high and the consequences ranging from bone-shattering to fatal, there was little room for error.

I led out across the face, heading for the notch in the summit ridge, well over 3,000 feet away. My vision of the route we would take to the notch was precise. Patches of snow clung to the face of the mountain, and I would try to climb from one to another, hoping that the points of my crampons and the picks of my ice axes might be able to gain purchase in this snow.

The climbing was extremely technical, involving the most delicate weight transfers to keep the snow from calving off the bare granite slabs. Where the snow was slushy, it would slide off unless I carefully molded it into a tiny ledge. Holding my breath, expecting to fall, I would ease onto each clump of the slush. The ledge would slide, sometimes for only inches before compacting a bit more into the rough surface of the granite. If it held, I moved onto it. When it didn't, I set off upward, downward, or laterally in search of my next foothold. Occasionally, I found cracks in the rock and would lever my ice axes or crampon points into these.

Each pitch—a 330-foot section in our case because of the rope length—took me at least ninety minutes to climb. When I neared the end of the rope, I scraped in the snow in search of a crack to which to anchor the rope and myself before allowing my partners to climb up to me. Then I would lead out again. The snowstorm came and went throughout the day. At times, the blizzard conditions nearly tore me off the wall. Small avalanches of soft powdery snow hit me without rhythm. Occasionally, I could see and hear Dan and Austin. Other times, I felt totally alone in the center of the storm.

Amazingly, it was when I felt most alone that I felt most competent, focusing solely on the objective at hand. I quickly shed the burden of fear. I didn't have the time or emotional energy for it if I was going to do my job, and worrying about falling to my death seemed unproductive. As long as I kept persevering, I was making progress. In the process, I was receiving direct and immediate feedback, and it was positive and encouraging. I was in the flow state, and being there made me emotionally and intellectually stronger.

Twelve hours and a dozen rope lengths later, the terrain changed. The route took us up a thin icicle that hung over a section of the granite face. Fourteen hours had passed since our last Twix bar meal, during which time there wasn't even a ledge big enough for us to stop and rest on. Exhausted, we either stood on our crampon points or hung in our harnesses the whole time.

The icicle was physically the hardest section of the route we faced that day. Luckily, in the rock wall behind it I was able to hammer a piton into a crack, allowing me to safeguard against a fall. The icicle was no bigger in girth than a telephone pole, and it seemed like thirty vertical feet of struggle would get me through the toughest part. I'd gotten halfway up when the ice narrowed. I tried to reach past the thinnest section and blindly scraped around for an ice axe placement. Tiring, I swung the pick of the ice axe into the ice. The icicle split in two, and I fell thirty feet through the pitch-black sky. I landed on a steep patch of snow, kept from falling further by the rope that was attached to the piton.

Life's most defining moments demand perseverance. If we are ever to reach the summit or achieve success in business, we must keep moving. Of course, we need to catch our breath, but we mustn't linger in the danger zone or let opportunity pass us by while we're resting on old laurels. When obstacles seem most impossible, any step is better than none. Action brings feedback, and the feedback lets us know if our solution has merit or stinks. The trick is to listen and alter course if the route we've visualized might be fatal or reckless.

Unhurt by my thirty-foot fall, I climbed back to my previous high point, hoping that I could force my way past the difficulties and onto the top of the granite face. Once again I swung the ice axe into the remaining bits of ice, and once more I fell thirty feet into the soft snow below me.

I was spent, physically drained after more than fourteen hours of leading out with the rope. My exhaustion was now slowing the team. We were at the very top edge of a 5,000-foot cliff face, and a mistake here could kill us all. Yes, I visualized myself climbing that icicle. Yes, I attacked it, falling twice. But now I was becoming a liability to the team. The time had come to pass the responsibility of leading on to a partner so he could persevere.

This tactic of putting one foot in front of the other has also served us well at Earth Treks, as cash-flow crises are rarely solved by a miracle sale or brilliant entrepreneurial vision. The only method that seems to work for us is perseverance: keep doing the right thing over and over and over again until the crisis passes.

We built our first indoor climbing gym within subleased space, renting a mere 7,300 square feet in a 622,000-square-foot warehouse. Soon, the building was sold to new and ambitious owners, and they began to renovate. Our tranquil work environment was turned into a war zone by the construction of additional floors, the refacing of the building, the paving of the parking lots, the landscaping, and the sewage and electrical upgrades. Power was shut off at odd hours and for up to two days at a time, usually on weekends when we were most busy. Piles of garbage, mountains of dirt, scaffolding, and bulldozers hid our entrance and threatened the safety of our clients. Sales dropped by 25 percent each month. By the sixth month, we were having difficulties making our loan payments.

We worked patiently and closely with the new owners, and they were quick to patch the new roof leaks and replace the damaged sewage pipes. They apologized for the inconvenience, but pointed to the fine print in the lease. It didn't help that we did not have a direct lease or that we were the smallest tenant. To make matters worse, the tenant we were subleasing from took legal action against the landlord. In short, our future was bleak. We owed nearly $300,000 to an old client, and we were about to default on that loan. The landlord decided to evict the tenant we subleased from. Revenues were at an all-time low and our savings were depleted.

Besides our belief in hard work, three things were in our favor as month six ended: The contractors were finished and cleaning up around a much-improved building, the busy season was approaching, and a local bank was anxious to win our business (based on the success of the previous year and a favorable Small Business Administration program). After battling for half a year against declining income, we could see the summit and just needed to struggle upward to reach it.

The staff had dug deep for the first six months; now, seeing the end in sight, they put in even longer hours while thinking creatively to cut expenses just a bit more. Two months after construction ended, operating profits returned. The bank stepped in with a better loan package, lowering the interest rate and extending the terms. And the landlord, after evicting the tenant we subleased from, crafted a new, long-term lease directly with us. We persevered through the crisis.

In retrospect, our responding to this problem by simply working harder and smarter was critical to our eventual success. (We saw the results of the other side of the coin—getting angry and pursuing litigation resulted in the eviction of the company from whom we subleased.) And our commitment to and friendship with our regular clients paid off because they never abandoned us, despite not knowing if we would even be open as they drove from work to our door. We just kept putting our best foot forward, over and over and over again, each step cementing our bond as partners.

PARTNERSHIP

Climbers can't stop talking about their partners. The rope so obviously links us together that partnership defines the experience. Every time I have pushed my technical limit, my partner fed the effort with enthusiasm, coaching, and devotion to my safety. Partners make you better, whether they are obvious during the battle or not.

Few experiences in life place so high a premium on partnership as high-risk Himalayan climbing, but many experiences reinforce the partnership lessons I've learned there. When we built our first gym, our core team members transcended themselves and became a high-performance unit, as so often happens with bootstrap start-ups. We were so committed to the vision that we literally stayed at the site for the final nine days of building, collapsing into forty-five-minute naps every few hours but never compromising on quality. In fact, our best work came in the final weeks of the six-month project. That business experience was the most intense "expedition" in which I have ever participated, and in some ways the most enduring. To this day, the pride that each of us feels is incredible. Each partner who made it to that level of commitment and performance—and quite a few did not—experienced the flow state for hours and days at a time. The team members who built that gym know that they have the seeds of excellence in them forever.

With the gym, our money was at stake. On Shivling, it was our lives. At midnight, Dan Jenkins took the climbing protection from me and began to lead climb up a steep cliff band. I had dismissed this path in favor of the ice route, but while I was high above them, failing, Dan and Austin saw possibilities where I saw none. Dan inched up the wall as Austin fed him the rope. After fourteen hours of leading, I hung from my harness, waiting for Dan to reach the top of the wall and gathering my strength back.

By 2 A.M. we had regrouped on a narrow ledge, just below the ridge crest of the summit plateau. A cornice—a wave of wind-sculpted snow—hung over us. Below, a flake of rock had jammed the ropes. Unable to budge them, Dan lowered himself back down the route, freed the rope, and climbed back up to us. Now he was spent.

I resumed the lead, searching for a weakness in the cornice. As I traversed further and further to the right, I remembered a classic photo from the early days of Scottish winter climbing. These climbers had literally drilled a tunnel up and through a cornice; the photo was of the second climber popping his head through the hole. The bottom of our cornice was within reach, so I figured I could do the same thing. Of course, it was dangerous. If the cornice broke, more than a ton of densely packed snow and ice would collapse and carry me down the face.

Swinging my ice axe, I chopped until the hole was a bit wider than shoulder width. I crawled up into the shaft, leaned against the back wall, and dug some more. I then pulled my feet up into the shaft and braced myself against both sides, so I could dig even higher into the overhang. Beneath my feet, the egg-shaped shaft in which I was encased framed the 5,000-foot East Face of Shivling.

After eight feet of digging, I broke through the surface and crawled toward the safety of the summit ridge. With shaky legs, I walked for the first time since we started up the mountain six days earlier. As far from the hole as the rope would allow, I created an anchor. Since there was neither a convenient rock to tie to, nor a patch of ice for an ice screw, I dug a hole and sat in it, the rope still tied to my waist. Dan and Austin climbed safely through the hole and sat beside me.

With the sky beginning to lighten and the clouds thinning, we pulled out the stove and remolded the tin foil into a pot. On the morning of the sixth day, we each ate a Twix bar and drank half a cup of water.

The actual summit seemed so close, but Austin had no desire to go any higher, so Dan and I set off without our packs to tag the top. The ridge above us twisted toward the summit, but just a few feet below it, and a hundred feet before the true peak, we ground to a halt. The remaining few feet were too dangerous for us to traverse. After all we had gone through, we couldn't even touch the summit. Dan and I huddled together on a tiny hump of snow and rock, taking in the almost unbelievable view. Still, we couldn't relax, knowing we were so far from safety.

Our partnership began with our collective desire to test our limits and prove our abilities on a remote and difficult mountain. Dan, Austin, and I were young and ambitious. We had no idea that we were embarking on an epic battle for our lives. High on the slopes of Shivling, our long friendship entered a phase rarely experienced. We were completely dependent on each other for our survival. The personal strengths we brought to the team were magnified. The extreme situation demanded that our weaknesses be controlled. Forged by the severe circumstances we faced, we sculpted a culture up there that quickly shifted burdens to whomever could best shoulder them at the moment. I am certain to this day that most teams would have died on Shivling.

I took this lesson on the importance of partnership to heart when building Earth Treks. I wanted to mold the employer-employee model into a climbing partnership. When fighting through business challenges, the boss is usually out in front, leading the troops and waving the corporate flag. The same is true in climbing. The leader takes the greatest risks, stretching out the rope and protecting the followers from a fall. That's the role I play at Earth Treks: I sign the loan documents, the leases, and the contracts. If cash is short, I don't get a paycheck. If we default on a loan, it is my house the bankers will own. In return, I get the biggest piece of the pie.

That's Management 101, but a climbing partnership changes the dynamic in subtle yet important ways. If I lead us to the first ledge, you lead us to the next. This balance creates a relationship based not on hierarchy but mutual dependence. The very act of climbing, with its inherent risk, also makes the relationship more intimate. When we enter into a climbing partnership, we know that we will see each other wrestle with self-doubt and struggle against the pull of gravity and the discomforts and brutality that are part and parcel of adventuring in extreme environments. But for every weakness that is exposed, we also see the beauty of personal triumphs. We bear witness to limits being pushed and expectations exceeded. We share moments of awe and majesty that can be felt or seen only in the natural world. Through the journey, we play a crucial role in each other's growth.

I've tried to do that at Earth Treks. I stress partnership where many other business owners stress leadership. To create this partnership approach, we took first hires very seriously, because together we would be creating the corporation's cultural legacy. We spent hours outlining our values. Staff training sessions and end-of-season debriefings focused on questions such as "What extra things can each of us do for our clients that will make their experience the best it can be?"

Guided by these conversations and by a few early hiring mistakes, we refined our hiring and training processes. Today, a team interviews each candidate, and no full-time employee is hired without being interviewed at least three times. We want to be certain that whoever we bring on board shares our values and has the desire needed to contribute to our organization's growth.

In part, the need for a good fit is driven by the economics of the climbing industry. Almost every manager at Earth Treks took a significant pay cut to join the company. They came to us because they wanted a career built around their love of climbing and because they were confident they could help us grow sufficiently to return to the salary range they once enjoyed.

Our focus on partnership pervades all of the organization's operations and decision-making processes, from open-book management to our profit-sharing plan. Twenty percent of all profits are split among part- and full-time staff. The bonus checks are just one of many ways to celebrate our successes. A business partnership, much like a climbing one, can be difficult to maintain. The intensity can burn people out. We've had to fire underachievers and the less-than-zealous. On a long and difficult climb, a bad climbing partner can kill you faster than a bolt of lightning or an avalanche. But in both venues, those who survive thrive.

COURAGE

Dan, Austin, and I had to descend from the summit of Shivling via a route we did not know, through terrain that might be even more avalanche prone than the faces of the south and east sides. We shouldered our packs and headed across a giant glacial plateau at 21,000 feet. When the edge appeared abruptly, we rappelled down a 300-foot wall of dense glacial ice. Below this, the face dropped down a 1,000-foot cliff. On the sixth rappel, Dan and Austin waited below as I leaned back on the ropes. We had anchored them to a loop of thin nylon webbing that had been flipped around a large, icy rock.

I leaned back. The rope slipped off the rock. I fell through the air.

In the eight or so seconds I was airborne, I focused on just one thing: survival. Instead of fear, I was bathed in calm. My mind was in complete control, seeking a solution. First, it confirmed that I was falling. Then a mental map of the mountain presented itself. I was flying past hundreds of feet of rock, heading for a fifty-five-degree snow slope. A thousand feet down the snow slope, a jumble of ice cliffs fanned out into a sea of crevasses. To stop myself while my body was still on the snow slope, I would need to dig my mittened hands into the snow, spreading my legs wide apart to keep from flipping and tumbling.

While I was falling through the air, Dan started to scream, and Austin dove for the ends of the rope. He hadn't told us, but before starting the climb, Austin had had a premonition that one of us would die. Now it looked as if this fear would prove true. As my arcing body flew past, then drew taut on the rope, Austin was yanked from his stance. The rope flew from his hands, along with his ice axe, and he, too, tumbled down the slope, out of control.

A few hundred feet below him, I was being pulled toward the face of the mountain, my trajectory altered by the momentarily taut rope. After falling through the air for 450 feet, I slammed into and bounced off the steep snow slope. Fifty feet later, I was propelled like a dart right into the face of the mountain. A small avalanche started by my initial impact swept over me and threatened to pry me from the slope.

As the snow hurled past, I looked up to see Austin tumbling down the face, heading straight for me. In a flash of a second, he whipped himself around and stopped. His ice axe bounced past me.

Buried to my knees but alive, I felt a rush of security sweep over me, even though I knew that overconfidence at this point would be more dangerous than the fall. This absurd delusion told me that my partners were going to get me off this face alive. In reality, each of us was fighting, separately and together, for survival. The terrain and situation were simply too desperate.

I wanted to cry: not a little whimper, but a full-on wail of fear. I wanted to let go of every restraint, to give in to self-pity and despair, but I wasn't willing to accept my death. I wasn't ready to give up after so long and hard a battle to make it down alive. I reached for my ice axe, unclipped it, and swung it into the snow, and that simple step allowed me to take back some control, to reassert my will to live. The moment that ice axe struck, the need to bawl like a baby subsided, at least momentarily. (It welled up repeatedly—at first, by the second. After a few hours, I could go a minute without the need to cry. Within days, a few hours might pass.)

We were still high on the mountain, at just over 19,000 feet, but at least we were physically whole. I had one small scratch on my nose, my crampon hung loose from my right foot, and a pile of avalanche debris was piled on my chest. Thankfully, no bones were broken or ligaments torn despite my 500-foot fall.

Austin righted himself and climbed down to me. We didn't need to speak. Dan gathered the ropes as he climbed toward us. It was his turn to take complete control of the situation. He was now our leader.

Darkness caught us as we traversed the giant face for hour after hour, aiming for a flat place on the ridge to camp safely. Once we found a good ledge, Dan, in a tremendous display of partnership and perseverance, melted a round of hot drinks. Late that evening, we huddled together in our tiny nest of snow, carved from a step in the ridge. After more than forty hours of nonstop technical climbing, in desperate conditions, we were spent. At dawn, the hanging glacier above us collapsed, sending tons of ice down the cliff face we had rappelled only twelve hours before. When it hit the snow face that had stopped me, it triggered an avalanche. Within seconds, a cloud of snow dust rose beside our camp, covering us with an inch of powder while wiping away every sign of the fall and every footstep we'd carved while climbing to the safety of the ridge.

We spent the next several hours climbing down the ridge and hiking the easy terrain back to Base Camp, occasionally glancing upward to the face of the mountain. We were hungry and thirsty—but most important, we were alive. In the midst of a dire situation, we had been left with three basic instinctual responses: fight (stand up to the problem and try to defeat it), flight (run away from the problem), or freeze (simply ignore the problem and suffer even worse consequences). We chose to fight, and that's why we made it through.

Our climb of Shivling was a fight for our very survival. Everything was going wrong, from the storm, to the dropped pot, to the 500-foot fall. Any one of those events could have killed us. But somehow, when things seemed out of control, the stress inhuman, I felt stronger and more capable. I became more courageous with each challenge, thinking, "Well, if we survived that, we can certainly survive this."

On Shivling, acts of courage inspired the team. As long as one of us was willing to fight, we moved toward safety. I see this phenomenon play itself out in business all of the time. When we decided to build our second gym, we pulled together the Earth Treks team and laid out the risks and the rewards. Just a few years ago, I had been running the business out of a condemned warehouse, and now we wanted to borrow $960,000 while our collective and ambitious vision was for a $1.5 million facility. We decided to roll the dice, build the greatest gym, and supplement our debt with a lot of sweat equity and creative financing. We were constructing the gym using alpine-style climbing methods like we used on Shivling. A group of us shouldered minimalist equipment and set off into the unknown. The staff rallied to the cause, some of us working seven days a week, fourteen to forty-eight hours straight. We sold the vendors on our vision, persuading them to extend terms and deeply discount their products.

Despite our commitment, we ran into a giant hurdle: We needed to change the zoning for the site, from manufacturing to recreational. We hired a lawyer who told us the bad news. Clearly, we did not meet the recreational code requirements: Baltimore County demanded at least

10 parking spots for every 1,000 square feet of space. We needed 160 spots and had fewer than 40.

Our zoning lawyer shook his head and said, "This project will never, ever be approved by the zoning commission."

I was shocked by his willingness to admit defeat. "We have to be approved. I've already torn the roof off the building. I've spent over $360,000 on this site already. We have to be successful."

I prodded him to nearly his breaking point, forcing him to come up with a crazy scheme, though he proclaimed, "Thirty years of zoning work in this county and I've never seen it done." The solution: a landlord within 500 feet of Earth Treks' front door had to give us a fifteen-year lease for more than 100 parking spots. The problem was that in reality, the parking lots surrounding the building didn't have any spots to spare. Each parking spot was like a bar of gold, fought over by tenants in overcrowded buildings. Could I convince someone to sign away 120 of her most valuable assets, assets that were pledged to rent-paying tenants?

Solving this problem required me to use passion, vision, perseverance, and partnerships that I had developed within the Baltimore business community. But none of those things would have mattered had I not had the courage to act on them and pursue a solution to the problem. I remembered speaking to an executive M.B.A. class and meeting someone there who managed more than a million square feet of commercial space in Baltimore. His company owned a neighboring building. A phone call, an offer to go to lunch, and an Everest story or two led to his staff crafting just the finely balanced and creatively worded document we needed. Two days later, I sent our zoning lawyer the documents and signatures he said couldn't be obtained. At the zoning meeting, the commissioner had but one question: "Would it be possible for my child to have a birthday party at this climbing center?" With a quick "Yes, sir," the papers, along with a handful of special exemptions for parking, were signed. It was a small step in the long climb toward completing the gym, but it was a good reminder to not accept failure.

The Shivling expedition was the most valuable learning experience I've ever had, and it is one I hope to never have to repeat. Shortly after surviving that climb, I felt an intense sense of pride at having pushed myself so far beyond my imagined abilities and limits. But it took years for that pride to progress into a conscious and reusable source of wisdom.

When we applied the lessons learned on some of the world's largest peaks to the culture and operations of Earth Treks, we found ourselves standing on not one summit but many. Creating an organization that consistently exceeds our customers' expectations demands that we apply these lessons with discipline. Given the company's rapid growth, we face a lot of challenges, and cash-flow issues and personnel difficulties always remind us that there is a lot of work ahead. We are constantly relearning that after every summit, the team needs to return to the valley floor. Of course, you may be superhuman enough to "enchain" multiple summits, but most teams are incapable of enduring such abuse. In the Himalayas, those who linger to celebrate on the summit often die on the descent. Leaders must make sure their teams have enough in reserve to get back to the valley and should take advantage of forced rests to celebrate recent successes, assess resources, and mend wounds.

Guiding clients to the summit of Everest and building the highest-grossing climbing gyms in the United States are big goals. But simply declaring the pursuit of such goals could lead a company to disaster. Teams should not attempt to climb a metaphorical Everest without first developing the philosophical foundation of the company and increasing the depth of corporate courage it has to draw on. Consciously applying the lessons of passion, vision, perseverance, and partnership strengthens our foundation and gives us the courage we need.

5

Scaling Up:

Ridge Walking from Silicon Valley to McKinley's Summit

PAUL ASEL

Notice: Men wanted for hazardous journey. Small wages. Bitter cold.
Long months of complete darkness. Constant danger. Safe return
doubtful. Honor and recognition in case of success.

—Advertisement posted by Ernest Shackleton
for his last Antarctic expedition (the ad drew 5,000 applications)

JUNE 1998. A BLIZZARD RAGED ACROSS THE WINDSWEPT crest of the Kahiltna Glacier on Alaska's Mount McKinley. Drifts leaped the eight-foot snow-block wall that encircled us, submerging our tent. For the next twenty-four hours, Doug Heroux, Fred Mauren, and I took turns shoveling snow and reinforcing our position. We battled exhaustion and cold, struggling to secure our shelter against the storm.

We rarely talked in the tent that evening, retreating instead to our own solitude as we steeled ourselves for the ordeal ahead. Both Doug and Fred had climbed McKinley before. Fred had reached the summit two years earlier in benign weather, while ten years earlier Doug had made a harrowing escape along the West Buttress after a week of gale-force winds and whiteouts at high camp had depleted food supplies and ended the expedition without a summit attempt. Now, Doug stared blankly into space, reliving that week at high camp and summoning strength for this new ascent.

The tent door zipped open, and Fred plunged into the tent. It was my turn. Back in the blizzard, I held the shovel in front of me with outstretched arms. It was barely visible. So this was McKinley at 10,000 feet. What would it offer at 20,000? During the previous week, reports from high camp at 17,200 feet rarely varied: temperatures ranging from minus twenty degrees Fahrenheit to minus thirty, and winds exceeding forty miles an hour. The mountain had already claimed three lives in the last week, and weather had forestalled all summit bids until now, early June, in the middle of the 1998 climbing season. Our commitment to complete the climb without blackening toes or friendships now seemed in jeopardy. How much were we willing to risk in a summit bid if marginal conditions prevailed? The question now seemed more pressing and the answer less resolute than when we nonchalantly signed waivers at park headquarters in Talkeetna after watching a vivid documentary portraying McKinley's many hazards.

The challenges of mountain climbing provide a powerful metaphor for business. While investing in and advising start-ups for the past fifteen years, I have often used lessons from mountaineering experiences. Like climbing, starting a business is a risky endeavor in which the difference between success and failure is narrow and the consequences extreme. Entrepreneurs walk unconstrained by ropes, unconcerned about the danger of snow and ice disappearing underfoot, and unimpeded by layers of clothing designed for arctic conditions. Nevertheless, they guide their companies along narrow ridges, reconciling competing forces within and beyond the firm.

On a mountain or at the office, the quest for peak performance is a balancing act. Both entrepreneurs and climbers require:

- Tolerance for risk while pursuing uncharted opportunities
- A combination of team competence and compatibility
- Clear vision despite limited visibility (the "summit mentality")
- Responsiveness to changing conditions while steadfastly pursuing the ultimate objective

- Standards of practice while fostering innovation
- Sufficient speed to seize windows of opportunity while building strength to pursue new heights
- Unstinting perseverance tempered by prudence under pressure
- A broad perspective to exploit expanded horizons upon reaching the initial summit
- Managing the sometimes competing prerogatives of getting to the top and surviving to pursue other summits

As we climb Mount McKinley together, let's look more closely at how the lessons from mountaineering reinforce the balance necessary to reach our business summits.

THE ENTREPRENEURIAL MIND-SET: ON RISK AND OPPORTUNITY

Perhaps no mountaineering book has been more widely read and evoked more visceral reactions than *Into Thin Air*, Jon Krakauer's first-hand account of an ill-fated 1996 assault on Mount Everest in the spring of 1996 in which eight climbers died. The tragedy became a poster child for the dangers inherent in climbing and crystallized a debate about the merits of promoting expeditions to the world's highest mountains. Many were appalled by Krakauer's vivid account; it reaffirmed their worst impressions and squelched any interest in climbing. A second, smaller group had precisely the opposite reaction. Cognizant of the risks but intrigued by the challenge and sense of adventure, many have since become avid climbers.

Mountain climbing attracts those who enjoy stretching beyond perceived limits, and whether a deterrent or a welcome feature, risk is integral to the calculus of climbing when testing these limits. A supremely physical sport, mountain climbing requires not only a strong body, but also a level head to manage the mental stresses of risk.

The hallmark of elite climbing is a first ascent, which pushes new generations of climbers to attempt ever more challenging and risky routes. Mountains progress through a well-defined life cycle: climbers claim virgin peaks by the simplest means available, then they attempt increasingly technical routes, and, finally, they do them in the winter. The expansion of the Yosemite Decimal System, which rates the difficulty of North American free-climbing routes, reflects the escalation of climbing standards and raises the bar for top climbers. Class 5 climbs ranged from 5.0 to 5.9 until the 1950s, when 5.10 was added and then divided into 5.10a, 5.10b, 5.10c, and 5.10d to distinguish the newly blazed routes that accumulated in the most difficult categories. In recent decades, these same divisions have arisen in new categories 5.11 to 5.14. This escalation demonstrates the human capacity to push past old limits while managing the concomitant risks and increased dangers.

A tolerance for risk is also essential for entrepreneurs. Entrepreneurs have learned to embrace risk as the catalyst for new business opportunity for one simple reason: Uncertainty is the handmaiden of opportunity. Disruptive economic or technological change is a greenhouse for new companies, as entrepreneurial initiative, innovation, and nimbleness can overcome the traditional advantages of established firms during these uncertain periods. The venture capital industry, generally a barometer for new business prospects, has experienced three cyclical highs since the 1960s, corresponding to the emergence of the semiconductor, the personal computer, and the Internet industries. These brief windows of opportunity produced many of the leading technology companies of today, including Intel, Dell, Sun, Apple, Microsoft, Oracle, and AOL/Time Warner.

While disruptive change is a catalyst for new companies, the odds of long-term survival remain daunting. In 1929, there were 247 U.S. automobile manufacturers, including several dozen public companies, but only three survived the Great Depression and World War II. In the early 1980s, more than 80 data storage and 60 computer systems companies were established. Only Bell Micro, Iomega, Komag, and

Overland Data remain as independent data storage companies. Apple, Dell, Silicon Graphics, and Sun are the only surviving computer systems companies started during that period.

The yin-yang of the entrepreneurial culture in Silicon Valley is that it tolerates failure while celebrating its many successes. For example, John Doerr, a leading venture capitalist, has invested in such winners as Sun Microsystems, Cypress Semiconductor, Symantec, Citrix Systems, Intuit, Netscape, and Amazon. But Doerr's investment portfolio also includes defunct companies such as Cimlinc, WaveFrame, Go, Dynabook, and MNI Interactive. In consistently swinging for the fences, Doerr accepts strikeouts as a by-product of a process that has produced one of the best track records in Silicon Valley.

The balance between risk and opportunity is often mitigated by the tangential benefits of failure. Go, for example, was a laudable effort that was well ahead of its time. Founded in 1987, Go sought to make pen-based portable computers. The company did not last, but the concept did. Pen-based portable computing led to future successes such as notebook computers and personal digital assistants. Go's management team also gained experience that later served them well as executives at Intuit, AOL/Netscape, and elsewhere.

IDEO, a leading design firm, has incorporated the benefits of trial and error into its design process with a principle that founder David Kelley labels "Rough, Ready and Right." Kelley encourages designers to fail early and often to succeed sooner, recognizing that early prototypes may be incomplete yet still contain worthwhile aspects of the final product.

Embracing risk and managing uncertainty is critical in situations where the opportunity is enormous and the margin between success and failure is slim. In these "high-beta" environments, the winners are likely to emerge in companies with cultures, like those of Silicon Valley and IDEO, where risk taking is encouraged, well-intentioned failure is tolerated, and overachievement is expected and highly rewarded.

Doug Heroux, the strongest climber on our McKinley expedition, talked little about his failed attempt on the mountain ten years before, but it was clear that the ordeal had steeled him psychologically and physically for our current attempt. In the many long days and evenings in the tent together, he occasionally gave us snippets of his week at high camp: He referred to sleep deprivation from a constant wind ripping at the tent that sounded like a 747 flying too close overhead; ennui induced by three days without food at 17,000 feet; and battered nerves from descending along an exposed West Buttress in gale-force winds that buffeted him like a blade of grass. Whenever these thoughts resurfaced, he played his *Rocky* sound track to blot them out. Throughout the climb, he and I did push-ups together to maintain arm strength while waiting out storms. After I stopped from exhaustion, he would finish off the workout with five one-arm push-ups with each arm. His iron will and blockbuster build earned him the nickname "Alpine Rambo." Failure had made him stronger; it was clear from the outset that nothing short of impenetrable weather would keep him off the summit this time.

Both entrepreneurship and mountain climbing demand a capacity to stretch beyond perceived limits, envision possibilities where others see impregnable obstacles, and execute on a daily basis to maximize the likelihood of success despite slim odds. In the balance between risk and opportunity, Silicon Valley and climbers have accelerated innovation by tipping the scales of the traditional risk/reward equation. Silicon Valley has fostered an entrepreneurial climate by reducing the stigma attached to business failures; entrepreneurs and executives who acquit themselves well with investors will have future opportunities though their businesses may not succeed. Climbers have conquered the world's highest peaks and blazed increasingly difficult routes by competing intensely to notch first ascents, expanding the perceived realm of possible climbs with an ever-growing rating system, and using failed summit bids as fuel for future successes. By changing the frame of reference, the two communities have adjusted the traditional tendency toward loss aversion—the propensity to play it safe in uncertain situations as potential losses loom larger than gains—to encourage prudent risk taking.

* * *

AN ENTREPRENEURIAL ATTITUDE enabled most of the climbers in our group to work full-time and pursue their love of climbing. Fred Mauren was a financial executive at Kmart but had an agreement allowing him four weeks off per year for an annual climbing venture. Susi Kriemler had focused her practice on high-altitude medicine, allowing her extended forays in the Swiss Alps. Others owned their own businesses or practices and organized their schedules around summit bids. For those who balanced professional careers and climbing, the mind-set transferred well, though the venues differed significantly.

CHOOSING YOUR TEAM:
ON COMPETENCE, COMPATIBILITY, AND CULTURE

In preparing to climb McKinley, I wanted to enlist the best guide on the mountain. A friend who had spent two years on McKinley doing search and rescue recommended Brian Okonek, a twenty-year veteran who had led fifteen successful ascents in seventeen attempts. His reputation was impeccable. Brian exuded enthusiasm for climbing balanced with respect for the mountain. A couple of conversations convinced me that we were compatible and that his experience, leadership, and judgment were first-rate. We agreed on a McKinley traverse approaching along the West Buttress and descending Karstens Ridge to the Muldrow Glacier.

As a partner in a venture firm, a husband, and a father, I have experienced partnerships in a variety of forms, yet no situation rivals the intensity of climbing with a companion in exposed conditions. The "sacred bond of the rope" intertwines climbers in a shared fate. Etched in my mind and stomach is that sense of mutual reliance—and vulnerability—when leading sections along narrow ridges with thousands of feet of exposure on either side. If I fall off one side of the ridge, I depend on my partner to instinctively jump over the other side to counteract the fall. The bond becomes intuitive over time as experi-

Climbing on Karstens Ridge on Mount McKinley

ences are shared. Sometimes one must sense a partner's peril without seeing him, or else both will be dragged off the mountain.

Successful expeditions require a delicate balance of competence and compatibility. James Whittaker and Sir Chris Bonington are the most experienced American and British expedition leaders, respectively. Based on their varied climbing experiences, their emphasis differs regarding the trade-off between skill and teamwork, with profound implications for the teams they assemble.

For his 1978 American K2 Expedition, Whittaker drew on lessons learned from the uneven skill and determination levels demonstrated by an aborted 1975 attempt on the mountain and selected the "best, meanest, toughest climbers in the United States" from a broad pool of applicants, according to his introduction to Rick Ridgeway's *The Last Step: The American Ascent of K2*. The expedition's fourteen men and women endured the Savage Mountain for sixty-seven days as they waited out storm after storm. Schisms emerged as conditions toughened and climbers coped with unfamiliar partners, yet the expedition weathered its differences through shared determination and a commitment to success. Despite some rocky moments, the expedition eventually placed four climbers—John Roskelley, Rick Ridgeway, Lou Reichardt, and Jim Wickwire—on the summit by two different routes. In the process, Roskelley and Ridgeway became the first Americans to climb an 8,000-meter mountain without oxygen.

Bonington has led more expeditions to the Himalayas than any other Western climber: He boasts more than twenty first ascents in the Himalayas as a climber and expedition leader. Having once seen two ill-matched climbers fall to their deaths on the North Wall of the Eiger in Switzerland, Bonington made trust and team chemistry his foremost criteria in selecting climbing partners. For his expedition to the South Face of Annapurna, he looked for climbers "who could climb at a very high standard on rock and ice, with plenty of endurance, and an ability to subordinate their own personal ambitions to the good of the expedition as a whole. Most important of all, they would have to get on together." Bonington's expeditions have encountered tragedies along with many successes, yet accounts invariably attribute their ability to endure difficulties to the camaraderie and trust that arose from having climbed together over many years.

Businesses are similarly reliant on teams that combine complementary skills, tenacity, and chemistry. According to an old adage, valuing real estate involves five key criteria: location, location, location, location, and location. The corollary when investing in early stage companies is management. At Telos Venture Partners, our partnership invested first and foremost in management teams. We devoted considerable time to assessments of management strength, unique skills, appetite, and balance. Every investment required a founding team that could build and sustain a differentiated product or service. Since key executives would be added as the company grew, understanding how the team would evolve over time was essential. Complete teams with complementary skills reduced risk and accelerated the timeline to fulfill business milestones.

Bill Hewlett and David Packard are the gold standard of business partnerships. Classmates at Stanford University in the early 1930s, Bill and David began Hewlett-Packard with the encouragement of professor and mentor Fred Terman. From its humble origins in a Palo Alto garage in 1938, Hewlett-Packard grew steadily under their joint leadership, gaining a reputation as a progressive, well-managed company that turned out high-quality engineering products. Only in 1964, when Hewlett-Packard was a public company with $126 million in revenue and 7,000 employees, were David and Bill formally elected CEO and president, respectively. Nearly two decades into their partnership, David and Bill were asked how they had managed a large company over a long period as equals. According to Silicon Valley lore, they both looked at each other and asked simultaneously, "Would you like to answer the question?" Then they turned to the interviewer and suggested that perhaps he had his answer.

The Bill Hewlett–David Packard pairing was unique in that it combined extraordinary engineers and superior managers who also happened to be good friends. Most businesses must compromise in the trade-off between competence, compatibility, and culture. Intel and Microsoft, for example, feature overtly competitive and confrontational cultures that would clash with the collegial "HP Way" of managing by walking around. Nevertheless, Gordon Moore and Andrew Grove at Intel and Bill Gates and Steve Ballmer at Microsoft established effective, enduring partnerships based on a passionate drive to be the best, mutual respect, complementary skills, and sometimes brutal candor. The lesson from James Whittaker's 1978 American K2 Expedition and Chris Bonington's Everest expeditions is similar. Regardless of style, successful partnerships share complementary skills, a zeal for a common objective, and a personal commitment to the group to realize the goal.

BRIAN OKONEK ASSEMBLED THE EXPEDITION in Talkeetna near the Denali park headquarters (McKinley was formerly known as Denali, and still is in mountaineering circles). The team, which Brian had screened and interviewed for both skill and compatibility, included two New Zealanders, one Swiss, and five Americans. Most were veterans of the Alps, Andes, and/or Himalayas, and three had previously climbed McKinley. All were in good physical condition and were anxious to get on the mountain. All systems were go as we waited for the weather to clear and the airport to open.

BASE CAMP:
ON CLEAR VISION DESPITE LIMITED VISIBILITY

The turboprop hesitated and then whirred into motion, and we were off. Our pilot lifted our heavily loaded plane off the runway and guided it over a bull moose that grazed serenely in the verdant marshes beyond Talkeetna. The plane labored over a steep rise before nestling into a valley at the tongue of the Kahiltna Glacier. Soon only the azure blues of yawning crevasses and rocky clefts of the surrounding ridges interrupted the white sea of snow that surrounded us. The plane banked hard right and fluttered onto a stretch of hard-pack snow, and we stepped onto the glacier that would serve as our living room, bedroom, and kitchen for the next month. A peaceful silence replaced the hum of the plane as it disappeared around the ridge.

For the past several months, our team had focused on preparations for an ascent of McKinley. Anticipating twelve-to-eighteen-hour days of uninterrupted climbing at high altitude, we had trained rigorously. Scott Hissong regularly walked six miles to and from work shouldering a 130-pound backpack, Fred Mauren recorded a personal best marathon time, and Thai Verzone had just returned from winning a 150-mile extreme orienteering race between Hope and Homer, Alaska, that he completed in three days. Susi Kriemler had trained in the high Alps for much of the winter. Peter Lethbridge had trained extensively on Mount Cook in New Zealand. We also voraciously read accounts of prior climbs on McKinley. Early explorers such as Fred Cook, Hudson Stuck, Henry Karstens, and Brad Washburn left indelible impressions and were the subject of frequent debate during the climb. John Waterman's account of a 1982 winter ascent along Cassin Ridge served as a particularly haunting reminder of the focused endeavor on which we were embarking. Ten days into his climb, stuck on a ridge at 13,500 feet with minus forty degree temperatures, he lamented: "We were married, chained, and bonded to Denali because a lesser dedication would have been dangerous luxury. Once we climbed higher, retreating during a winter storm, or even just surviving a storm, seemed unthinkable. We had to get up."

Now that we were on the mountain, our lives were simplified, shielded from the din of daily events, and stripped to bare essentials. For the next four weeks, our sole focus was the summit of McKinley, rarely visible but always top of mind. Every activity and each ounce of energy expended brought us closer to our conquest. Our concentrated energy seemed to generate its own momentum, which would be vital when the mountain eventually retaliated.

Mountaineers share one clear objective—the summit. The vision is clear, though the view may be obstructed for days or weeks. Climbers brave bitter cold, withstand wind and whiteouts, spend days huddled in cramped tents, ascend for days or weeks with little oxygen and less food, and risk life and limb to stand on the world's highest peaks, often for less than fifteen minutes. No matter how much climbers enjoy the freedom of the mountains and the camaraderie of their companions, the ultimate goal of months of preparation is the peak experience.

Clarity of purpose is equally important in business. Unfortunately, the uncertain business environments in which start-ups flourish discourage focused objectives. Clarity of purpose must be carefully and continuously cultivated in an environment in which daily signals tend to scramble business activities. Starting a business requires a summit mentality, which identifies a clearly defined initial business objective that entrepreneurs can marshal resources to attack, seize, and defend against entrenched, better-capitalized competitors. Given limited capital and a brief window of opportunity, start-ups must attack this single promontory point with precision and force.

Paul Asel near the summit of Mont Blanc

The evolution of the computer market demonstrates how start-ups used a series of focused attacks to compete against IBM and create today's dynamic, multifaceted industry. In 1952, IBM produced its first computer and leveraged its experience in calculators and tabulators to establish a dominant position. By 1963, the company held a 70 percent market share with mainframe computer sales of $1.2 billion, nearly nine times those of its nearest competitor. Not a single mainframe competitor survived intact. Frontal attacks on Big Blue were no longer viable, but a series of focused flanking attacks proved successful. In 1965, Digital Equipment Corporation established a beachhead with a mass-produced minicomputer called the PDP—a smaller, less-expensive computer with reduced functionality. Compared with IBM's sales and market position, DEC's entry seemed insignificant, but not for long. DEC sold $15 million worth of PDPs in 1965, but expanded revenues to $135 million by 1970. In the decades since, minicomputers, now divided into servers and workstations, have become so pervasive that mainframes have been relegated to a relatively small number of extremely computation-intensive applications.

Other companies replicated DEC's focused strategy in computer niche after niche. Wang Laboratories developed a computer focused on office automation in 1972, the first of a series of application-specific computers developed during the decade. Tandem followed with fault-tolerant computers for the financial sector. New markets developed as semiconductor technology improved, and nimble start-ups were the first to seize on these opportunities. Apple Computer emerged in 1977 to champion personal computers, and Compaq began promoting portable computers in 1982. Dell Computer added to the specialization trend in the late 1980s with made-to-order computers. Sun Microsystems applied advances in networking technology to develop workstations, which eventually led to the networked computer. The computer industry spawned numerous other information technology markets, including software, peripherals, and services. Start-ups identified and rapidly moved to establish themselves in these new markets as well. By 2000, IBM had $88 billion in revenues, but the information technology industry had grown to more than $900 billion.

Articulating a vision is integral to a summit strategy. The relationship between clarity of vision and company success is striking. Joe Costello, CEO of Think3, offers an explanation: "Articulating a complete vision enables one to rationalize it, make it internally coherent, live in that environment, and develop a comfort level with the ultimate objective as if it were already a reality." Clarity of purpose also allows others—employees, customers, and investors—to share, reinforce, and propagate the vision.

Microsoft is abuzz with activity; its vision infuses everyone. Employees talk openly about their passion for their jobs and a desire to change the world through software, a business culture that dates back to the company's founding days. Bill Gates left Harvard early in 1975 to focus on developing desktop software for the Altair computer. While the computer establishment focused on large systems, Gates envisioned a computer on every desk. He viewed computing as pervasive and wanted Microsoft to lead the charge to ubiquity. Microsoft got its big break in 1980 when it won a contract to develop IBM's operating-system software. While IBM focused on hardware, Gates realized that it was software that breathed life into the machines. His vision was infectious. Microsoft products are now used to generate most of the spreadsheets, word documents, and presentations created worldwide. Nevertheless, the atmosphere on its campus suggests that Microsoft's mission is incomplete. Microsoft's recent forays into WebTV and Xbox play stations continue to enhance the versatility of computer hardware while the .NET initiative is Microsoft's attempt to adapt its software to the Internet era.

WE LEFT BASE CAMP and began the long march up the Kahiltna Glacier to the base of McKinley. The weather was fine, the route well trodden, and the slope gradual as we moved from Base Camp to Camp Two at 8,000 feet and Camp Three at 9,500 feet. Nearly two weeks would pass before we glimpsed the summit of McKinley, yet our vision of the peak framed our activities and propelled us forward. We encountered our first challenge—route finding—when the first storm arrived at the head of the Kahiltna Glacier.

ROUTE FINDING:
ON STEADFAST RESOLVE AND ADAPTIVE EXECUTION

Geometry teaches us that the shortest distance between two points is a straight line, but approaching the summit by the shortest distance rarely prevails in mountain climbing. Instead, climbers focus on the path of least resistance—the most efficient route offering the highest likelihood of success. Contouring, traversing, and occasional backtracking are both practical and a matter of survival. In this process, climbers balance a steadfast resolve to reach the summit with the flexibility to adjust to weather and climbing conditions along the way.

Our route on McKinley was well known, yet navigation remained a constant concern. We were well aware of the disconcerting opacity of snowstorms and spindrift on featureless slopes that sometimes confounded climbers within 100 feet of their camp. Accordingly, we placed wands—thin, two-foot-long wooden stakes adorned with small red or dark-blue flags—one rope length apart to mark our route. These wands proved essential when a blizzard moved in while we were carrying a load to Camp Four at 11,000 feet. The storm forced us to leave our cache 500 feet below the intended site and retreat to Camp Three using the wands as our guide. Though thwarted temporarily, we were undeterred, remaining at lower altitude and returning to establish Camp Four when the storm subsided.

The need for flexibility regarding means of ascent while remaining steadfast on the ultimate objective is more salient on first ascents, where the climb is a process of discovery. In 1950, Maurice Herzog sought to become the first man to summit an 8,000-meter peak. His goal was Annapurna, a 26,504-foot peak in an unexplored region of Nepal. Unlike climbs that draw on prior reconnaissance, the routes up Annapurna, like other first ascents, had never been analyzed. Herzog and his team had to locate the mountain using sketchy maps, pick out a single, untried route, and go for the summit—all within a two-month climbing season that ends when the monsoons arrive. The team unsuccessfully attempted the northwest spur, detoured to explore neighboring Dhaulagiri, then changed course again and settled on a route across the North Annapurna Glacier to the summit. In developing his ever-changing route to Annapurna's summit, Herzog skirted avalanche falls, navigated through crevasse-laden glacial debris, and identified a bridge spanning a wall of seracs that he called the Sickle.

Entrepreneurship has much in common with the discovery-driven planning and adaptive execution that Herzog demonstrated so effectively on Annapurna. In *Only the Paranoid Survive,* Andrew Grove describes the founding, growth, near failure, and ultimate success of Intel Corporation as a series of critical tests—or "inflection points"—on which the survival of the company depended. He described one critical juncture in 1985 when lower-cost Asian producers were forcing American manufacturers out of the semiconductor memory business, a market that Intel had led and that still constituted the vast majority of its revenues:

After this aimless wandering had been going on for almost a year, I was in my office with Intel's chairman and CEO, Gordon

Moore, and we were discussing this quandary. Our mood was downbeat. I turned to Gordon and I asked, "If we got kicked out and the board brought in a new CEO, what do you think he would do?" Gordon answered without hesitation, "He would get us out of memories." I stared at him, numb, then said, "Why shouldn't you and I walk out the door, come back, and do it ourselves."

Grove and Moore not only saved the company by exiting memories but led a transition that freed the company to focus on microprocessors, an emerging market at the time that has since become the computer industry's most important component.

The dynamic process that Grove described at Intel is common among early stage companies, sometimes leading to destinations markedly different from the point of origin. Matsushita was formed in 1918 to make electric bicycle lamps. Motorola began as a maker of car radios in 1928, and Texas Instruments started as a producer of geological instruments for the oil industry in 1930.

The Matsushita, Motorola, and Texas Instruments of today bear only moderate resemblance to their origins, yet each business developed an area of expertise and followed a path of learning that allowed the company to respond quickly to threats and evolve as changing business conditions required. Matsushita built retail distribution, consumer marketing, and electronic design and production capabilities while focusing on bicycle lamps in the 1920s, then used those skills to expand into electric irons, home heaters, batteries, radios, and tubes in the 1930s. Matsushita was well positioned for the emergence of television in the 1950s and, through its Panasonic brand, has established itself as one of the leading consumer electronics companies today. Motorola built on its expertise in mobile radios in the 1930s and became a broad-based, integrated communications manufacturer during and after World War II. Motorola recognized the potential of the cellular market in the 1980s and moved quickly to become the leading provider of cellular telephones in the 1990s. From its roots in geological instru-

ments, Texas Instruments leveraged expertise in seismology to provide
radar and sonar equipment for the military during World War II and
transistor radios starting in 1952. After developing the first silicon transistor in 1954, TI established a commanding lead in silicon-based products through the 1970s. TI continued to evolve its business in response
to the Asian threat in the 1980s by focusing on digital signal processors,
a market in which it retains a worldwide lead today.

Intel, Matsushita, Motorola, and Texas Instruments all used similar
pathfinding strategies to grow from inception to leadership in their respective industries. They established core competencies, employed a
process of continuous evaluation and course correction as markets
evolved, and moved rapidly to solidify their positions as significant opportunities emerged that leveraged their core strengths.

The ability to navigate through strategic inflection points while
balancing a clear vision with adaptive execution remains vital today. In
calm conditions with a clear field of vision, climbers may use distant
points on the horizon for guidance, altering the course only for crevasses
and other nearby obstacles. In whiteout conditions, however, the field
of vision narrows, forcing climbers to navigate blindly from wand to
wand. The same narrowing of focus and adaptive execution applies to
companies in turbulent times. The NASDAQ stock market crash in
2000 has dramatically impacted all technology markets, forcing businesses to trim costs and refine their strategies. The survivors may
emerge as quite different companies, yet the core competencies and vision must remain steadfast as a foundation on which to build.

AS WE CLIMBED SQUIRREL HILL and crawled around Windy Cor-
ner, we were careful to both avoid the traditional avalanche paths and
skirt the crevasses, both seen and unseen, that lurked below. The slope
steepened as we ascended Motorcycle Hill onto the West Buttress ridge.
The exposed, narrow ridge dissuaded us from pitching our tents; we
dug snow caves instead and established camp quickly. Nestling into our
icy confines, we prepared a hot meal and enjoyed the orange hues of
the low summer sun reflecting off the tundra ponds 16,000 feet below.

With several thousand feet of exposure on either side, balance was required in our every movement.

RIDGE WALKING:
ON ESTABLISHING STANDARDS OF PRACTICE
WHILE FOSTERING INNOVATION

Mountains have manifold countenances. They are serene when placid, but brutally tempestuous when stormy. They are enticing yet intimidating, august yet austere, inspirational and provocative. Mountaineering also contains a duality. Mountaineering celebrates rugged individualism and our quest to tame nature's most formidable edifices, yet this quest often requires ascetic discipline. *Mountaineering: The Freedom of the Hills*, a classic handbook devoted to instruction on recommended climbing practices, contains in its title the essence of this climbing paradox. Mastery of the technique—and repeating standards of practice until they are rote—liberates one to experience the freedom of the hills.

From small rocks do avalanches begin. Having volunteered for search-and-rescue missions on Mount McKinley for more than twenty years, Brian Okonek has observed most every kind of mountaineering mishap. Out of his experience came a philosophy that he described early on our climb: "In extreme conditions, mental faculties diminish and instinct is the only reliable resource. Trivial oversights at sea level may prove fatal at high altitude. When the weather deteriorates, the situation can unravel quickly as small mistakes precipitate larger, more costly errors."

The mere mention of Marty Hoey's death was all Brian needed to illustrate his point. An accomplished, cautious climber, Marty fell 6,000 feet to her death off the Great Couloir on a 1982 Mount Everest expedition. The fall occurred at a rest stop when she leaned back against the support of her rope, only to have her waist harness come unbuckled. Unable to stop herself on the steep, icy slopes, Marty disappeared in seconds without a sound, leaving only her unstrapped harness as evidence of her mishap. Her elementary yet fatal error: failing to thread the end of her belt back through the buckle to assure that the harness would not come loose.

Okonek established routines and prescribed procedures at the outset of our climb to minimize the potential for human error and enable us to safely climb the mountain. Before encamping, we probed the entire campsite for crevasses and established borders that clearly demarcated safe and untested ground. Only within these borders were we free to walk around unroped. Setting up camp required digging snow caves or building fortifications to secure the tents against high winds. We were only free to rest without concerns about the weather once the camps were fully established. Decamping in the morning involved roping up among climbing teams, checking partners for correct gear assembly—including checks that the belt was threaded back through the buckle—and belaying each climber out of and into camp. Only after these safety checks were we free to begin our climb. Daily drills on techniques for self-arrest, crevasse rescue, and use of protection assured that we executed our regimen with military precision and were prepared for the exposed ridges and extreme conditions that awaited us.

Standards of practice—corporate policies supported by management processes and financial controls—are also essential in business. The high-profile demises of Continental Illinois, the Barings Group, Long Term Capital, Enron, and WorldCom show that even venerable firms are vulnerable to rogue business practices if adequate controls are not established and enforced. But the role of process and procedure in early stage companies is controversial. Standards of practice promote operational efficiency, but bureaucratic oversight can become cumbersome, undermining the flexibility, innovation, and speed required as start-ups seek to outmaneuver better-capitalized competitors. Yet the rise of Compaq Computer demonstrates that process and procedure are not incompatible with innovation in early stage companies.

Compaq used well-implemented standards of practice to streamline innovation, accelerate growth, and scale its operations faster than any U.S. company before it. In 1982, Ron Canion founded Compaq to exploit new opportunities in the personal computer market. Although Compaq enjoyed a first-mover advantage in portable computers, Canion realized that economies of scale were necessary to eventually compete with DEC and IBM. Accordingly, Canion laid the foundations for a big company at the outset. He developed strong financial controls, an operating infrastructure, and a forecasting system before production began. He raised a record $30 million in venture funding and recruited senior executives from Texas Instruments and IBM, which is common practice now but was unusual at the time. Meanwhile, Canion used Compaq's potential scale to establish a network of authorized dealers and accelerate development of technologies complementary to its portable computer model. He persuaded Intel to adjust its 80386 chip to meet Compaq's requirements and Bill Gates to develop software for the computer. Compaq leveraged its timely entry in the portable computer market, industry partnerships, and operating infrastructure to grow to $1 billion in revenues within four years.

While Compaq demonstrates that standards of practice can accelerate growth among start-ups, established companies such as 3M, Rubbermaid, Disney, Microsoft, and Intel have maintained a culture of innovation as they have grown. These companies, which generate a significant portion of their revenues each year from new-product introductions, have found that standards of practice may reinforce innovation through processes that engender and implement creative ideas in useful products and services.

One of the longest-standing examples of continuous innovation in corporate America is provided by 3M. Since 1937, when CEO William McKnight established the Central Research Laboratory, 3M has developed a system of amassing expertise in an area and then leveraging this knowledge to create and commercialize new products and applications. The simple tape business, for example, led to more than 300 products, including new opportunities in electrical tape, reflective tape, magnetic tape, duct tape, and Scotch tape. Through intensive development efforts, the company expects to generate at least 25 percent of sales from new products created in the last five years.

Essential to innovation at 3M is a lead-user process, a systematic method of identifying, learning from, and jointly developing products with companies and individuals who are at the forefront of its markets. Project teams dive deeply into target markets and network their way up pyramids of expertise to identify lead users and experts, first in the target market and then in other key fields to which they are referred. The medical-imaging team, for example, began by finding expert radiologists, who referred them to experts in semiconductor imaging and pattern recognition. The company sponsors lead-user workshops that assemble identified experts, product developers, marketers, and technical and manufacturing people to vet user requirements and new product ideas. Then 3M seeks to convert selected lead users into early adopters who can test and refine new products that emerge from this process.

When James McNerney took the helm of 3M in December 2000, he faced the challenge of reviving the bottom line without sacrificing its innovative corporate culture. In addition to cost controls, McNerney has sought to accelerate innovation by streamlining 3M's development pipeline of 1,500 products and funneling R&D funding to high-potential projects. McNerney's initiatives at 3M are works in process, yet they illustrate the healthy tension between financial discipline, process, and innovation.

FOR THE NEXT TWO DAYS, we ferried supplies along the West Buttress ridge to high camp. Now two weeks into the expedition, each pair on our team had developed a well-honed routine. The lead climber used ice stakes as anchors to secure himself and his partner as they traversed the narrowest portions of the ridge, while the trailing climber retrieved the anchors and returned them to the front during rest breaks. We kicked our crampons with each step, locking ourselves firmly into the snow and ice and using deeply planted ice axes to provide balance. Our focus on these practices helped stave off the languid effects of altitude. Recalling that two climbers had fallen to their deaths here a week earlier after an experienced lead climber had inexplicably unclipped to assist his partner, we now realized that our regimen early in the climb served us well at this time, when we needed it most.

OPERATING AT 20,000 FEET:
ON SPEED AND PREPAREDNESS

Step, step, breathe. Step, step, breathe. It is remarkable how much easier the altitude seems when climbing in rhythm. The rest step was an old friend and constant companion on McKinley.

Our group left Talkeetna with more than 100 pounds of food and equipment per climber, anticipating as many as thirty days on McKinley. As the air thinned and the slope grew steeper, our loads seemed heavier and our pace slowed. Once past Camp Two, we divided our loads and settled into a routine of carrying the first load—generally consisting of food and gas that would not be needed until later in the trip—to a site higher on the mountain, caching it, returning to camp for the evening, breaking camp the next morning, retracing our route to the cache site, and establishing camp with the rest of our gear. The two-day routine, weather permitting, allowed us to acclimatize while easing the burden of climbing with heavier loads. We established successive camps at 9,500 feet, 11,000 feet, 14,000 feet, 16,000 feet, and 17,200 feet in this manner.

Dr. Charles Houston, an early authority on the effects of altitude on human physiology and an avid climber who made a first ascent of Mount Foraker in Alaska, wrote this in a research report during World War II: "There is nothing critical, physiologically speaking, about the summit of Everest." Reinhold Messner and Peter Habeler proved Houston's assertion more than thirty years later, in 1978, when they became the first climbers to ascend Everest without supplemental oxygen. Still, if a person living at sea level were placed on the top of Mount Everest, he or she would die within minutes.

The key to coping at high altitude is packing light and acclimatization. Both strike a balance between preparedness and speed. Rapidly changing conditions at high altitude require extra gear, yet each additional pound slows the ascent and increases time spent on exposed ridges. Acclimatizing, the process by which the body adjusts to less oxygen, is time consuming—above roughly 8,000 feet, the body typically adjusts to higher altitude at a rate of about 1,500 feet per day—but necessary. However, at high altitude, where the weather is particularly unpredictable and physical and mental faculties deteriorate rapidly, dashes to the summit followed by rapid descents are common practice.

Entrepreneurs face similar challenges in determining how fast to grow their businesses. Moderate growth risks missing the window of opportunity and allowing a rival the chance to seize the competitive advantage. Acutely aware of the importance of timing and the fickleness of capital markets, a leading venture capitalist, Tom Kleiner, advised start-ups to "eat when served." Amazon, Ciena, eBay, and Yahoo are examples of companies that achieved leadership by seizing a first-mover advantage and growing aggressively in new markets enabled by the Internet. But aggressive growth places strains on management and often requires an unsustainably high burn rate if market adoption is slower than anticipated. Reflecting on more than fifty years of business experience in his book *The HP Way*, David Packard noted that more companies die of indigestion than starvation, an observation dramatically reinforced during the Internet era. Exodus Communications, Excite/At Home, eToys, Priceline, Webvan, and WorldCom were "red giants" that together raised billions of dollars but imploded under the weight of excessive burn rates and premature expansion on unproven business models.

As Kleiner's and Packard's comments suggest, there is no universally applicable rule for the pace at which early stage companies should grow. But climbing provides useful guidance. Companies must observe sustainable growth rates just as climbers yield to the physiology of acclimatization. Dismissing the siren call of first-mover advantage and pacing growth as business "muscles" strengthen may be appropriate during formative market stages, much like acclimatization builds a base for climbers as they approach higher elevations. Raising additional capital as a buffer for market or product delays is worth additional dilution, just as some redundancy is prudent at high altitude. At the same time, preparing for rapid growth after achieving market traction is essential in seizing the window of opportunity, just as dashes to the top from high camp are common in climbing.

MOVING METHODICALLY UP THE MOUNTAIN, we arrived at high camp early on our seventeenth day on McKinley. The calm, clear weather belied the normal conditions that prevailed at this altitude. The bullet-proof hardpack on which we pitched our tents and with which we carved ice-block barricades forewarned us of the windy tempest to come. Conditions boded well for a summit attempt the next day. But it wasn't long before our preparations were interrupted.

HIGH CAMP: ON PERSEVERANCE AND PRUDENCE

We heard the *thwack-thwack-thwack* long before the helicopter emerged on the horizon. Help was on its way. Two British climbers had been seriously injured in a fall at 19,500 feet two days earlier, but bad weather had thwarted their attempts to descend, along with other efforts to rescue them. As the helicopter plucked them off the mountain, we were reminded of the fate of last year's expedition sponsored by Brian Okonek. Caught in a storm at 19,000 feet and lost in a white blur of wind and snow, the climbers had to burrow in for the night. Everyone survived, but the mountain had excised its bounty in lost fingers and toes. Now it was our turn. The summit stood tantalizingly close—just 3,000 vertical feet away—yet the rescue reminded us how quickly things can go wrong at this altitude.

Our guidelines were clear as we prepared for the summit: Our turnaround time was not to be overlooked. Rob Hall's ill-fated expedition on Mount Everest in 1996 reinforced the consequences of such a folly. Hall had given 2 P.M. as the latest possible turnaround time on summit day: All climbers were to start descending to high camp at that time regardless of proximity to the peak. Yet Hall, spurred by rival guide Scott

Fischer and aware of his client's go-for-broke desire to reach the top, ignored his own limit and guided Doug Hansen to the peak. By the time they began their descent after 4 P.M., both men suffered from depleted energy and oxygen reserves. The onset of a blizzard sealed their fate. Hall and Hansen died high on the mountain.

The balance between prudence and perseverance is the tightrope of climbing. At high altitude in the "death zone," the margin for error is razor thin. Fatigue, failed footholds, fast-breaking storms, or faulty protection can quickly turn acts of valor into preludes to tragedy. Few places on earth have potential consequences so acute yet are less conducive to rational decision making. Hypoxia strips the mind of clarity, while each step forward heightens the lure of the summit. Climbing demonstrates that the body can be pushed far beyond perceived limits if circumstances require, but the forces of nature must be equally respected. Risk is manageable if one controls the dice. But climbers roll only one die; nature controls the other.

Determining when to hold or fold is one of the most vexing challenges in managing or investing in struggling ventures. A never-say-die attitude is critical to success. But it is not the quick deaths that kill venture investors; it is the living dead that drain capital and management resources. Investors are taught to ignore sunk costs such as prior investments or expenditures of time and resources; but initial commitments create a bias toward ongoing commitment (after all, one's reputation is at stake), so sunk costs are never really sunk. This tendency may explain statistics indicating that stock market investors tend to hold losing investments too long, that companies receiving seed investments have a higher likelihood of success than restarts, and that companies requiring additional venture financing after the third investment round have a lower likelihood of success on each subsequent round. In each case, additional information about company performance and better understanding of the market as it develops should improve decision making, yet a bias to persevere dulls receptivity to market signals.

As mountain climbers use clear guidelines such as turnaround times to determine whether to push to the summit or turn back, managers and investors rely on clear milestones established at the outset. A company's ability to make annual forecasts, budgets, key product delivery dates, projected customer sales, and competitive performance targets serves as an early warning system for companies, enables timely course correction, and, when the situation is dire, helps investors determine when to hold and when to fold. Yet, as the example of Hall and Hansen on Everest suggests, clear milestones are often insufficient to counteract the bounded rationality inherent in evaluating ongoing commitments. Instead, a separation of roles may be necessary to ensure the appropriate balance between perseverance and prudence. New investors in subsequent financing rounds and arms-length advisers help provide objectivity as a company progresses and free executives to focus on the task of persevering.

AWAKENING EARLY THE NEXT MORNING, we found the weather had held. We melted snow for hot drinks and cereal and consumed as much as our altitude-starved bodies would allow, aware that if all went well, this would be our last meal until our return sixteen hours later. We felt strong and well acclimatized; the remaining unknown variable was the weather. As we set out, we glanced anxiously at the clouds hovering far below in the valley, knowing how quickly storms can boil up at this altitude. The clouds appeared benign, but their hovering presence lurked like an alarm bell. Weather aside, we plodded ahead, determined that nothing but a storm would deter us from reaching the summit.

A VIEW FROM THE TOP: ON MAINTAINING PERSPECTIVE

Hey! Hey! The summit was ours today! The weather was spectacular. The wind eased and frosty morning conditions gave way to relatively balmy temperatures of zero degrees Fahrenheit as we climbed the headwall and traversed the final ridge to the top of McKinley. We lingered atop North America for almost an hour, enjoying hundreds of miles of visibility in all directions. Mount Foraker and Mount Hunter, which had dominated our views early in the climb, hovered far below around the shoulders of McKinley. From this angle, the solution to the intricate maze of the jagged, low-lying Kichatnas seemed deceptively simple. On the horizon hundreds of miles away stood the stately Wrangell and Chugach Mountains. The vast expanses of Alaska suddenly seemed much more accessible.

Barry Richmond, professor of systems dynamics at Dartmouth and founder of Hi-Performance Systems, advocates "10,000 Meter Thinking" in problem solving. Richmond believes that executives suffer from too much depth and not enough breadth. A broader, integrative perspective helps decipher how changes far afield impact the company and how new business initiatives may alter market dynamics.

General Electric's "boundaryless" initiative illustrates one practical application of the benefits of such higher-level thinking. After nearly fifteen years of emphasizing the need to be number one or number two in every market, GE undertook a "mind-set change." Believing that division leaders had overlooked larger opportunities by defining markets too narrowly in their quest for preeminence, Jack Welch mandated that all markets be redefined so that no business had more than a 10 percent market share. The market-expanding exercise became a mind-expanding breakthrough. The new market definitions offered plenty of headroom for growth. Over the next five years, GE doubled its revenue growth rate from the same newly energized portfolio of businesses, going from $70 billion in sales in 1995 to $130 billion in 2000.

Entrepreneurs, unfortunately, do not have the luxury to undertake boundaryless initiatives like GE does. With limited resources, early stage companies must expand their horizons incrementally. Mountain climbing provides a useful analogy. Views expand gradually as one gains altitude. Cresting a ridge offers a new, broader view of surrounding peaks. Reaching the summit opens the route to the next peak on the mountain range; one can walk along the ridge from summit to summit in this manner. Similarly, a summit mentality focuses initially on winning the first target market. Thereafter, the company may enlarge its business scope to encompass adjacent markets.

Siebel Systems, for example, began offering sales force automation (SFA) software in 1994. Focusing on SFA software shortened the sales cycle and simplified implementation requirements. As a result, Siebel grew to $410 million in sales by 1998 and won the SFA market, beating rivals Clarify, Vantive, Aurum, and Scopus. In 1999, Siebel expanded its market definition to customer relationship management (CRM) software and began selling enterprise software applications for sales and marketing. The expanded software product and market definition enabled Siebel to quadruple sales to $1.6 billion in 2002.

Executives must exercise judgment in determining when and how far to expand the business scope. While the location of the summit and route to the next peak is generally clear for climbers, entrepreneurs lack such objective markers. Expanding the scope may be necessary to achieve a defensible position, but expanding too quickly risks causing a two-front war. Managing this tension requires breadth of perspective as well as deep-domain knowledge. One does not have to go to 10,000 meters to find that; business guru Peter Drucker takes many of his insights from his reading Greek literature. Regardless of source of inspiration, all leaders need changes of venues that offer a view from the top.

WE RETURNED FROM THE SUMMIT to high camp exhausted but exhilarated. It was midnight, but the summer sun still shone bright on the horizon as we ate dinner before retiring for the evening. Stormy weather kept us tent bound for two days, but the anxiety had dissipated with the satisfaction of having reached the summit. Finally, on the twenty-second day of the climb, we left high camp, traversed to the Muldrow Glacier, and descended toward Wonder Lake.

OVER THE TOP: ON SUSTAINING THE SUMMIT EXPERIENCE

"The rest is a walk in the park," exclaimed Brian Okonek. Moments later a high-pitched splitting sound interrupted our short celebration. A hanging serac at the top of Pioneer Ridge had given way, scattering thousand-pound blocks of ice down the slope and launching an avalanche that obliterated the tracks our snowshoes had made just minutes earlier.

Over the last three days, we had descended down an exposed Karstens Ridge and across the Muldrow Glacier. The descent had been painstakingly slow as we maneuvered through icefalls with "cracks of such dimensions that a whole railway train might disappear into them," according to Erling Strom, an early explorer in the region. On this morning, the twenty-sixth of the expedition, we had broken camp at 3 A.M., hoping to pass through the lower icefall while conditions were still firm. Even then, unstable conditions frequently forced us to retreat to the slopes of Pioneer Ridge, which offered surer footing but left us vulnerable to the hanging seracs that lined the

Paul Asel, left, establishing camp on Karstens Ridge on Mount McKinley

rocky clefts above. We occasionally surveyed the twin treacheries of the serrated glacier to our right and the ridge above us on our left, hoping for some alternative to the loaded gun under which we walked. Now, the mountain had taken a parting shot. Though a misfire, the avalanche had delivered its message: This was not a walk in the park. Five more miles of glacier and the swollen, glacial strands of the McKinley River awaited us before we arrived at Wonder Lake. If Denali had its way, there would be no easy days.

The culmination of a successful climb—the summit—is only the halfway point. Descents are as treacherous as ascents; indeed, descents have higher casualty rates, especially when resources are depleted and exit strategies are poorly worked out. Chris Bonington worried aloud that prior to the final summit attempt on the long, exposed, unclimbed Northeast Ridge of Everest, his team had still not established a line of retreat down to the North Col. Worrying that he was climbing "out of control," Chris made the difficult decision to forgo a summit bid. Half the team decided to go on without him. A week later, Joe Tasker and Peter Boardman left Advanced Base Camp, never to return.

Long-term success and survival, whether on a mountain or in a business, depends on sustained vision, focus, initiative, and execution. The 1994 business bestseller *Built to Last* struck a nerve for two fundamental reasons: We all want something to show for a career of hard work, yet we all know that sustaining success is no walk in the park, either. The lessons in *Built to Last* were often overlooked during the "new economy" of the late 1990s, when money flowed easily and companies were frequently built to flip. During this frenetic period, initial public offerings were often viewed as destinations—liquidity events for founders and early investors—rather than funding milestones en route to critical mass, market leadership, and long-lived businesses. Such companies rose weightlessly in a buoyant market, only to falter and dissipate amid turbulent conditions. As a result, the survival rate has been poor. Of the technology companies that went public in 1996, fewer than half remained independent five years later, and less than 20 percent had increased in value over that time. Early indicators suggest that survival rates will be lower in IPOs from 1997 to 2000.

Companies that are built to last are generally well constructed at the outset. Though the challenges may change as the business grows, the fundamental traits that lead to success vary little over time. The skills that get climbers to the top of the mountain are the same that get them down. And so it is with businesses: The foundations established at the founding of a company—its vision, culture, and organizational processes—are similar to those that will sustain it.

Charles Schwab & Company was an unlikely candidate for a built-to-last company. Charles Schwab launched in 1974 after the SEC mandated a thirteen-month trial period for the deregulation of certain brokerage transactions. While most established firms used deregulation to raise commissions, Schwab undercut the competition. His prospects seemed dim in a low-margin business dominated by large, well-capitalized firms, but focusing on the retail investor enabled Schwab to offer superior service while streamlining operations. Schwab's initial vision also proved remarkably resilient. A commitment to "offer individual investors useful, ethical services at a fair price" served the company well initially as a discount broker and later as a full-service financial adviser. Its commitment to service and low costs made Schwab an early adopter of computer systems technology in 1979 and online trading in 1996. Having withstood competition from the securities industry, averted consolidation of the banking industry, and led online trading, Schwab has evolved against all odds from renegade to a mainstream industry leader.

CROSSING THE MCKINLEY RIVER, we stopped to survey the massive expanse of the Denali range. For twenty-eight days we had tarried in the shadow of McKinley, learning lessons that would fortify us upon our return. Now the rest truly was a walk in the park. As we turned and walked the last few miles to Wonder Lake, thoughts of work returned and the foothills of the American Professional Range emerged on the horizon. Standing between McKinley and the professional journey ahead offered a unique view, highlighting ways to sustain the summit experience. A balanced approach that applied mountaineering guidelines for teamwork, a summit mentality, adaptive execution, standards of practice, preparedness, perseverance, and perspective would serve us well elsewhere. As we prepared for our next venture, we realized how deeply these standards had been ingrained. For as any climber knows, the mountains never really leave us—even when we leave them.

Strategy at the Crux:
Life-and-Death Choices on Everest and K2

RODRIGO JORDAN

No end is visible or even conceivable to this kingdom of adventure.

—GEORGE LEIGH-MALLORY

AT 9:30 A.M. ON AUGUST 13, 1996, FOUR MEMBERS OF THE Chilean climbing team I was leading reached the summit of K2, the second-highest mountain in the world and the deadliest of them all. Climbers call K2 the "Savage Mountain" for good reason: of those who reach the 28,253-foot summit, about one in seven perish on the descent, a death rate perhaps five times greater than on Mount Everest.

K2's summit juts into the death zone, the unfriendly terrain above 8,000 meters. The environment above this height is so inhospitable that the human body begins to physically deteriorate from dehydration and lack of oxygen. Prolonged exposure to this altitude will gradually but inevitably lead to cerebral or pulmonary edema, and thus to certain death. Throw in sheer exhaustion—our team had been climbing for nearly sixteen straight hours—and the pressure of traversing the most difficult terrain on a mountain known for sudden, treacherous weather changes, and the dangers of remaining long on the summit should be obvious to climbers. But above 8,000 meters, the brain requires more oxygen than the air offers, making the simplest movement a huge mental effort. In its oxygen-deprived state, our summit team chose to celebrate with a glass of Chilean wine while the clock was ticking off fateful minutes.

News of the celebration worried me inside the mess tent at Base Camp, 9,840 feet below, where I had been glued to the radio for the last ten hours. I knew the most hazardous section of our entire expedition—the descent to Camp Three—lay ahead. Then, at 2 P.M., shortly after the team left the summit, I received a dreadful call. "Miguel is exhausted," his climbing partner, Cristián, told me. "He sat down and does not want to continue walking."

Miguel, Cristián said, had stopped 650 feet above an equipment cache where, on the way up, they had stashed fuel, pots, and a stove for melting fluids. Reaching it would greatly increase Miguel's odds of survival, as just half a liter of water could make him recover his energies enough to descend for a few hours to the relative safety of Camp Three. That was his only hope. Only minutes ago, just 90 feet above where he and Cristián now stood, Miguel had tossed aside a partially filled oxygen cylinder—the only other aid to survival at that altitude—because he found it too "cumbersome." Thin air was wreaking havoc on his brain.

The options for help were limited. The two other members of the climbing team were still on the mountain, but I had lost radio contact with them, and Cristián couldn't see them and had presumed they had continued to climb down. Although nearly exhausted himself, Cristián was still able to help Miguel, but he wanted to work through with me every decision about what should be done and when. Ultimately, I knew, Miguel would have to find the will to come down on his own, but if I could keep Cristián involved and rally the other climbers to help, we could exponentially increase the chances of Miguel's deciding to help himself. As the summit team tackled its most serious challenge of the climb, I faced one of the most serious tests of my career: Had I built a team that could stand up to this unexpected challenge?

A DECADE AT VERTICAL

I started climbing while studying for my engineering degree at Universidad Católica de Chile in Santiago sixteen years earlier, in 1980. By graduation, I had committed myself to pursuing two parallel careers: industrial engineering and extreme mountaineering. I was able to continue along both paths in graduate school, pursuing a doctorate in management at Oxford University and attending mountaineering courses at the National School for Outdoor Activities in North Wales.

After returning to Chile, I participated in three expeditions to Mount Everest, leading two of them. Shortly after my third trip, a successful summit by the demanding East Face in 1992, I decided to undertake a different type of adventure: starting a nonprofit educational foundation. A decade of climbing in the Andes and the Himalayas had convinced me that physical and technical skills alone were not enough to guarantee success. Without social skills, all the technical talent in the world couldn't create a high-performance team. What was true of the mountains, I had come to believe, was true of other organizations. The elementary schools that I was familiar with focused almost exclusively on cognitive topics such as physical and social science, language, and mathematics, yet without social skills such as leadership, teamwork, communication, and entrepreneurship, children would have trouble succeeding in adult life, especially underprivileged kids who already had two strikes against them. That's where I decided to focus, not only because I could do society a good service but also because an opportunity was there to be exploited.

Since I knew that starting a foundation was going to be as difficult as climbing a high-altitude mountain, I searched for a partner to accompany me in this new venture. Marcelo Grifferos, who had been crucial in organizing the expeditions to Mount Everest and was a trusted friend, enthusiastically jumped into the plan. Together, we expanded the original concept into universities and the world of business management. Thus, instead of starting one organization, we launched two: the original nonprofit foundation—Fundación Maitenes—and a for-profit company—Vertical S.A, which focuses on delivering high-quality outdoor education and training services to large multinational and domestic companies and institutions in Chile and elsewhere in South America.

Vertical offers adventure-based experiential learning programs and workshops on leadership, communication skills, high-performance teamwork, and entrepreneurship. Courses range from three days to two weeks, including lectures, outdoor exercises, and discussions. The idea is that people must learn, leave, and transfer their knowledge. Since 1993, Vertical has grown into a company of fourteen full-time employees and fifty part-time instructors, running training programs for more than 270 companies and institutions in nearly all South American countries. Clients have included Shell, Unilever, Coca-Cola, Exxon, Nestlé, Procter & Gamble, and Pfizer, among others. Vertical has also put together programs for institutions, such as the ministries of education, health, and labor in Chile.

Overseeing these training programs and courses, as well as guiding the nonprofit side of our business, has given me the unique opportunity to study leadership and team building within a vast variety of organizations, from big multinationals to small domestic companies, government agencies, sport teams, public hospitals, and nongovernmental organizations. I've seen company presidents, government ministers, and impoverished children struggle to master the issues and skills out of which I believe high-performance teams are built:

- Clear objectives and a shared vision
- Individual responsibility
- Positive attitude
- Strong leadership and consistent decision making
- Trust

In 1986, 1989, and 1992, I had the chance to test my own skills against Mount Everest. In 1996, it all came to a head on K2: I felt that every last bit of my business management and mountaineering experience was being challenged at once. Our summit team had been training for this expedition for two years. I had insisted on building a peak-performance team—one that excelled not only in its technical capacities but also in its social skills and, above all, one that was bonded together by a strong core of shared values. But had I built it right?

In mountaineering, "the crux" is the single most difficult point in the climb. Successfully negotiating the crux move on a climbing route requires great physical strength, technical ingenuity, and emotional resolve. In a sense, this would be my crux move as a leader—a final measure of the strength, ingenuity, and resolve of the team I had put together. Would the lessons I'd learned on Everest be enough?

THE TEACHINGS OF EVEREST
Clear Objectives and a Shared Vision

In 1992, after two failed expeditions and the loss of a dear friend in the first of them, I returned to Everest on a lean expedition with a very tight budget, leading a small team of six very strong climbers, two Sherpas, and a physician. This time, we chose one of the most difficult routes up the mountain: the Neverest Ridge on the Kangshung, or East Face. The eastern side—known as the "Forgotten Face"—is arguably the mountain's most difficult approach, and unquestionably the least often tried. Only three expeditions had attempted it before us, and only two had succeeded.

As a team, we had set ourselves the objective of climbing Everest, but we had also firmly agreed not to do so by an easier, more heavily traveled route. Today in the climbing world it is recognized that under the right circumstances, *every* mountain can be beaten by a great deployment of resources and technology, and so a new style has been introduced in world mountaineering, a new "ethic": Peaks should be attempted by their hardest routes and using the least resources possible. We would therefore attempt the ascent of Everest in this spirit, by one of its hardest faces—an extremely technically demanding and dangerous sweep of rock, ice, and snow—using minimum gear. In this way, the mountain would have the greatest chance to deter us from its summit.

We also firmly agreed that we could not solely concentrate on reaching the summit; tagging the top *and* coming back alive was our goal. This objective—clear, common, and challenging—focused our minds.

In retrospect, this proved an extremely important issue: A common goal and a profound agreement on the means to achieve it bonded us strongly together. Although we didn't realize it at the time, this agreement was the basis for our transformation from a group of people merely working together into a high-performing team.

So many times when I visit a company for Vertical, bosses will complain that their teams are not committed enough. When I ask if their objectives have been clearly set, I nearly always get the same answer: "Of course the employees know them; they were presented very openly in the annual company meeting." But when I go down to the factory floor, the opposite is generally the case: The front lines lack a common vision and therefore approach tasks as very short-term goals. Medium- and long-term objectives—and even the means to achieve them—are a mystery to the people who are being asked to accomplish them.

At Vertical, I continuously try to use every opportunity—formal or informal, individually or collectively—to talk about our company goals and vision. For example, because our seminars and workshops are generally delivered in the outdoors, there is plenty of time to discuss these topics with our instructors while preparing for our clients, be it on long hikes, in tents, or during meals. I feel confident that these conversations help instill a sense of community, assuring our people that they are an integral part of maintaining the quality, contents, and philosophy of our programs. This has resulted in our clients ranking our instructors as the highest-rated element of our seminars.

Individual Responsibility

At the very outset of our Everest expedition, I asked each of the team members about his interests and skills, and then assigned the various responsibilities accordingly across the entire small group. One climber would be in charge of food, another of clothing, somebody else of transportation, and so on for equipment, financial matters, communications, and health. Unlike previous expeditions I had been on, each of us would be made accountable to the team—not the leader—for our individual responsibilities.

Heretofore, we had all valued ourselves mainly on our climbing abilities. Now we would be required to master a roster of managerial skills: Each of us would be exercising leadership over our area of responsibility. This generated a much-greater conscientiousness in dealing with every aspect of managing the expedition. Each issue had to be resolved to the utmost level of quality because human lives were at stake, and it would have been impossible for me as a leader to do this with such attention to detail. Breaking up the leadership roles allowed us to better lead ourselves as a team.

Furthermore, the firm conviction that every single person added important value to the expedition increased our sense of belonging to the endeavor. Each of us knew deep inside that the team's failure or success would be the product of each and all of us.

In the case of Fundación Maitenes, where we are out in the wild, working with children on the critical issue of education, the extra risks confronted require extreme care and competence from our instructors. (Our programs include adventurous activities such as crossing a white-water river on a rope bridge or making the kids descend a 100-foot cliff by means of a rope.) Instilling in our instructors the individual responsibility for their groups has been not only vital in the true sense of the word, it has been an essential ingredient in producing excellent results. The quality of our programs is recognized throughout the elementary schools we have worked with, allowing the foundation to increase the number of children serviced every year from 300 to 6,000 in ten years. An unexpected though extremely gratifying auxiliary result is the sense of achievement and triumph over personal responsibility our instructors have felt and expressed, which has brought the foundation tremendous interest among Chilean outdoor specialists and produced a permanent waiting list of applicants.

Positive Attitude

On March 18, 1992, we arrived in Nepal. After rushing up and down the streets of Kathmandu, purchasing last-minute items, we crammed ourselves into a small bus—seven Westerners, two Sherpas, a cook, the driver, and his assistant; with our equipment, maybe two tons in all—and lumbered off toward the border with Tibet.

A few days later, we began our final sixty-mile leg to Kharta, a tiny rural Tibetan village, where we would leave the vehicles and start the fifty-mile trek to the foot of Everest. For this walk, we had hired the use of fifty-one yaks. In Kharta, though, a village official informed us that the year's heavy snowfalls had made the mountain passes we had to cross impassable for yaks. We would have to hire Tibetan porters to carry the equipment on their backs instead. The official said we needed 120 porters, an expense that broke our budget, and we had no choice but to shed part of the load to reduce the number of porters by about a third, to a more manageable 84.

Reflecting on this situation today, I realize how an initial positive attitude meant all the difference to the climb. Reducing our load meant reducing our chances of success. We all knew that, yet no one openly complained. Quite the contrary: Everyone went around assuring everyone else that this might be for the best. Less weight meant fewer people, fewer people meant smaller teams, and smaller teams were flexible and fast.

At Vertical, we have come to consciously search for this attitude when selecting our instructors. Sometimes the person with the most positive approach might be less qualified in a specific teaching skill, but I have discovered that it's easier to train someone in how to teach rock climbing than it is to modify his or her attitude toward life. This strategy has ensured that the ambience at Vertical is a fun one, thus making it a place where every employee, executive, or instructor likes to work. In addition, the positive atmosphere has translated into high productivity.

Strong Leadership and Consistent Decision Making

Instead of looking to one person to make all the critical decisions on Everest, every team member was prepared to make difficult choices on his own. Others would not always be present to help in the decision-making process, and we had to be ready for that. This awareness helped all of us to step up when we had to. Every team member made tough calls while climbing—calls that had implications for the safety of the whole team. Those decisions, in turn, built the ladder that was our final route up the mountain.

By April 27, the expedition had slowly moved up the mountain. We had stocked Camp One with the required equipment and had fixed ropes up to 22,000 feet, where the most critical technical difficulties ended. The weather had remained quite favorable, but we feared it might change. It was time to make an assault on the summit.

The plan called for six of us to make the final push: Three would establish Camps Two and Three; another three would then use the camps en route to making the actual summit attempt. Since there were eight of us in all—six Chileans and two Sherpas—two would be left behind at Base Camp. Whom should the team choose?

One of our Sherpas, Ngima, was scared of the route and did not want to keep on working. Chuldim, though, appeared to be in excellent condition. A seasoned twenty-nine-year-old Sherpa, he had worked very well with us and was extremely keen on reaching the summit. He would be the first Sherpa to do so by this route, and succeeding would open up excellent work possibilities for him in the future. But including him would mean leaving Claudio Lucero behind. Claudio was the mentor from whom all of us had learned our mountaineering and with whom I had been climbing for thirteen years. But at age fifty-nine, he had diminished physical strength, and strength was what was most needed for the summit bid.

Leading the group in making that decision was one of the most difficult tasks I have ever undertaken. Claudio and I had scaled dozens of peaks together; indeed, he taught me all I knew about climbing. This was his fourth and surely his last attempt on Everest. After thirty-five years of mountaineering, he was the one who most deserved the summit. It took me two days to find the courage to sit down and speak to him. I tried to show him what he had always taught us: that as a team, we had to play the best cards available; there was no place for sentiment in doing so; and I was firmly convinced that leaving him and Ngima behind would give us the best chance of success.

Claudio was silent for a long five minutes and then said, "The important thing here is the final goal of this enterprise, not the personal or individual desires of a certain member of the expedition." Although I sensed Claudio had been deeply affected, his reaction was a lesson to everybody, useful on or off the mountain. If a leader ensures that the final goals of his enterprise are clear to all the team members, and if he acts consistently in accordance with those goals, even the hardest decisions become easier to accept.

Our first try failed utterly. At Camp One, bad weather battered us, Chuldim developed a skin infection, and another member suffered a severe pain on his ribs that prevented his climbing further. We withdrew to Base Camp and planned a new attempt with only five Chileans. It would be the last, as we had only packed supplies for a forty-day expedition, and they were almost gone.

On May 12, the five of us climbed to Camp Two in a sixteen-hour ordeal, trudging through deep snow that buried us up to our waists. We needed another four hours to build a terrace on which to pitch the tents; but while protected, it was not a great site. Windblown snow submerged the tents so quickly that we had to clear them off every forty-five minutes. At 24,130 feet, these small defeats were heartbreaking. Before splitting up to our respective tents, we made the final decision on the summit team. Cristián García-Huidobro, a thirty-one-year-old computer engineer, extremely intelligent and probably the strongest of us all, and I would attempt the summit, while Christian Buracchio, twenty-eight, a mechanical engineer and our expert on technical climbing difficulties, and Juan Sebastián Montes, a twenty-six-year-old lawyer, the youngest of the team and probably the strongest in terms of willpower, would support us to Camp Three. Claudio Lucero would wait for us at Camp Two.

Surprisingly, perhaps, I wasn't the one who made the final decision on who would summit. The five of us discussed the matter and decided collectively. Again, individual desires took a backseat. We had all committed to the common goal of achieving the summit and coming back, and we were willing to support whichever climbers seemed strongest at the moment. That's what happens when everyone buys into the program: Decision making becomes so much easier and straightforward.

As mentioned before, at Vertical and Fundación Maitenes, the conscious decision of the executive group has been to hand individual responsibilities to the employees and instructors. This cannot be achieved if power is not given to them to make their own decisions. To allow for this, we have designed a permanent training program—there are three workshops a year held in the wild—that gradually train the members of these organizations to make ever more difficult calls. Again, this has ensured that when it has been required (for example, in a program with executives held in a remote and isolated area) our instructors have been able to make appropriate decisions. Many times, due to environmental conditions and safety concerns, they have chosen on their own to modify the scheduled itinerary of a defined program, changing a route or moving a campsite. Once more, the quality of our program is enhanced and assured.

Trust

At 19,700 feet, we encountered a particularly dangerous section: a nearly vertical cleft of ice that was exposed to avalanches from above. In the previous days, my teammates had anchored rope to aid all of us in our successive ascents of this section. As I climbed the rope, using an ascender joined by a sling to my harness and a second ascender-sling to my foot, I thought about how my life was depending on a one-third of an inch rope that one of my team members had anchored 130 feet above me days before. I couldn't help but ponder the profound role trust plays in mountaineering. In the many days and hours of this trip, we all had climbed together, working on this trust. This quality is such a valued asset of a team, but it requires great effort and time to build it to its utmost.

On our climb to Camp Three (the last camp at 26,000 feet), as night quickly fell and temperatures plummeted, Christian Buracchio told us that he felt tired and was nearing hypothermia. Just 650 feet below Camp Three, we shoveled a terrace on the steep snow slope and stopped for two hours to help him recover.

Christian knew that for us to have the required equipment, food, and fuel to attempt the summit from the South Col, he and Juan Sebastián would have to carry it up there. That was not an option. The expedition members had given him this responsibility, and though he was near exhaustion, Christian was not going to let us down. The expedition trusted him, and he trusted the expedition. Slowly but firmly, he stood up and started climbing again. By midnight, after sixteen hours of continuous work from Camp Two, the four of us reached Camp Three on the South Col. We were now, thanks to the work of Juan and Christian, in a position to attempt the summit.

I don't know of anyone who has developed a foolproof method for developing such trust, in mountain climbing teams or in any other organization. My experiences in the high peaks of the Himalayas, conducting training programs for executives, and hiking with schoolchildren have taught me that a very good way of doing this is by encouraging people, especially yourself, to reach for excellence in every task, including simple, everyday ones. Doing so is contagious. Demand excellence in yourself, in every way, and the people around you will start doing so as well. Whom do you trust? The person you have seen again and again performing to his utmost capacity. Whom will I trust on the mountains? The climber I've seen checking and rechecking and checking again the batteries of his torchlight before a climb or putting on sunscreen in the early morning. Excellence is in details. Trust is in excellence.

All the characteristics I've just mentioned helped build a degree of trust that was deeply embedded in each of the members of our Everest expedition. To climb the highest peaks on earth, places where the threat to life is real and constant, trust is absolutely essential. We had built up our trust after years of climbing together, but in the expedition of 1992, we were able to take our trust to a deeper level. It was trust above all that allowed Cristián and me to reach the summit of Mount Everest on May 15, 1992. It was trust, more than anything else, that convinced me we were ready to attempt K2.

From the summit of Mount Everest on May 15, 1992,
Rodrigo Jordan displays a photo of his wife, María Paz,
and daughters Sofía and Natalia

THE ULTIMATE CHALLENGE: K2

K2 is 782 feet shorter than Everest, but it poses some of the most formidable challenges a mountaineer will ever meet. For one thing, there is no easy route to the top, and no easy way to get down once you are up there.

We had committed ourselves to climbing K2 by an especially challenging route. The south-southeast spur had been climbed only twice before we tackled it in 1996: by a Basque expedition in 1994 and by a

Catalonian one in 1995. Tragically, two of the Catalonians had died during the descent.

K2's danger is a large part of its allure. If there were no risks, if the summit were easy to reach, if the climbing were not so difficult or exposed, then K2 would be of little interest to us. A crucial element of the experience we seek when attempting the great mountains of the world is to explore new challenges and confront them with passion, but at the same time with discipline and preparation.

Five climbers joined us who had not been on Everest: Misael Alvial, a thirty-four-year-old mountain guide who had climbed solo the extremely difficult south face of Aconcagua, in Argentina; Aldo Boitano, twenty-nine, a married engineer who would later become programs manager at Vertical; Waldo Farías, twenty-six, a lawyer-in-waiting who had postponed his graduation exam to participate in the expedition; Alberto "Tito" Gana, a twenty-five-year-old architect who was to be married after the expedition; and Miguel Purcell, thirty-four, a botanist and former member of the Chilean National Olympics Ski Team. Also on the team were Everest "veterans" Cristián García-Huidobro and physician Alfonso Díaz. Collectively, the eight of us had climbed in places as remote and varied as Antarctica, the Himalayas, Patagonia, the Andes, Africa, and Alaska.

The team also included a film crew—our Everest partner Christian Buracchio and Ralf Oberti—as well as physical trainer Tomás Grifferos, age thirty-five, and our "manager," Marcelo Grifferos, thirty-one, both of whom are dear friends and partners at Vertical. As we climbed up the Baltoro Glacier, I was convinced our team was up to the challenge. I didn't know, though, that we had hidden virtues that would help to save one of our lives.

As on Everest four years earlier, it took us fifty days to establish the route. We fixed ropes up to 24,900 feet, establishing Camp One at 20,700 feet and Camp Two at 23,300 feet. Again as on Everest, our first attempt failed; at Camp Three, we were hit by severe bad weather. Once again, we were running out of time. Twenty-five hundred pounds of food and fifty gallons of fuel that had been meant to last sixty days

Camp One at 20,700 feet on the slopes of K2 in 1996, a hazardous perch for sleepwalkers

had been stretched to seventy. As before, we had one last opportunity to make the summit before we had to abandon the expedition.

Because conditions faced above 8,000 meters are extremely demanding and draining, we always keep an experienced mountaineer back in a lower and safer camp. Only from the lower vantage point is it possible to remain sufficiently calm in order to clearly visualize the environment in which the men above are risking their lives. Claudio Lucero had taken the job on Everest, but he was not with us this time. I was now the "veteran" and the most suitable candidate, so I hunkered down in Base Camp to assist those above in their decision making.

On August 10, at three in the morning, the six members of the summit group left Base Camp to confront 10,000 feet of fixed ropes. After two days, four climbers were at Camp Three, ready to make the summit attempt, while two others waited at Camp One to assist them. Communication between Camp Three and Base Camp was almost constant that day as we worked out the details. The team left at 8:00 P.M. on August 12, intending to climb through the night.

They started off in two rope teams: Cristián and Miguel, and Misael and Waldo. Each man was carrying a twenty-pound backpack. Nor-

mally, mountaineers set out from the last camp for the summit traveling as lightly as possible to increase their speed—some even not taking
a backpack at all and only stashing a few candies and a water bottle in
their down parka pockets—but we didn't want to compromise the
margin of safety. Our team decided to completely prepare for the unexpected and took not only two oxygen cylinders to share among the
four climbers, but also a portable stove, two cylinders of fuel, a cooking
pot, juice and food, four bivouac sacks, and a shovel.

Near midnight, the team cleared the Shoulder—the characteristic
high-snow plateau on the southeast ridge of K2 that leads into the
summit pyramid—and reached the base of the Bottleneck, a dangerous, steep ice section that is the only passage to the summit ridge and
that marks the most difficult part on the summit attempt. The climbers
knew that they would find ropes there that Japanese climbers had put
in place the day before. Nonetheless, they had taken along 300 feet of
additional rope just in case. Cristián led them past the Bottleneck. Then
they all carefully but quickly negotiated the Traverse—a lateral 300-
foot move that was required to weave around the front of a hanging
glacier.

By three in the morning, the climbers were above the more technical parts of the climb and reached the Triangular Rock, the distinctive
last rock outcrop before the final summit ridge. The team surpassed the
Rock at 5:00 A.M. and began fixing rope where the Japanese had left
off, another 300 feet up the trail.

At 5:45, they stopped for a hydration break, using the portable
stove to heat juices that had turned to slush. They knew they had to
reach the summit early and descend quickly because bad weather was
expected to close in at 3:00 P.M., a pattern we had seen repeated over
and over. In order to dash quickly to and from the summit, they decided to jettison the portable stove, fuel, and cooking pots and pick
them up on the way back.

The temperature by now was hovering around twenty degrees
below zero, but the weather was clear and the team could see the summit. Everything looked to be on track. Little by little, the team gained

Miguel Purcell, Cristián García-Huidobro, and Waldo Farías
on the summit of K2 on August 13, 1996

the final feet. Back at Base Camp, I was following their progress via regular radio contacts.

Cristián reached the summit at 9:15 in the morning. Over the next hour and fifteen minutes, the rest of the summit team arrived one by one.

Tears, happiness, and photos followed: on the summit, at Camp One, and at Base Camp. Our joy was overwhelming; the emotion, uncontainable. Remarkably, Cristián had managed to carry a crystal wineglass to the top of K2. He took it out, splashed a bit of Chilean wine in it, and toasted our victory. The gesture was magnificent, but time was at a premium. The team spent the better part of two hours snapping pictures, sipping water, and contemplating the view. They talked and talked over the radio to us down at Base Camp, and it took ages for them to get ready to leave. By the time they started down, it was already 12:30. We estimated they still had at least eight more hours ahead of them before arriving back in Camp Three, including the delicate descent of the Traverse and the Bottleneck.

Ninety minutes later came the message that no one wanted to hear: Miguel had, in effect, gone on strike. Too exhausted to go on and still a perilous 650 feet above the cache where the portable stove, pots, and fuel cylinders waited, he sat down and refused to budge. The climb had taken its physical toll, as it always does, and Miguel had doubled as our high-altitude cameraman. That extra effort produced outstanding footage, but it also seemed to have carried him beyond the limits of human endurance. For Cristián, who had called with news of Miguel, the first question was whether to climb back up 90 feet for the oxygen cylinder his partner had discarded in his confusion or to climb down 650 feet for water.

Back at Base Camp, I knew the moment had come. The performance of our team was to be tested in the ultimate crucible. Above 8,000 meters, even the most physically and mentally fit climber is on the razor's edge of survival. Would Miguel be able to summon his will and spirit? Would we be able to help him down if he could not?

This crisis was heightened by the fact that nobody knew where Misael and Waldo were. Cristián couldn't see them, and we presumed they had managed to climb down. That is the first instinct: to descend as swiftly as possible to lose altitude. If Misael and Waldo had already descended the ropes of the Traverse and the Bottleneck, they would be too exhausted, too far down, and lacking enough time before dark to climb back up again to assist Miguel.

In Base Camp, Alfonso decided that although hydration should be the first priority, the effort needed to climb down and then return 650 feet was simply too great for Cristián. Instead, he advised Cristián to climb up 90 feet for the oxygen. To suggest this is easy, of course; to actually do it was a Herculean task.

As Cristián went up for the oxygen cylinder, a sense of helplessness began to overwhelm us in Base Camp. Even if Cristián managed to retrieve the little oxygen left, Miguel would still have to get on his feet and descend another 3,000 feet to Camp Three, an effort that takes five hours under normal conditions. Only 650 feet further below lay the replenishing oasis where the climbers could prepare liquids, but that, too, was an infinite distance at such an altitude. Still, Miguel had to get there somehow. Otherwise, he would remain at 28,000 feet forever, sitting and staring at the eternal snows of K2.

"He looks optimistic, but he won't decide about going down," Cristián radioed us after watching Miguel take some oxygen, then stumble, stagger, and sit down again. Cristián's words were still hanging in the air when Misael's voice burst through the static. Risking their own margins of safety, Waldo and Misael had stopped to wait for their companions at the equipment cache, where they had been preparing water. When we told them what was happening 650 feet above them, the response was immediate. In a show of superhuman strength and self-sacrifice, Misael climbed back up to deliver the water, while Waldo stayed behind and melted snow in order to have as much liquid as possible when the others arrived. The level of sacrifice this act involves is difficult to comprehend from the standpoint of an urban citizen. At that altitude, after several hours of extreme hard work, all of your body is screaming for a rest. The only element that keeps you moving is utter willpower, and this is to climb *down*. Climbing up seems like sheer insanity.

At about three o'clock, Miguel took some more oxygen and began sipping water mixed with hydrating salts. He seemed to recover somewhat and finally rose to his feet. Slowly and deliberately, he began to descend with Cristián and Misael.

Worn out by the effort, the three joined up with Waldo at about four in the afternoon. By 9 P.M., they had reached the Shoulder, thankful that the night ascent had given them light to work by on the way down and that the weather had not turned as vicious as it so often did in the late afternoon. Now, in the darkness, the team could walk over relatively easy terrain to the tents. At 10:30 P.M., the summit team reached Camp Three. They had logged twenty hours of work above 8,000 meters.

Although all four were extremely exhausted and weak, we urged them by radio to stay awake for a few more hours so they could take in liquids. The climbers still had the trek to the lower camps ahead of them. We also instructed the climbers in Camp One to prepare to go up to meet the summit team the following day.

At 5:00 in the morning on August 14, Cristián woke up and began guzzling tea, trying to hydrate himself. He gave Miguel tea while urging Misael and Waldo to prepare more. At 11:30, the team began the descent.

Our original goal had been to leave no equipment behind on the mountain, as a show of respect. Now, I told the team to abandon anything that wasn't vital to their survival. They didn't. Even in their extreme fatigue, the team managed to bring down everything but the tents.

At 2:00 in the afternoon, the four finally descended through the clouds, and we could make visual contact with binoculars. An hour later, Tito and Aldo, climbing from Camp One, met up with them. All six climbers were in good condition and able to continue down. Just as on Everest, the descent was made in ten straight hours with the help of everybody on the mountain. It had been a very close call.

In Base Camp, as we prepared a good hot soup and awaited their arrival, I thought of something Claudio Lucero had once told me: "The real summit photograph is the one showing everybody safe and sound back at Base Camp." So it was with us. Getting to the top of K2 had been important, but getting everyone back down had been far more important to all of us.

After all my Everest work, I thought I had identified every issue required to build a high-performance team. K2 taught me that I had missed one thing. Technical skills are, of course, vital for a highly effective team. Social and managerial abilities are also indispensable—so much so that I sometimes think this should be a strategic line of work for human resource departments. But while both sets of qualities might produce a tremendously effective team that could work like a precise machine to generate beautiful and impressive results, the team will still lack something fundamental if it is not humane.

Friendship, mutual consideration, affection, humility, and caring about your teammates are not just important qualities: They are essential. These are the traits that allow a team both to perform at its peak and to reach a new dimension of satisfaction and joy in so doing.

At Vertical and Fundación Maitenes, instilling and teaching these values has brought me some of the greatest satisfaction I've ever experienced. On K2, our emphasis on such human fundamentals also saved a life.

Lessons from the Top:

Mount Fuji, Mount Sinai, and Other Peak Paradigms

EDWIN BERNBAUM

"AS CEO, I'M GOING TO QUARTERBACK THIS TEAM TO victory—we're going to crush the competition!" "This division is going to bring home the gold for the shareholders in the fourth quarter." We've all heard these rousing statements before—there's nothing like a crisp, vivid metaphor to put a common goal into perspective, especially in business. The prevailing source of these metaphors, thanks to television, is competitive sports such as football and baseball. For me, though, summiting a mountain peak is the clearest, most powerful and accurate symbol I know for attaining a goal or objective. A touchdown, a game-winning three-pointer, or a bases-clearing home run cheered by tens of thousands is nothing compared to standing on top of the world. Indeed, the mountain-climbing metaphor has a number of advantages over many other sports metaphors used in business.

Baseball, basketball, football—they all play on until someone loses, in overtimes or extra innings. On the mountain, however, everyone can win: All members of the expedition can reach the summit together. The mountain-climbing metaphor has greater flexibility to model cooperative business ventures and win-win scenarios in which nobody has to lose. Mountain climbers can and often do compete with each other or the mountain—human nature gets exaggerated in extreme conditions, after all—but the best climbers also know that they don't have to compete and, in fact, often succeed most easily when they don't.

In addition, mountaineering expeditions emphasize team efforts even as they allow for individual initiative and leadership. No matter how close the group, ultimately, one or two members will have to go out in front to establish the route for others to follow, but they're doing it—or should be doing it—so everyone who is able has a chance to get to the top. As Ida San, the Japanese leader of a Mount Fuji society, puts it, "The most important thing in climbing is the inner strength to help each other, so that not just the strongest but all the members of the group reach the goal."

Climbing also takes place not on a neatly controlled playing surface but out in nature, an unpredictable setting where potentially fatal changes can sweep in out of nowhere. We've all been hit by unforeseen storms and avalanches in life: a sudden death in the family, a fatally flawed product, a court decision against our company that seemed to come out of the blue. Geologically exposed to the extremes of weather patterns, mountains prepare us for the unexpected—in business and in life.

And, of course, mountains are deeply inspiring in and of themselves. As the highest and most dramatic features of the landscape, mountains inevitably come to represent humankind's highest and most central values and aspirations. Mount Sinai occupies a special place in the Bible as the imposing site where Moses received the Ten Commandments, the basis of law and ethics in Western civilization. The remote Himalayan peak of Mount Kailas, rising aloof above the Tibetan Plateau, directs the minds of millions of Hindus and Buddhists toward the utmost attainments of spiritual liberation. Expeditions to Mount Everest stand out in Western culture as inspiring models of the initiative and determination needed to overcome seemingly impossible obstacles.

Over the past five years, Mike Useem and I have been leading mountain seminars for graduates of the Wharton M.B.A. program for executives and other Wharton programs. Our search for peak paradigms—mountain metaphors that evoke a whole new way of looking at some critical aspect of leadership and teamwork—led us to the Himalayas and other mountains. These spectacular natural settings are some of the best environments for teaching effective lessons about leading successful organizations in today's challenging world of diversity and change.

Every mountain has definable characteristics that distinguish it from other mountains, both physically and culturally: Mount Everest is singled out as the highest peak in the world, Mount Kailas is revered as the center of the universe, and so on. Each of the following peak paradigms that we use in our programs exemplifies a different aspect of leadership and teamwork that we need to cultivate to lead successfully.

MOUNT EVEREST:
SETTING AND ATTAINING MOTIVATIONAL GOALS

It's no wonder that business corporations commonly hire Everest climbers to give motivational speeches to their employees. As the world's highest peak, Everest places a premium on the leadership tasks of setting and attaining goals and building a team that makes full use of its skills and resources. Just as Everest stretches people to do more than they thought they could, so companies want to stretch their employees to help the organization reach the loftiest goals—to be number one in the field, to provide the best product or service in the industry group.

Two kinds of expeditions to Everest mirror management models commonly used in business. The siege-style expedition moves large amounts of material slowly up the mountain, establishing and stocking many camps in a pyramid of dwindling supplies that fosters the summit attempts of a few climbers. This style emphasizes logistics, organizational teamwork, and a military command-and-control style of leadership. Ross Perot has run both Electronic Data Systems and Perot Systems along these siege-style lines, complete with military terminology, an abundance of retired military personnel, and a corporate structure in which the CEO is viewed as a general commanding his troops.

In the other kind of high-altitude mountaineering expedition, the alpine style, a small party of climbers goes quickly up the mountain in one push, using a minimal number of camps and traveling as lightly as possible. This style emphasizes speed, flexibility, and individual initiative, combined with a diffuse leadership spread over each member of the team. It corresponds in the business world to a small innovative company or a skunk-works operation within a larger organization. A classic example is the team that Steve Jobs set up apart from the rest of Apple to experiment with ideas and develop the new Macintosh computer.

A siege expedition allows climbers to weather storms and setbacks and have a surer, safer chance of reaching the summit. For this reason, the Royal Geographical Society at the last minute chose John Hunt, a military colonel, to lead the British expedition that made the first ascent of Everest in 1953. There's a price, though, for ratcheting down risk. Siege climbers lack the speed and flexibility to take advantage of short bursts of good weather and other fortuitous opportunities— important windows in the always-changeable climate at the highest altitudes. The siege style suits a more mature corporation with a well-established product line that requires good logistics to sustain its operations.

Alpine climbers are ready to go at almost any moment. The disadvantage of this lighter, more flexible style is that if the weather turns bad, the climbers will not have the resources to wait out a storm and reach the summit—and may not be able to get back down the mountain safely. The alpine style of mountain climbing works well as a model for entrepreneurial leadership in starting a company, especially one that needs the quick response and flexibility to develop new products, but it doesn't hold up well over the long term.

The first time I went to Mount Everest, I climbed a neighboring ridge for a view of the highest mountain on earth. From my perch at 18,000 feet, I could see, in the last golden light of the day, the West and Southeast Ridges converging on the summit with its characteristic plume of snow veering off in the jet stream. The first American ascent of Everest in 1963 climbed both ridges, using an assault strategy that combined the siege and alpine styles in one expedition. While the major, siege-style effort focused on making sure an American would get up the already-climbed Southeast Ridge, a smaller party was given minimal resources to attempt the unclimbed West Ridge in alpine style. Because the leader, Norman Dyrenfurth, was successful in reconciling the divergent objectives and needs of the two teams, his expedition not only got the first American to the summit of Everest, but also accomplished something of greater value to mountaineers—the first ascent of a new route.

One of the members of our first Wharton trek to Everest asked me to apply this combined model for a new corporate division he was heading up. He had been given a team and charged with developing a new approach for his applications hosting company, but his employees were encountering resistance from the company's larger division, which feared that any new approach would draw resources and business away from their established way of delivering software to clients. We used the American expedition to Everest to get his team members to think of themselves as entrepreneurial, alpine-style West Ridgers accessing new customers for the greater good of the company. They could then present themselves as extending, rather than threatening, the market share of the rest of the corporation, which used the standard, siege-style approach. As happens in mountain climbing, one side didn't have to lose for the other to win. Both could ascend to their own peaks by different methods, each contributing to the overall benefit of the company and its bottom line.

MOUNT SINAI: CALLING, SERVICE, AND TRANSFORMATION

Who is the most famous and influential mountain climber in Western history? The answer, I would maintain, is not Sir Edmund Hillary, the conqueror of Everest, as one might expect, but the biblical prophet Moses. The revelation and covenant made on Mount Sinai are considered the most important events in traditional Jewish history, while the Ten Commandments Moses brought down from the summit form the basis of law and ethics in Western civilization. Did it actually happen?

The Monastery of Saint Catherine at the foot of Jebel Musa, or Mount Sinai

That's for scholars and faith to decide, but true or metaphorical, the story of Moses' ascent has had an enormous influence on billions of people over the centuries.

In the biblical account, Moses climbs Mount Sinai in response to a call in order to receive something of benefit for others—the first five books of the Bible and the Ten Commandments. Upon hearing the directives of God on the heights of the mountains, Moses comes down, his face transfigured with light, to transform his people into "a nation of priests."

When I climbed Mount Sinai, I was struck by the brilliant, crystalline light shining on the sun-scoured rocks of the desert summit. In that hauntingly translucent setting, I could easily see how the experience of the mountain might alter a person's perceptions of reality, revealing a higher clarity and meaning that one would then feel compelled to share with others. Only a rare few of us in history are summoned to anything approaching Moses' calling, but Mount Sinai still shows us how a leader can transform people and organizations by fostering a sense of vocation and a commitment to service.

When Roy Vagelos was the CEO of Merck, he was faced with what might have seemed a crippling dilemma to someone with less of a commitment to service. By serendipity, one of his research teams had developed a new drug, Mectizan, that could cure the scourge of river blindness for millions of Africans. The problem was that those who would benefit from the drug were among the world's poorest people, utterly incapable of paying for the medication. Vagelos agreed with his director of clinical research that supplying Mectizan to the Africans was a matter of professional calling. Although this leadership decision cost the corporation in the short term, it gave Merck priceless publicity and attracted the best scientists in the field to come work for a company whose values they respected. This influx of highly motivated talent transformed the research department and led to the development of new products that more than made up for the loss of revenue incurred by giving Mectizan away for free.

Appealing to a sense of vocation gives meaning to work and helps to draw out the best in individuals and organizations. When people dedicate themselves to something more meaningful than the bottom line, they come out of the experience enriched with fuller and deeper lives. They also discover resources and skills they didn't know they had. For example, the dedication of companies such as Ben & Jerry's and Tom's of Maine to quality and service has transformed them into leaders of their industries.

As participants on our Wharton treks are quick to point out, CEOs of publicly owned companies have a primary responsibility to their shareholders. Appealing to higher values at the expense of the bottom line requires extraordinary leadership, but such courage can often produce even greater rewards. Moses, after all, didn't do a bad job for the people he was called to lead.

HUA SHAN:
FINDING INCLUSIVE SOLUTIONS, EMPOWERING OTHERS

With sheer walls of polished granite meeting in sharp ridges and delicate peaks, Hua Shan is one of the most spectacular sacred mountains
in China. The shaded and sunlit sides of this dramatic mountain are in-
timately tied to a concept that underlies almost all systems of Chinese
thought—the idea of complementary opposites, such as dark and light,
cold and hot, female and male. Indeed, yin and yang, the Chinese
terms for these opposites, originally referred to the shaded and sunlit
slopes of a mountain, which depends on both sides for its existence.
Take away either one and the mountain ceases to be.

On our treks, we use Hua Shan to illustrate a powerful way to resolve or manage conflicts: Look for a fuller, more inclusive picture that
transforms conflicting views into complementary opposites—different
sides of a greater whole. A story told me by a doctor working on a
Navajo reservation demonstrates how to put this principle into practice. An elderly woman who was going into a medical clinic overnight

Hua Shan, one of China's five most sacred mountains

for a routine checkup wanted her traditional medicine man with her. She insisted that without him she would die. The doctor and her husband refused, saying it was superstitious and unnecessary. She didn't need the medicine man; Western medicine was better. The woman died the next morning. "Since then," the doctor said, "I've always let the medicine men come and work with me." Instead of insisting that modern scientific medicine was the only way to treat people, he learned through painful experience to view traditional Navajo medicine as another side of a fuller treatment focused on the greater good of what was best for his Native American patients.

Hua Shan was once a favorite haunt of Taoist hermits, who would meditate in caves carved into the vertical faces of the mountain and in temples perched on the crests of narrow ridges. They sought to follow the teachings of Lao-tzu, the sixth-century B.C. sage and founder of Taoism, one of the three principal religious and philosophical traditions of China, along with Buddhism and Confucianism. The *Tao te Ching*, or "Way of Life"—the principal text of Taoism, composed by Lao-tzu—is basically a leadership manual for wise rulers. It includes a powerful lesson on the value of drawing attention away from yourself and empowering others so that when the goal you have set is accomplished, they will feel they have done it themselves.

Asian cultures tend to value this style of leadership—empowering others while minimizing one's own profile—more than Western cultures, where the cult of the CEO has become so prominent. But on our treks we find time and again that American executives, exposed to examples of quiet empowerment, come away deeply impressed by its ability to accomplish complicated goals. Everest trekkers, for example, routinely single out Ang Jangbu, the leader of our large Sherpa staff, for his low-key, invisible style of leadership in which, as one person put it, "You never see him doing anything, but everything gets done."

This kind of leadership also lies behind the famous Hewlett-Packard style of "management by wandering around," in which managers give their subordinates free rein and wander around unobtrusively to provide encouragement and keep tabs on what is happening. In fact, on our first leadership trek to Everest, we had an executive from Hewlett-Packard who was assigned the task of running back and forth along the trail to make sure everyone was keeping together to accomplish a particular group task. At the end of the day, he commented that it felt exactly like managing by wandering around at his corporate office back home.

MOUNT KAILAS:
ESTABLISHING CORE VALUES, IDEAS, AND COMPETENCIES

Nearly a billion Asians from different cultures and religions revere the remote Tibetan peak of Mount Kailas as the center of the universe. Buddhist and Hindu pilgrims come thousands of miles not to climb the mountain, but to pay respect by walking around it. For them and for many others in Asia, the peak functions as a cosmic axis that unifies the world and gives it meaning and order. From its location at a high point of the Tibetan Plateau, four rivers—among them the Ganges—flow out to the four directions of the compass, providing hundreds of millions of people with the water that sustains their lives and economies.

Mount Kailas illustrates the need for a leader to establish and promote a central value, idea, or competency that can hold an organization together and make sense of what it does. Walt Disney Productions organizes all its operations at Disneyland around a drama metaphor. Employees are called "cast members." Those who work directly with the public are "on stage." The personnel department is referred to as "casting." The metaphor helps everyone see how the different divisions of Walt Disney relate to each other and the overall mission of "putting on a show." It also promotes the company's central value of providing service by having employees treat customers as "guests."

The management at Sony realized that the company's core competency lay not in manufacturing transistorized pocket radios, its first product, but in miniaturization. They were then able to identify and develop many different, innovative products that could make use of their basic skill in making miniature components. In effect, Sony was also using the Kailas model: With the center in place, new products and services could flow like the rivers issuing from the different sides of the mountain. Recognizing and making use of its core competency enabled Sony to branch out into related areas, rather than continue with one successful product, and played a key role in helping the company to survive and expand over the long term.

In 1991, I took the long journey across the Tibetan Plateau and followed the traditional pilgrimage route around Mount Kailas. As we circled the peak in the company of Tibetan and Indian pilgrims, it

gradually revealed its different sides, each with its own distinctive character. From the south, where we started, Kailas took the form of a white dome of polished snow set on a pedestal of rock, eliciting a smooth sense of tranquility. From the north, halfway through the circuit, it shot up in a fierce, austere face of ice-streaked rock, soaring 6,000 feet above its windswept base. The high point of the route, the Drolma la, or "Pass of the Savioress," looked out on a vast landscape of peaks and ridges that evoked a sense of mystery and openness. At the end of the three-day pilgrimage, I felt that I had come to know the mountain and its surroundings in a much fuller and deeper way than if

A Tibetan pilgrim circumambulating
Mount Kailas

had simply climbed straight to the top.

Thus it is with any organization. The more we view its central competencies and values from all sides, the more we can unlock the different possibilities inherent in each of them. Some companies institutionalize this process by setting aside regular times for employees of widely varying skills, responsibilities, and knowledge to brainstorm ideas for new products and services.

MOUNT FUJI:
BUILDING TEAMWORK, IDENTITY, AND STABILITY

No mountain is more closely identified with a nation and the spirit of its people than Mount Fuji, the highest peak in Japan. The elegant volcano is both a symbol of the quest for beauty and simplicity that lies at the heart of Japanese culture and a rallying point for national pride. Among major corporations, only perhaps Prudential gets to claim such a deep association with a mountain of its own—the company's longtime Rock of Gibraltar logo. Other companies, though, can and should profit from the lessons of Mount Fuji.

An evocative corporate symbol, name, or slogan can bring people together and make them feel part of a team with a clearly defined mission and a shared set of values. It also can provide the public with a memorable image of what an organization stands for. Symbols of corporate identity and the associations they evoke are especially useful for positioning a company and selling its products and services.

Participants in the Wharton treks get a direct experience of how symbols can build teamwork and establish corporate identity. A hiking exercise divides them into small teams with rotating leadership. The first leader of each team works with his or her members to come up with a group theme, the second a name that expresses that theme, the third a motto or a slogan, and the fourth a logo. One team decided they wanted to walk slowly, so they named themselves the Funeral Procession and came up with the memorable slogan "Arrive alive!"

When trek members gather at the end of the day to discuss their experiences, they inevitably turn to the business world for comparisons. Pondering Mount Fuji and all it stands for, one participant noted that Hewlett-Packard spent $1 million to come up with an evocative name for its new spin-off company, Agilent, with its implied associations of agility in developing innovative products. Prudential's long and extremely effective use of its logo to elicit brand recognition and convey a sense of dependability is invariably mentioned, too. Everyone knows you can trust in the "Rock."

Often, in fact, we'll use the Rock of Gibraltar to launch us into another aspect of the Fuji paradigm. Perhaps the most famous work of Japanese art outside the country, the block print *Great Wave off Kanagawa*, by Hokusai, shows Fuji as the still point in the midst of swirling waves about to overwhelm a boatload of frightened people. To help their organizations survive the turbulence of the marketplace, leaders need to seek equivalent points of stability. Symbols and ideas of corporate identity that reflect enduring values and competencies can help hold corporations together over the long term and provide a solid base for managing change and innovation. A wise leader also knows that he or she needs to look beyond immediate objectives and use their attainment to build enduring, committed teams that will ensure future success.

Once, on my way back from a trek in the Himalayas, I stopped in Japan to see Fuji. It was hidden in clouds, as usual, and yet, even in the mist, I could feel the mountain's presence, looming invisibly over the Japanese landscape. As I stood there, I was reminded of a haiku by Bashō, one of Japan's most famous poets:

> *Delightful, in a way,*
> *to miss seeing Mount Fuji*
> *In the misty rain.*

The central role of Mount Fuji as a symbol of Japanese culture makes it a tangible reality, whether we see it or not. A leader who knows how to build and use a well-established identity for his or her organization makes it a continual presence, even when it's not noticed, bringing people together and giving them a sure sense of purpose and direction.

THE MOUNTAIN JOURNEY:
DEALING WITH DOWNTIMES, LEADING FOR THE LONG TERM

Although each mountain has its own lessons to impart, the trek itself is a valuable teacher; after all, its peaks and valleys mirror those in the business world. Halfway through the Wharton Everest trek, we reach our high point—the summit of an 18,000-foot peak beneath Mount Everest. Mike and I always remark, as we all stand transfixed by the sight, that we can't stay long because the most dangerous part of the climb lies ahead: the descent. Tired and no longer focused on a goal, in a hurry to get down, we are most apt to slip and fall. We also note that we still have half the journey ahead of us—a succession of ridges and valleys to cross with many challenges and experiences along the way. Until we have finished the whole trek, we won't know whether we have completely succeeded or not.

Mike and I use the descent to focus attention on the critical period following a major business success. Too many leaders succumb to overconfidence, certain they can stand on their summits of achievement forever. As they begin to come down—pulled by the gravity of business cycles, market changes, and simple fluctuating luck—depression and fatigue often replace feelings of euphoria. No longer driven by the vision of a goal ahead of them, many leaders tend to lose focus and make mistakes. The fall of Enron after its rapid successes in the energy market is a stunning example of the consequences of pride and carelessness. The leadership overextended the company and failed to plan for the slowdowns and setbacks that were sure to follow. Enron's spectacular success made them feel they could get away with questionable—even illegal—business practices. In the end, everyone suffered, from CEO to data clerks and shareholders.

Whether you choose an alpine- or siege-style approach, the most rigorous mountain climbing involves dreary days of building supply lines and maddening waits for the weather to break, punctuated by brief but glorious moments when everything is in place and the terrain just seems to glide by. So it is in the lives of individuals and corporations. The critical test of leadership is how one deals with the long downtimes between the high moments of achievement. Can we recognize what those times have to offer and use them to build more robust, enduring organizations? Aaron Feuerstein, the CEO of Maiden Mills Industries, faced just such a long, dark time when his main factory for producing the popular Polartec fleece burned down. Rather than lay off employees while he struggled to rebuild the company, Feurstein kept his workers on the job and rebuilt the company around them. This decision won him both national acclaim and the loyalty of a dedicated team whose support helped Maiden Mills survive a subsequent period of bankruptcy.

The metaphor of trekking through the Himalayas adds a horizontal dimension to our consideration of organizational growth. How do our goals and the values we develop fit together as high points of a longer, fuller journey? Do we have a vision of where we are going that can guide and sustain us as we traverse the peaks and valleys that lie ahead? A key ingredient for negotiating the long-term journey will be the flexibility to change and grow. In our group discussion on the trail, one participant realized that the out-front, hands-on style of leadership that he had used to start his company no longer worked: With the growth and maturation of his corporation, he needed to move back and delegate more responsibility—a difficult transition for him to make and one that has stymied the growth and long-term prospects of many organizations. Finally realizing that he could no longer immerse himself in day-to-day details, he learned to let others take over tasks he had thought only he could do and focus instead on his new role of directing the overall course and operations of the company.

BEYOND THE SUMMIT:
BRINGING HOME THE LESSONS OF SUCCESS AND FAILURE

John Muir, the American environmentalist who founded the Sierra Club and played a major role in establishing Yosemite National Park, wrote in *Our National Parks:* "Climb the mountains and get their good tidings. Nature's peace will flow into you as sunshine flows into trees. The winds will blow their own freshness into you, and the storms their energy, while cares will drop off like autumn leaves."

The late Supreme Court justice and outdoorsman William O. Douglas saw mountains as a source of inspiration for developing national character, writing in *Of Men and Mountains:* "A people who climb the ridges and sleep under the stars in high mountain meadows, who enter the forest and scale peaks, who explore glaciers and walk ridges buried deep in snow—these people will give their country some of the indomitable spirit of the mountains."

We all need those good tidings, a renewal within ourselves of that indomitable spirit. One participant in our Wharton treks, the CEO of a software firm, sat alongside an Everest trail and told us that when he has a problem he can't solve at work, he goes off into the mountains. It's there, he said, among the peaks and rock faces and whistling winds, that the solution comes to him, almost as if it had been waiting for him to arrive.

Leaders who want to enhance the productivity of their staffs need to give them the opportunity to clear their minds so they can come up with fresh approaches to seemingly intractable problems. Perhaps the answer is as simple as encouraging a few minutes of meditation. Perhaps it's a team meeting at some coastal retreat. Winston Churchill famously relaxed from the pressures of governing by taking his paints and easel and finding a quiet spot in the countryside. Mountains aren't the only place to find the peace of mind that can recharge our batteries and renew our determination and vision. But mountains, I believe, are almost unique in the lessons they have to teach.

We know from mountains that we cannot remain long on the summits of success and that the elation we feel there soon dissipates. Mount Everest is not only the world's tallest peak; it may also be the world's best leveler of hubris. What can we bring back from those brief high points of achievement? Some of our other peak paradigms offer valuable pointers here. Mount Kailas shows us that in reaching the summit of a mountain we also reach its center—and the sense of centeredness we experience there, unlike momentary feelings of elation, is something we can bring down to the rest of our work and personal lives. Like the still point of Mount Fuji in the print by Hokusai, a leader who is centered has the inner stability needed to weather the conflicting demands of the workplace and respond to people and situations more objectively. Grounded in this way, he or she can more effectively apply the models of Hua Shan and Mount Sinai to resolving conflicts and empowering subordinates, as well as motivating others with a sense of calling and service to a higher, more meaningful purpose.

One way to develop centeredness and stability in the midst of work is to focus on the work itself—the process of climbing the mountain. One Wharton trekker realized, after many days of hiking, that his reluctance to take on leadership roles—a reluctance that was holding him back in his career—stemmed from his fear of making a wrong decision that could lead to failure. When he stopped worrying so much about the negative consequences of his actions and concentrated more on what he was doing at the moment, he found himself steadier and freer to make even tough calls. Back in the United States, he undertook a major career change, accepting a challenging leadership position at a riskier, more entrepreneurial company.

In fact, taking a positive attitude toward failure and seeing what we can learn from it encourages us to take the risks that we need to take to become dynamic, effective leaders. A leader who doesn't fail or make mistakes from time to time is not out front, leading the way toward innovative solutions. Effective leaders realize that they need to encourage their subordinates to take risks—and support them when they fail. As a 3COM executive puts it: "We tell our folks to make at least ten mistakes a day. If you're not making ten mistakes a day, you're not trying hard enough."

Failure itself can be a valuable source of insight and growth, as I learned when an enormous ice avalanche in the Himalayas swept me down a thousand feet and buried me in rock-hard snow. Although convinced I was going to die, I somehow managed to free myself and helped a companion get out. At the time, the expedition seemed a total failure—I had lost everything and we had to turn back—but later reflection prompted me to think more deeply about why I was climbing mountains in the first place. Why do we do what we do in our lives? I concluded that at that stage I was seeking unusual experiences, and surviving the avalanche was certainly more unusual than reaching the summit! With that realization, I was able to view my apparent failure in a positive light and learn valuable lessons from it.

One of those lessons I recall most vividly didn't take long to arrive. In the middle of the night after the avalanche, I woke up, and for the first time on the expedition I felt like climbing the mountain for the sheer joy of it. We had to go down the next day, but over the years I have come to realize that when I have done things simply for the delight of doing them, I have done them best, have felt most fulfilled, and have had the most positive influence on others. A leader who inspires others to take this kind of joy in their work frees them to fulfill themselves even as they fulfill their goals.

First Mover Advantage:
Tenacity and the Business of Adventure

AL READ

THE WEST FACE OF GASHERBRUM IV IN PAKISTAN. THE SOUTH Face of Lhotse in Nepal. "Blood from a Stone"—the East Face of Mount Dickey in Alaska. Serious mountaineers proudly view the most audacious climbs, especially difficult first ascents like these, as badges of achievement and courage sought out by the elite and daring. Inevitably, high-standard climbs require tremendous physical perseverance, but they also demand the focused mental tenacity both to overcome fear (or most of it) and to use that fear to hone the self-preservation instinct and so prevail on the climb. As you've read often in this book, even the best climbers can meet with disaster. They fall, or things fall on them—rocks, ice and snow avalanches, even other climbers. When climbing at your limit, especially over unknown terrain, it's this electric conflict between fear and controlling fear that sets you on a razor's edge of concentration, creativity, and excitement. It takes climbing beyond a physical sport, to a form of art. It's the absence of that conflict and creativity that can make life back in the valleys seem mundane and unsatisfying. Taste the experience once in its undiluted state, and it's hard not to return to the mountains for a new adventure. Climbing to some can almost be an addiction.

But there is much more to technical climbing than the singe of excitement. For most who pursue mountaineering throughout their lives, there is a respect—indeed, a reverence—for mountains. An enormous force in nature, mountains hold great power and enchantment over those who approach them. They evoke the conflicting auras of exquisite beauty and the dreaded unknown. And with good reason—their countenances can be peaceful and serene, or they can unleash powerful storms of tumultuous and lethal avalanches, floods, and landslides. Barely 200 years ago, humans approached the mountains with terror and only attempted their summits in pursuit of a religious pilgrimage or sacrifice. Today, though, ever more people satisfy their craving for climbing.

The mountains have held me in their grip for decades now—as long as I can remember—driving me to carve my life's work from them. My career spans Exum Mountain Guides, a technical mountain-climbing company operating in Grand Teton National Park in Wyoming, where I have guided off and on since 1959 and where I am president; Mountain Travel Nepal, where I served as managing director; Himalayan River Exploration, the first adventure rafting company in Nepal, which I helped found; and Geographic Expeditions (formerly InnerAsia), one of the major adventure travel companies in the United States.

My partners and I, together with a magnificent staff, capitalized on the lure of the most respected and daring explorations in founding and building Geographic Expeditions. The adventure-business marketplace is crowded and full of competent competitors. In order to create our niche and then to maintain an edge, we enticed clients by offering trips to the most remote and previously unreachable areas, places our competitors did not have the knowledge or interest to pursue. Our travels have culminated in the first commercial crossing of the Turugart Pass between Xinjiang Province in western China and Kyrgyzstan; the first American crossing of the Patagonian Ice Cap, which straddles the frontier between Argentina and Chile; the first commercial treks in northern Vietnam; and the first successful commercial crossing of South Georgia Island, repeating the route of Sir Ernest Shackleton's epic adventure.

Because risks are best understood by those who have taken them, it helped me tremendously in understanding and developing such a business that I myself was drawn to the fever of first ascents and the tenacity, drive, and concentration they require to be done successfully. During my early mountaineering years, there was nothing so exciting as climbing at the top of my ability, and because so few people had taken up the sport back then, first ascent opportunities abounded. Like many other young climbers, I tried to emulate contemporary heroes such as the French climbers Lionel Terray and Gaston Rebuffet and the Austrians Heinrich Harrer and Herman Buhl. The pioneering first ascents that they and others had made in the Alps were models of high adventure, daring, and sacrifice. Those climbers are still my idols.

The first ascents I did in Colorado and the Tetons paled in comparison to those of my European heroes, but for me those years were the most exciting period of my life. Every time I went climbing, I was able to experience a real adventure. Our equipment was crude. There was no down clothing then, no sticky rubber; only malleable iron pitons for protection. Carabiners were iron (not today's high-tech anodized aluminium alloy); there were no nuts or cams. Nylon rope was new to mountaineering, but often the material was so stiff that it was difficult to tie a knot.

In 1955, I first climbed the North Face of the Grand Teton, then considered a major ascent. I wore heavy army surplus World War II ski mountaineering boots, cotton army surplus pants, and a cotton sweatshirt, and carried a long wooden ice axe, canvas and leather packs, iron pitons, piton hammers, and heavy steel crampons. (The same climb today would be done in Goretex outer clothing, warm fleece, and lightweight sticky rubber footwear, while carrying cams, aluminium nuts, short and lightweight technical ice axes, and state-of-the-art internal frame packs.) Halfway up the face, we encountered a serious storm and had to bivouac under a small overhang, which barely protected us from the barrage of rockfall the storm generated and exposed us to much of the rain, snow, and wind. The next morning, we had to make the call whether to retreat or press on. Despite the unstable ice and snow plastering the rock face, we chose to force our way to the top. My companion quit climbing completely after that experience, but we both took pride in the tenacity and perseverance that resulted in success. The easier and safer option of a long rappel descent to the glacier 1,500 feet below would have been no substitute for the summit. Even though the North Face had been climbed before, it was my first ascent of this intimidating route and I was hooked on that feeling of personal pioneering.

Now, the first ascents have nearly all been done. Most of the great peaks and mountains of the world have been climbed by multiple routes. The cutting edge of mountaineering now is to make the best time, climb the most radical, often dangerous routes, and ski, snowboard, hang glide, or paraglide down. Even the great adventures remaining will likely be supported by the ultimate in technical know-how and equipment. True self-reliance disappeared with the advent of cell phones, radios, GPS systems, and massive rescue organizations. Yet intangibles still make the difference, and I believe that tenacity is a key factor for success in adventuring and in business.

Turning adventure into a way of life requires far more tenacity than reaching a summit does. Only through perseverance and at some considerable sacrifice have I managed to create a career out of my love of the mountains. Maybe because my father was a scientist, I never contemplated a career in business, especially entrepreneurial business. None of my college courses taught me anything about finance and accounting, and only a little bit about business law. But even though I lacked the seal of an Ivy League M.B.A. to back me up, no M.B.A. program could have prepared me for business the way the mountains did.

DISCOVERING A CAREER

I trace my own passion for mountain adventure back to my early years. At the age of six, I read my parents' Book of the Month Club selections of James Ramsay Ullman's *High Conquest* and *The White Tower*. Ullman's sagas of high adventure among the peaks of the world riveted me. I was raised in part on the Navajo Indian Reservation in Arizona and on ranches in the mountains of northern New Mexico, so the peaks were never far away. I have been fascinated by climbing ever since, but when I was about thirteen, I had the opportunity to learn the technical skills. I soon began serious mountaineering. I had no idea that it would serve to build the foundation of a career that would be a continuous search for adventure.

During my early days of climbing in the Tetons, I met Glenn Exum, the famous owner of Exum Mountain Guides. Glenn had tremendous charisma and a commanding presence, but he also had an innate kindness about him. I came to admire him deeply. His presence and amazing guiding history and traditions made me want to be a mountain-climbing guide more than anything else, but I was only in my mid-teens. Still, I simply could not forget the images from *The White Tower*, which portrayed guiding as a demanding leadership role in the face of danger, requiring honor and self-sacrifice to protect the clients who placed their lives in trust with their guide. It seemed in my youth the most valiant and exciting of professions. After five more years of climbing, doing what were then the most difficult routes in the Tetons (mostly to impress Glenn and his guides), I finally won Glenn's trust enough that he asked me to become one of his five guides. I was twenty-two then, and it was the greatest honor of my life. But I had also learned a valuable lesson: I had decided that I wanted to do something very specific—to guide for Exum—and I then pursued it doggedly for years until I achieved it.

Glenn trained me himself, making sure that I learned to be exacting, to hone in on details, and, most important, to anticipate problems and dangers before they occur (in climbing, once dangers do arrive, it's often too late to do much about them). He transferred his tenacity to me, demanding that I get the guiding techniques and protocols right. Glenn was forgiving, and as I learned from him, I became intensely and unwaveringly loyal. In time, he made me the first chief guide at Exum and later enabled me, with several of my colleagues, to become a partner.

My first high-mountain expedition, in 1963, was to Mount McKinley in Alaska, the tallest peak in North America. A guide colleague at

Al Read climbing on the Exum Ridge on the Grand Teton

Exum and I had been passed over for a slot on the first American Mount Everest expedition because we had not yet been on a major high-mountain climb. Yet several other Exum guides were asked to go (one Exum guide, Jake Breitenbach, was killed on the expedition in Everest's Khumbu Icefall). I was intensely envious of their adventure and vowed never again to be denied a place on an expedition I wanted to join. But to ensure that, I needed some big-mountain experience right away. My colleagues and I set our sights on the unclimbed East Buttress of McKinley. (The route has only been climbed a few times since.)

For the six of us on the expedition, this was a perfect adventure. We drove the Alaskan Highway in late winter and then flew into the Ruth Gorge with the legendary bush pilot Don Sheldon. Our six-week expedition included everything we could have wanted: avalanches, bitter cold, hideously hot days on the glaciers, falls into crevasses, steep technical climbing, complex route finding, unknown terrain, and storms and winds so strong we had to stretch our bodies against the insides of the tents to prevent them from shredding and collapsing. No one else

Al Read on the first ascent of the
East Buttress of Mount McKinley

was on that side of the mountain, so we were alone in a splendid Arctic wilderness. Mount Huntington, the Moose's Tooth, and all the peaks lining the Ruth Gorge were unclimbed. It was as exciting as adventure gets, and our expedition was monumentally successful.

McKinley taught me that high-altitude climbing is in reality a grueling slog upward with a heavy pack and inadequate oxygen—arduous, exhausting, and unpleasant. Many times on that expedition and those in the Himalayas that followed, I've said to myself, "I will take ten steps before I stop," and then been able to take only eight. Often I've seen a feature in the snow ahead—just a ripple or a shadow—and made it a goal to reach that landmark, only to have to stop short and double up over my ice axe gasping for air before I could go on. You challenge yourself, and you tell yourself that the next time you will be more physically prepared and better able to achieve the smaller goals. Then you drive yourself harder still; you make the small goals bigger ones, the hard route even harder. Achieve this goal, and you empower yourself to achieve higher, larger ones in better style, and often in a shorter time.

Whether in business or in mountaineering, or in the business of mountaineering, the tenacious will always be striving to achieve the next goal and setting the bar higher as they go along. That's what you build success on, and how you compound your success as you move forward.

A CONFLUENCE OF CHAOS

In 1961 and 1962, I served as the first climbing and expedition instructor at the Peace Corps Training Center in Puerto Rico, where I taught survival techniques to Peace Corps volunteers bound for overseas assignments. The training was designed to serve as a metaphor for achieving excellence through self-esteem and tenacity and to help the volunteers cope with severely underdeveloped conditions and radically different cultures. The training also introduced me to the director, Bill Delano, who urged me to enter the diplomatic service. In 1964, I enrolled at the Georgetown University Graduate School of Foreign Service.

At Georgetown, I really had to apply myself and study. I even had to learn another language (German), no easy task for me, but the tenacity I had cultivated in my mountaineering helped me through the long hours of reading, dogged memorization, and sedentary toil.

After two years of study, I was yearning for excitement. I traveled to Colombia and Nicaragua, working from 1966 to 1968 and getting my first taste of international political strife. The region was a confluence of chaos, and I found myself at the periphery of guerrilla warfare and political violence. I witnessed great poverty and extreme state brutality against threats to the existing political power structure. In Nicaragua, it seemed as though everyone had a gun; many women I knew carried derringers in their purses. Bullets flew at almost any provocation. In Colombia, the really severe political strife occurred in the streets of the big cities like Bogotá and under the cover of the mountainous jungles. I took no sides, finding both the government and rebel factions fascinating. Clearly, the mountains weren't the only source of great adventure—the high-stakes international political environment offered a new and electrifying intellectual rush. I wanted to learn more and become part of it.

After yet another year of ski instructing and guiding (I just had to go back to the mountains), I finally decided to use my graduate degree and took the Foreign Service exam. At the time, the U.S. government was supporting the Dalai Lama and the Tibetan army against the Chinese. Various specialized Foreign Service assignment opportunities existed in the Himalayas and on the frontier between China and the Asian subcontinent. Here was a real career adventure—in one of the best mountaineering landscapes on earth. Maybe I didn't have to abandon my climbing dreams to pursue a career . . . maybe I could combine the two exhilarating worlds. I was lucky enough to be among a handful of applicants selected in late 1969.

DHAULAGIRI AND DISASTER

I wasn't a stranger to the Himalayas. In the spring of 1969, I was asked to be the climbing leader of what became the American Dhaulagiri Expedition. The expedition had originally obtained permission for Malibuting, a peak in Pakistan, but at the last minute Pakistan closed its mountains for political reasons, and simultaneously Nepal unexpectedly opened its ranges after several years of closure. (After the 1962 Sino-Indian border war, the Chinese had diplomatically pressured Nepal to keep Indian troops and other foreigners out of the Himalayan frontier with Tibet and China. This included climbers. American mountaineers had aggravated the situation. In 1962, a small expedition under Woodrow Wilson Sayre had clandestinely crossed the Nepalese border into Tibet at the head of the Negojumba Glacier, near Cho Oyu, in an attempt to ascend the Rongbuck side of Mount Everest. It was an enviable adventure, even though it failed; but when Sayre returned to the United States and wrote a book about the illegal crossing and expedition, the Chinese forced Nepal to close its Himalayas to high-altitude mountaineering of any kind.)

Presented in 1969 with this unexpected opportunity to climb in Nepal, we chose as our goal the 26,810-foot Dhaulagiri I, one of the world's fourteen peaks that rise over 8,000 meters. (All are in Nepal, Tibet, and Pakistan.)

Nepal was fascinating then, not at all as it is today. There were few foreigners and cars, and no traffic, satellite phones, or electricity. The air was crystal clear, and the narrow streets and bazaars seemed as if they had been plucked intact from the Oriental Middle Ages. Shamans were treating people with dances and fascinating potions, and maimed beggars, many with leprosy, wandered everywhere, the disfiguring effects of smallpox and polio ravaging their faces and deformed bodies. Villagers sacrificed animals in front of the plethora of deity images, packs of dogs roamed the streets eating garbage and feces, and at night leopards prowled the outskirts of town, preying on goats and dogs.

Dhaulagiri itself was a very formidable mountain, probably more than we were prepared for. It offered up an important lesson on the unpredictability of Himalayan mountains and the dangers of pushing too far. Our expedition numbered fourteen, including two Sherpas and a government liaison officer. I moved forward in the advance party sent out ahead of the main group to establish a base camp and reconnoiter the route beyond. After climbing from 7,000 to 16,000 feet in a single day, I developed pulmonary and cerebral edema, a condition caused by climbing too high too fast and not acclimatizing. I had heard the medical warnings about altitude sickness, but I was naive and convinced I was too strong to develop the problem (I later learned that strength has nothing to do with it, just the body's ability to adapt to altitude). I lapsed into unconsciousness, and my companions wrapped me in our tent and slid me down the steep glacier, lowering me over the vertical seracs. Jim Morrissey, the expedition doctor, now a cardiac surgeon, climbed up 5,000 feet and met us near the foot of the glacier. By then I was in a decorticate posture (rigid, with flexed arms and clenched fists held in front of my chest), which indicated severe pressure on the pathway between the brain and spinal cord; I was about thirty minutes from certain death. Jim managed to save my life, but I remained in a coma for thirty-six hours. When I awoke, I was blind in one eye from retinal hemorrhages and could not walk. Sherpas and porters had to help me descend 5,000 feet to the village of Kalopani, at 7,000 feet.

When I was reasonably recovered, I walked to Jomosom, two days up the valley. Jomosom then had a primitive airstrip with occasional military or UN flights, and I hoped to get a flight to Kathmandu to have my blind eye checked. Unfortunately, there were no flights on the horizon. It appeared I would have to walk back, which would take about a week.

Two days after I arrived in Jomosom, Jeff Duenwald, one of the expedition members, walked into the house where I was staying.

"Avalanche," he said simply. "Seven dead." Numbly, he sat and we drank as he described the decimation of my climbing party.

Jeff had been in Base Camp when the avalanche occurred. It was late morning in the icefall. There had been clouds and early low temperatures, but by eleven the glacier was heating up. The advance party had just maneuvered a log across a crevasse and planned to descend just afterward. Then, from above, came a thunderous crack. A huge avalanche enveloped the party, filling the large crevasse that was being bridged. Lou Reichardt dived behind a hummock of ice, his pack torn off as the avalanche spewed over him. A huge roar filled the air and tumbling blocks of ice, some the size of refrigerators, rumbled past—and then there was silence. Lou stood up, expecting to see the rest of the expedition members emerge from hiding. But nobody appeared. He ran up and down, yelling names. Again, there was no movement. Only the silence of the glacier and the wind high up on the mountain. Because the avalanche had been ice and heavy snow, there was no way Lou could dig even if he had known where to start. Everyone was gone, disappeared, dead. It was one of the worst climbing disasters in the history of the Himalayas up to that time.

What is amazing about Lou Reichardt's survival is that he returned to Dhaulagiri on a later trip and was one of only two climbers to reach the summit. Lou continued with major Himalayan expeditions and reached the summits of Nanda Devi, K2, and Mount Everest, all via routes that were first ascents and major achievements. In the face of his very narrow escape and chance survival in the avalanche, Lou had the tenacity and courage to return to mountains equally dangerous and difficult as Dhaulagiri.

DIPLOMACY AND AN EXPLOSION OF OPPORTUNITY

Returning to Asia in 1971 as a diplomat was a compelling experience, but I was restless without mountain adventure. I was assigned to the U.S. Consulate in Calcutta, India, during the Bangladesh War, and later to the U.S. Embassy in Kathmandu. In Nepal, I had little to do on weekends because the mountains were too far away for a weekend trek or climb. However, I began to explore some of the country's great accessible rivers, most of which had never been run. My first raft was a four-foot inflatable given to me by Ron Fear of the 1973 American Dhaulagiri Expedition, who would later die running the Urubamba River in Peru. After much trial and error, I acquired a twelve-foot Avon raft, which was the perfect vehicle to descend Nepal's unexplored rapids.

Friends from an American adventure-travel company would show up in Nepal from time to time, leading treks for adventure clients and offering advice on rafting. Revered climber Skip Horner helped me fashion a rowing frame and make oars for my Avon, and Skip and I and other friends set out over the next few years to explore the high rivers. There was an obvious business opportunity in the rough waters. Nepal mountain tourism at the time was limited to game viewing, cultural tours, climbing, and trekking; the infrastructure for anything more didn't exist. There were, however, small aircraft to haul rafts up to air-fields near the heads of the great rivers, and plenty of porters who would gladly carry a raft.

Simultaneously, my tour of duty in Nepal was growing short. In the Foreign Service, officers are expected to return periodically to Washington to learn about new practices and the big picture of foreign policy, reacquaint themselves with America, and seek another foreign posting. I understood all that, but I also knew that there were no mountains worth the mention within thousands of miles of Washington, D.C. Luckily, I had rekindled my friendship with Jim Edwards, a charismatic British expatriate who had been with Pan American Airlines in Kathmandu during our Dhaulagiri expedition, and who ran

Tiger Tops Jungle Lodge, a famous big-game viewing lodge in Nepal's jungled Terai region.

Jim was looking to expand his business and was in the process of acquiring Mountain Travel, Nepal's original trekking and mountain-climbing outfitter. It was founded in 1963 by a British colonel named Jimmy Roberts after his final posting as military attaché at the British embassy in Kathmandu. Jimmy was the first to coin the word *trekking*, which now, of course, is a worldwide business. Jim Edwards proposed that I become the company's managing director. During the summer months—monsoon season in Nepal—I could return to the Tetons to be a climbing guide at Exum, and as an aside I could start the rafting company I had been contemplating.

The diplomatic service was a very coveted professional career that I had enjoyed and of which I was very proud. I had to gather the courage to leave—the prospect actually made me physically ill. I knew, however, that if I could muster the nerve to move on, my drive and perseverance would help me succeed in the unknown waters ahead. Resigning was one of the most difficult things I have done, but the timing seemed right. I just had to return to a job where the primary focus was mountains. It was the right choice, but when the world situation deteriorates I do look back and long to be in the middle of the action.

Soon, instead of writing political reports, I was organizing Sherpas for treks and climbing expeditions, reconnoitering routes, learning about the details of the Nepal Himalayas, and getting to know such celebrated clients as Chris Bonington, Reinhold Messner, Sir Edmund Hillary, Peter Habeler, Dougal Haston, and other famous mountaineers. I brought my friend Mike Yager over from Jackson Hole, Wyoming, to help create and manage the river company, which we named Himalayan River Exploration.

The river-rafting business was so difficult to get going that it was almost amusing. Rafts had to be brought in as personal baggage and declared as tents (there were no customs regulations for rafts). In addition, most Nepalese cannot swim because rushing mountain water is something to be feared and avoided in their culture. We placed an ad in the newspaper for "white water river guide trainees," and the few people that responded to the ad were more curious about what "white water" was than about the job, especially when they found out what the job entailed.

Mike did not give up, patiently gathering an excellent group of Nepalese guides. He taught them to be strong river swimmers, developed a weight-training program, and instructed them in first aid. We gradually built up a client base as trekkers heard about us. Most business consisted of day trips on the Trisuli River, which flows along the Kathmandu-to-Pokhara road (which was new back then). Many clients took a three-day river trip down to Tiger Tops.

One constant hurdle was vehicles. We had to rent different vehicles almost every day to ferry the rafts, clients, and boatmen to the drop-in point on the river, and most were broken-down trucks or Land Rovers. Often the clients had to push the vehicles to get them going. We encountered constant mechanical delays, breakdowns, exhaust fumes, and rattling metal, all on very treacherous mountain roads. But somehow lots of hard work, luck, and perseverance helped it all come together. Soon we had good vehicles, a smooth professional operation, and the growth of an industry. Our success bred competitors, and within ten years there were about 150 rafting companies in Nepal—the beginning of a new and profitable business for all of South Asia.

My efforts to grow the business also allowed me to personally grow my climbing career. With the resources and contacts generated by Mountain Travel Nepal, I was able to secure a coveted permit to organize and lead an expedition to the unclimbed Gaurishankar, a 23,440-foot mountain on the Nepal-Tibet border. The conditions that accompanied the permit were strict and administered by Kumar Khagda, a member of Nepal's royal family. (He was later killed in the 2001 palace massacre.) The expedition had to include an equal number of Nepalese and foreign climbers, and similarly equal numbers had to make the summit if it was reached. We prevailed and made the first ascent of the mountain—the last major unclimbed peak in the Nepal Himalayas.

Al Read at Advanced Base Camp
on Gaurishankar

Months later, the business also enabled me to travel to China and negotiate an expedition to Minya Konka (Gongga Shan), a 24,900-foot mountain in western Szechwan. (This was very bizarre to me, because a few years before, when I was with the diplomatic service, China was the enemy.) I also wanted to persuade the Chinese to allow Nepal-style trekking in Tibet, Qinghai, Szechwan, and Xinjiang, all remote mountain areas that had just opened up on a limited basis to foreigners. These areas had been closed for decades, and at the time were among the most sought-after adventure destinations in the world. I drew upon my diplomatic background and argued that if the Chinese allowed a limited number of trekkers to visit long before the government constructed hotels and other tourism infrastructure, they would earn badly needed foreign exchange and income that at least in part would flow to the local people. In trekking, I explained, clients need only put one foot in front of the other and foreign currency would come pouring in. The large capital investments needed for traditional tourism could come later. I don't think the Chinese ever really appreciated this concept, but we developed a personal bond, and they trusted us. We operated a few initial trips that went well and convinced them that we would abide by their regulations and be successful. They then allowed us to operate in many incredibly remote, previously restricted areas. There were a few issues—the Chinese were always embarrassed that they were not able to offer first-class accommodations to their foreign visitors. Also, while these areas were opening up to our foreign trekkers, traditionally closed societies got a glimpse of the rest of the world. At the time, this was not so welcomed by the Chinese.

GEOGRAPHIC EXPEDITIONS AND HARSH REALITY

I might have stayed on in Nepal for many years, but a serious business dispute over the use of the name Mountain Travel, among other issues, intervened. My experience in China paid off—eventually, Jim Edwards and I, joined by another former Pan Am executive, George Doubleday, purchased a tiny California travel-adventure company owned by Jo Sanders called InnerAsia. Jo had been in the adventure business for years and successfully negotiated and managed the first American climb in China since 1938: the ski ascent of Muztagh Ata. Jo's business had been built on permits to operate treks in four remote regions in China.

Our new incarnation of the company opened in San Francisco in 1983. We were primarily a marketing company—the half of the adventure business that creates, packages, and sells the adventure concept. Marketing companies select and communicate with the foreign operating companies, provide those organizations with business in the form of clients—either via group packages or individual tailor-made trips—and collect money, make payments, supply transportation and airline reservations, arrange visas, insurance, and information, and offer legal and financial recourse if anything goes wrong. Should a client experience an accident or illness, the marketing company is critical in arranging medical evacuation home, as well as activating insurance and notifying family.

At InnerAsia, we all had our individual expertise, but we had no idea how difficult it would be to leap into the United States in the middle of a very competitive market with low profit margins. Fortunately, George is a brilliant businessman and had sufficient investment funds to keep us going. We hired a small, excellent staff, but we struggled for several years while we networked among former Mountain Travel Nepal clients and did some location management. It took determination to discover our niche—private trips, something other adventure-travel companies discouraged. Our expertise enabled us to develop and create extremely innovative, unique excursions. We earned goodwill and developed a fine reputation, but we were still not profitable. And, unfortunately, like other businesses, adventure travel is about money.

You can offer all the excitement in the world, but if you can't make the bottom line come out right, you won't be in business for long.

The adventure market depends on disposable income. We target the upper economic levels because those clients have the money even in difficult times and because they tend to know enough history and politics to understand the images and dreams we are trying to sell them. But we also have to balance disposable income with disposable time. The more distant the trip, the greater the expense, but also the greater the expenditure of time, often our most precious possession. Most foreign trips need a minimum of eighteen days and often more. Even for the wealthy, that's a big chunk of time. We also have to consider physical capacity; we have to make sure we aren't overtaxing the strength and endurance of aging baby boomers. The young have the physical abilities to select a broad range of hard adventure trips, but they don't have the money. Those who have the money often can't spare the time. Those who have both time and money may not be physically able to handle a demanding adventure trip.

Cultivating clients with the right mix of qualities is an art, especially considering that regional conflicts, the threat of terrorism, and the reality of politics in the developing countries where so much of the best adventure travel is to be found all make adventure travel a perilous business. Growing a client base would be key to our success, as would quality control, customer service, and execution. While we sell romantic images, we survive by being deadline- and detail-oriented, fast moving, demanding, and highly competitive. Success demands creativity and innovative marketing—everything from stunning catalogs to courting the press—as well as insider negotiations with airlines and foreign political contacts at many levels.

The catalyst who finally put us over the top was Jim Sano. A one-time assistant to the superintendent of Yosemite National Park, Jim also came from a mountaineering background. He had led a major 1978 expedition to Mount Everest that we had handled at Mountain Travel in Nepal—during which he became perhaps the first person to use a computer to help manage a climb, even as he courted his future wife, the expedition doctor. Given his strong finance and computer background, Jim seemed a prime candidate to become our general manager, and eventually president. It was one of the best decisions we made.

A genius at organization, marketing, and finance, Jim also produced a wonderful brochure as our main sales piece, which played off our clients' dreams and romantic imagination. It called to mind images of those who struggled to make first ascents of the world's great mountains, those who set off across unknown seas to find new worlds. The intrigue of the great historic empires is part of the package, as are the struggles and, sadly, even the poverty of developed civilizations and Third World countries. Our brochures have won many industry awards.

Because of our staff expertise in the areas where we operated, we were able to come up with very detailed trip itineraries and could provide esoteric information to clients who called seeking a trip. We continued operating group departures and individual trips, and we expanded from Asia, which had been our original focus.

After various experiments with business models, we settled on one that centered not on what the market wants but what specific clients want. Since our goal was to provide high-quality client services, we delegated decision making to the staff, the ones closest to the clients, and provided them with incentive commissions. Opening up new frontiers was our specialty, providing that lure of the daring and audacious. Much of my own interest was beginning treks to what had once been "denied areas," countries that were behind the Iron Curtain when I had been a Foreign Service officer. We pioneered tourism in Tanna Tuva, a tiny region on the Russian border in Siberia, began U.S. travel in post-Khomeini Iran, and helped develop the remote Estancia Christina in Patagonia. We were the first foreigners since 1924 to visit the great bend of the Tsangpo River in eastern Tibet and to offer trips to Lhamo Lhatso, a Tibetan lake. (We've recently arranged for licensed—that is, legal—travel to Cuba, and we now offer adventure trips to Saudi Arabia, whose vast desert regions remain largely unvisited by Western adventurers.) Soon, various governments and private companies were engaging us as tourism-development consultants, and we were helping with foreign national media programs. As we expanded and became profitable, InnerAsia seemed too specific a name, so we broadened it to Geographic Expeditions, to represent our operations throughout much of the world.

IN RETROSPECT

I have been extremely fortunate to be able to turn my love of adventure and mountaineering into a career, and I have been lucky beyond measure in the people who have helped me along the way. Adventure and mountaineering both invite the human spirit to search the unknown, strive to achieve, and persevere till the end. What we in the business have done is simply to define and reflect that.

In business, in mountaineering, and in adventure travel, tenacity means nothing without timing, and I have been lucky there, too. As of the end of World War II, no 8,000-meter peak in the world had been climbed. (Annapurna I was the first—climbed by a French expedition in 1950.) Most of the world was still severely underdeveloped, and much of it was simply inaccessible. The places we send adventurers to now were available for nearly all of us only through the pages of *National Geographic* magazine. International mountaineering was reserved for the very rich. I entered the business—and I pursued my own adventures—in that fraction of a moment in time when someone like me could safely travel internationally, observe and experience many cultures in their ancient form, and afford to do so. It was a golden age.

Every time I wonder why I chose the business of adventure, I only have to climb high up a mountain in the warming morning sun, look down those many thousands of feet below, turn my face into the wind, and feel the force and power of nature. Then, once more, I understand.

Buried within us all is a curiosity about the unknown. To me, this is the essence of the human spirit, even if it is often masked by the distractions of everyday life. As long as one has the drive and tenacity and will to act on that curiosity, to look beyond, to learn, to see, and to know, the possible summits one can achieve, either professionally or personally, are limitless.

Thinking Like a Guide:
Making Grounded Decisions at All Altitudes

MICHAEL USEEM

WHETHER YOU'RE MANAGING A COMPANY OR A CLIMB, LEADER-ship demands that you instill a compelling vision of the future and then execute a strategy for achieving it. Good and timely decisions lie at the core of both. Customers want great products now, not next month. Investors require stellar results immediately. On a vertical rock face or in the middle of an alpine storm, the difference between success and failure—sometimes between life and death—is the right decision made in time to execute it.

Both venues subject leadership decisions to exceptional levels of uncertainty and stress. Disruptive technologies and human frailties recurrently upend intentions, and the price of placing the wrong bets or taking the wrong steps can be financially ruinous or physically disastrous. Decisions must be accurate and fast in environments that make reaching such decisions difficult.

Moreover, making accurate decisions quickly is inherently problematic. Good decisions require time, fast decisions allow little, yet managers and mountaineers cannot afford to compromise either quality or speed. "Shooting from the hip" buys speed but is predictably faulty. "Analysis paralysis" can get you to the right place, but at a woefully slow pace. Unless you can find a space between those two extremes, your prospects for leading successfully through a crisis are slim to none.

For leaders, the challenges are the same at sea level or above the timberline, but mountains raise the stakes. Critical decisions on mountainous terrain cannot be postponed, nor can they be flawed. Like sky divers, mountain climbers rarely get a second chance when things go seriously wrong. Because mountains impose such a high premium on both speed and precision, they provide an exceptional lens through which to prepare for leadership decisions on terra firma.

The observations that follow are the distillation of years of experience with both management development and mountain travel. As a business school professor, I've worked extensively with M.B.A. students on decision making in courses ranging from leadership and ethics to teamwork and organization. Decision making has been central as well in my work with managers in dozens of leadership development programs for enterprises ranging from Coca-Cola and Hewlett-Packard to the Marine Corps and the Presbyterian Church.

My mountain travel has ranged across the Alps, the Andes, and the Himalayas. Compared to other contributors to this book, my treks and ascents have been less daunting, the slopes less vertical, the altitudes less extreme. No killer avalanches, no hanging bivouacs, never above 20,000 feet—but I've still faced hundreds of moments when leadership decisions had to be made. Some were good, others flawed. From them and from my management programs, I've developed four guiding principles for making fast and accurate decisions, however thin the air.

THINK LIKE A GUIDE

To make a good and timely leadership decision, you need to sharpen the criteria for reaching it. No matter where you rank in the pecking order, imagine that you're the one responsible for the entire undertaking, whether it be a corporation or an expedition. What would you expect of a person in your position? Thinking like the CEO or the guide does not require brilliance, but it does necessitate strategic thinking—the ability to see ahead and see the whole. The more you appreciate the underlying forces that can drive success or trigger failure, and the opportunities and threats that the future may hold, the better you will be at decision making once your turn to lead arrives.

Such a moment to lead arrived for Enron vice president Sherron Watkins in 2001 when she confronted the company CEO, Kenneth Lay, on the afternoon of August 22. Watkins informed the chief executive that his company was in danger of collapsing from the partnerships that the chief financial officer, Andrew Fastow, was using to hide debt and enrich himself. Although Lay proved unable to challenge the ruinous practice, Watkins had spoken up, doing what she could to avert the impending disaster by acting as if she were accountable for the company's fate.

Similarly, on June 20, 2002, WorldCom vice president for internal audit Cynthia Cooper went over her boss's head to tell the board's audit committee that its chief financial officer had been improperly booking revenue to inflate profits by $9 billion. The Federal Bureau of Investigation's Coleen Rowley had done much the same when she wrote a thirteen-page memo to FBI director Robert Mueller and the Senate Intelligence Committee on May 21, 2002, outlining how upper-level FBI managers had failed to appreciate the early warning signs of what was to become the terrorist attack of September 11, 2001.

With no guidance from above and contrary pressures all around, these mid-level managers imagined themselves to be in charge and acted with the ultimate good of their organizations in mind. Despite angry responses and threats from superiors, they were thinking like their chief executives should have been thinking, and they spoke up accordingly.

In 2002, I accompanied a group of eleven M.B.A. students to climb Cotopaxi, one of Ecuador's massive—and still active—volcanoes. At 19,347 feet, Cotopaxi stands nearly a mile higher than any peak in the Rockies or Sierras. As we neared the top around 6 A.M. after a midnight start, one of our party—Jamie Hammond—became increasingly ill from the altitude. In spite of his condition, he also came to think like a guide.

Jamie badly wanted to touch the summit, just as the rest of us did, but he also knew that if he went for it, he would endanger everybody's chances as his illness worsened. At the same time, by stopping too soon, he would be prematurely forcing his ropemates down.

"I was exhausted, my head ached, and I was very dehydrated," Jamie recalled. Still, he pushed himself to climb within 700 feet of the

Climbers nearing the summit of Cotopaxi in Ecuador

summit. There, he found a tiny plateau where he could safely unrope and wait for the rest of his team to reach and return from the summit. As he later explained: "I wanted to get to a point where, if I couldn't reach the top, at least I wouldn't force the whole team to turn around."

Jamie had the same concerns as our mountain guide, but he chose not to leave them to the guide alone to resolve. When he heard the guide's description of the final stretch to the summit—"It will be the hardest hour of your life"—he decided on his own what should be done and then informed the guide of his conclusion. The guide concurred, and Jamie's clearheaded actions allowed the rest of his team, including me, to summit Cotopaxi and safely descend. We all knew that it was likely to be the highest point of our lifetimes, and we knew that Jamie had made it possible.

Developing the right criteria for reaching a good and timely decision isn't complex: In the mountains, think like a professional guide; in helping manage a company, think like a chief executive. Either way, you'll be developing the habits of mind that breed quick, clear decision making.

INFORMATION IS EVERYTHING

The right criteria for decision making open the door; the right information lets you walk through it. With timely data, a manager or a mountaineer is positioned to make an accurate and fast decision; but without the essential information, even the best decision principles are of little value.

The *Challenger* space shuttle disaster of January 28, 1986, illustrates the point about as well as any management failure can. The night before *Challenger's* scheduled launch, temperatures in central Florida plummeted to record lows. NASA flight directors called the top managers of Utah-based manufacturer Morton Thiokol to ask if its solid-fuel rocket booster would function reliably under the freezing conditions. Faced with the need for a fast decision—launch time was just hours away—the Thiokol managers recommended a go. At 11:38 the next morning, when the space shuttle lifted off with seven astronauts on board, the ground temperature registered just thirty-six degrees, fifteen degrees colder than on any prior takeoff. Seventy-three seconds later, an O-ring made brittle by the cold cracked in the rocket booster, causing the main rocket to explode.

Later analysis would reveal that ample information had existed in the Thiokol files that evening to tell its senior managers that the O-rings were almost certain to fail in the cold conditions sure to prevail the next morning. But the managers had not asked for the data because they had not known it was available—it was buried in a faulty filing system. They had made a fast decision, all right, but in the absence of good information, they had made a flawed one—the most fateful of their careers.

In business markets, quality information in the hands of key decision makers can influence the speed of the decision as well as its correctness. In her comparison of fast-moving and slow-moving computer firms in Silicon Valley, Stanford University engineering professor Kathleen Eisenhardt found vast disparities in the capacity to reach timely decisions. Though in the same industry, fast firms required half or less the time to reach decisions on product innovations and joint ventures than did their slower brethren: two to four months for the fast-movers versus six to eighteen months for the laggards.

A key difference, Eisenhardt found, lay in the use of real-time data. Managers at the fast-movers put a premium on having rich and reliable information on their products and customers, far more so than did the slower firms. They possessed fine-honed measures of their internal operations, and they met often to mine the data for fresh insight. They had better intelligence with which to appraise their own performance and appreciate where the market was going. The comparison firms, by contrast, tended to engage in tedious planning and forecasting exercises that sometimes required months for completion.

One of my own mountaineering experiences taught me a painful lesson in the value of good data for accurate decisions. Two of us had just scaled Monte Rosa, a long but not technically difficult Alpine climb. Eager for more action, we set out from our hotel in Zermatt, Switzerland, on a rainy August day to scale a nearby peak called the Dom. At 14,911 feet, it is the highest summit wholly within Switzerland—loftier than the Matterhorn, though not quite the height of western Europe's highest summit, Mont Blanc. Refusing to be deterred by worsening weather, we clambered aboard a cogwheel train from Zermatt for a ride down to the village of Randa, nestled in a narrow valley at an altitude of 4,623 feet. The Dom towered two miles overhead.

At noon we climbed quickly from Randa up a steep forested trail, lamenting the continuous rainfall and limited views but intent on our goal. As we climbed above the timberline, though, the rain intensified, the temperature plummeted, and the sky darkened. Our rain gear soon proved inadequate in the downpour, and by 6 P.M. we were wet, tired, and increasingly concerned about our ability to reach a high hut staffed by the Swiss Alpine Club. Our plan had been to sleep in that secure shelter and then depart at 3 A.M. for the Dom's magnificent icy summit. But the precipitation had now turned to snow, and the path to the cabin was becoming all but impossible to follow.

By eight that evening our circumstance had become alarming. We were many hours above the protective comforts of the valley. Half a foot of fresh snow obliterated the trail, darkness had fallen, we were drenched to the bone, and there was absolutely no indication of any hut ahead. The adrenaline of anxiety—still controlled but verging on panic—propelled us upward as fast as we could move on the rugged terrain. But still no sign. At 9 P.M., we began searching for crevices or any protective openings in the rocky canyon we were ascending. We had carried neither tent nor sleeping bags, certain that the Alpine hut would provide us with all the haven that would be needed. Now, we just hoped to find a bivouac site that would allow us to survive the night.

A futile half-hour search for a natural shelter left us even more desperate and lost, but then we spotted a tiny light high above us, barely visible through the driving snowstorm. We were so far up the mountain that we instantly knew that the light had to mark the hut we sought. It was a miraculous moment that we would never forget. Indeed, recalling it today still brings a rush of apprehension and relief.

Another hour of climbing later, we saw a kerosene lamp hanging just above the cabin door. The hut keeper had already turned in for the night, but to our everlasting gratitude, he had lit the lamp in case a beacon might be needed for anyone caught in the worsening storm. Caked with snow, we were such a sight that most of the cabin's guests rose to gape at the latecomers.

Like the Morton Thiokol managers, my friend and I acted in the absence of sufficient and timely information. We should have known more about the approaching storm, the time required to climb to the hut, and the mountain topography near the hut. Instead, we heeded our own optimism and left the valley floor late without adequate trail maps. We failed to anticipate the storm that hit or prepare for the conditions it brought. We were saved by the hut keeper's diligence, but if we had armed ourselves with the right knowledge before we set out, we would not have had to depend on a stroke of good fortune. I wonder—even now—about the consequences if the hut keeper had not shone the light.

We planned to sleep late at the hut, knowing that a summit attempt wouldn't be feasible in the fresh carpet of snow. But it stormed furiously through the night, and by morning the hut keeper had decided massive avalanches threatened. At first light, he announced that he was closing the cabin and that we would have to descend to the valley floor as quickly as possible. We did, severely disappointed that our terrifying climb up to the hut had been for naught but very much the wiser for it.

Whatever your field of endeavor, having the right data is a prerequisite for accurate and fast action. My climbing companion and I made our decisions quickly but not deftly, and save for blind luck and a dedicated hut keeper, we might have paid a hefty price for our failures. One lasting consequence is that I study more avidly and prepare more carefully before entering any terra incognita. I want to be certain that I have at my fingertips the information essential for real-time assessment of the situation at hand.

TRANSCEND YOURSELF

Fast decisions can be easy to make, but fast *and* accurate ones require us to subordinate our own self-interest to the collective objectives of the group. Until you transcend yourself, a snap decision is far too likely to be *about* yourself.

Rising above personal advantage in decision making is always a challenge, especially in an era of job-hopping and downsizing. When a firm has a history of frequent turnover and abrupt layoffs, managers are naturally tempted to give primacy to career over company, whether the subject is long-term expenditures or stock option allocations.

Adding to the challenge, free-market theorists have long elevated the pursuit of personal gain into public purpose. "The social responsibility of business," economist Milton Friedman has argued, "is to increase its profits." By inference, managers should act as micro profit maximizers themselves. The best decisions are those that optimize individual gain, and if all managers make decisions with that in mind, the resulting tide will lift all ships. Or so the theory goes.

In practice, such thinking is indefensible in a responsible leader. A leader's role by definition is to align and excite the group or organization to achieve the common purpose. Letting personal needs take precedence is a sure road to ruin, as witnessed by Enron prior to its collapse in 2001. Chief Executive Kenneth Lay was fast selling his own shares in the company while urging his employees to buy, and Chief Financial Officer Andrew Fastow was enriching himself through accounting chicanery that would later destroy the company. With self-interest running rampant, collective objectives and the common good circled the drain and disappeared.

Mountaineers face the same pull of competing interests, especially in the recurrent conflict between the teamwork required to reach a summit and the fame that is reserved for those few who do. Edmund Hillary and Tenzing Norgay won lasting renown as the first climbers to ascend Mount Everest on May 29, 1953. Far less remembered are the teammates who helped enable that triumph, or even John Hunt, the leader of the expedition. Climbing teams are often racked by discord when individuals push for personal glory even when their own summiting is less than optimal for the expedition as a whole.

Inevitably, those invested with power over others have the greatest chance to misuse their positions for private gain, when in actuality they should be the ones supporting the organization the most. Machiavellians tend to say "So what?" but most institutions deem such behavior pernicious and preventable. A Civil War dictum reminded cavalry officers of their priorities: "Feed your horses, feed your men, then feed yourselves." The U.S. Marines have a similar saying: "The officer eats last." Even those who don't have direct responsibility for others should keep the well-being of the greater organization in mind. John F. Kennedy offered much the same advice in his memorable inaugural address: "Ask not what your country can do for you—ask what you can do for your country." The norms of mountaineering have long emphasized an obligation to assist stricken climbers even if it means aborting one's own summit attempt.

Unfortunately, corporate America abounded in counterexamples near the time of the millennium. Dennis Kozlowski, chief executive of Tyco International from 1992 to 2002, should have reminded himself that the Tyco directors who had vested such extraordinary power in him expected extraordinary propriety in return. Instead, he misused company assets and shattered its reputation. Kozlowski ultimately was charged with looting Tyco of some $300 million, including several million for his wife's fortieth birthday party in Sardinia and household fixtures ranging from umbrella holders to shower curtains. He thought and acted like a thief, not a chief, with self-interest prevailing over any company interest.

To subordinate personal advantage to enterprise objectives, we must be able to identify what the venture requires, regardless of what we want. Then we must discipline our decision making to focus on the enterprise, not ourselves. My own appreciation for the latter point was strongly reinforced during a trek to Mount Everest. The trip began with our aircraft's sharp descent onto the sloped runway that is the gateway to the Himalayas—a tiny airstrip surrounded by snow-covered peaks in the village of Lukla, Nepal, elevation 9,350 feet. With fully laden backpacks and a keen sense of adventure, we began a journey into a legendary range capped by the highest mountaintop on earth.

We had gone to the Himalayas to learn about leadership in one of the outdoors' most stunning yet demanding classrooms. For the next eleven days, our team of twenty trekkers—M.B.A. graduates, mid-career executives, and my co-organizer, Edwin Bernbaum—would hike some eighty miles over rough terrain to reach a high point of more than 18,000 feet.

We departed from Lukla by mid-morning of our first day, wending our way along village homes, terraced fields, and valley walls. By late afternoon, we had arrived at our first campsite, in a deep valley with a roaring stream nearby and icy peaks above. That evening, we presented shirts emblazoned with a trek logo to each of the twenty-five Sherpas who would be our trail guides and yak herders in the days ahead. The act was more than just a token gesture. Guides, M.B.A.'s, yak herders, CFOs, and professors were part of a single team now, and the success of our expedition would depend greatly on how well we worked together and managed to subjugate our own needs to those of the group. That evening, we discussed how it was especially important that leaders not let their own interests on the trail ahead cloud their judgment when making decisions that would ultimately affect everyone.

Several days later, an American hiker whom we had met on the trail walked into our campsite at dusk. By then, we had pitched our tents at 14,150 feet, far above the timberline and the highest campsite of the trip. Our unexpected visitor reported that her brother was showing classic symptoms of altitude sickness: nausea, dizziness, and an uncertain gait. If untreated, we knew the condition could become fatal, but the only sure treatment was to walk him down to a far lower altitude—a harrowing prospect since night was falling and a descent would take hours.

I was exhausted by the day's doings, and the last thing I was fit for at that moment was to make a long nighttime descent. My physical instinct was to leave the problem to somebody else, since I was desperate for a night of rest in anticipation of a lengthy high-altitude hike the next day. But I reminded myself of a case that we had been debating along the trail—that of an investment banker who had passed a stricken Hindu holy man high in the Himalayas. The banker was so focused on his own destination that he rendered only the briefest of assistance to the stricken wanderer before resuming his own trek, and the stranded holy man may not have survived his plight. I made up my mind that if the hiker's health declined during the next few hours, I would simply have to make the difficult descent with him to a lower elevation, regardless of the personal hardships. That would be required, I reminded myself, regardless of who the stricken trekker was. But I also knew that it would be doubly demanded in this instance given the identity of the trekker: He was the son of one of my own colleagues.

Fortunately, the physician for our trek who specialized in emergency medicine had packed a yak-load of medicine. She treated the suffering trekker and placed him on an hourly watch to see if his symptoms worsened. He weathered the night, and the next morning he was able to walk himself down to a safer altitude. Several days later, we found him fully recovered in the thicker air of a village at 11,300 feet.

Though happily resolved, the incident strengthened my own determination to keep personal interests from taking precedence over what was best for others.

Our trekkers took turns being leaders for the day, each time gaining a renewed appreciation for how difficult it can be to put the needs of the group first. Like everyone else, the daily leaders arrived late in the afternoon at our camp, dog-tired, famished, and sometimes chilled or even altitude-sick. Their primary responsibility, however, called for them to ensure that everyone else had arrived safely and was recuperating quickly before addressing their own needs, no matter how hungry, weary, or cranky they might be. Leaders woke first and ate last, and in the process an abstract principle of decision making became an often exhausting reality.

Days later, this lesson was underscored in an unexpected way when we reached the monastery of Tengboche, home to the spiritual leader for the region's Buddhist population. We were able to receive a private audience with the high monk, the reincarnate lama, and with the aid of interpreters, we engaged in a freewheeling discussion of Buddhist concepts of leadership. Spiritual leadership, he said, can be built only by serving others. When leaders truly subordinate their private welfare to that of all others, their authority becomes unchallengeable. Near the end of our audience with the high monk, one of our trekkers asked him how he would respond if his authority were challenged. In implicit affirmation of the lama's revered status from a life of selflessness, our interpreters simply refused to ask the question.

Mountaineers and managers are often tempted to put their personal summits first. They may let their egos cloud their thinking or find convenient ways to rationalize self-interested decisions. Ultimately, though, the strength of an organization depends upon leaders who are concerned with doing what is best for their team regardless of what is best for themselves. That, in turn, requires that the venture's transcendent goals are embodied in every decision they take.

Trekkers at 18,000 feet near Mount Everest

SELF-CONFIDENCE, NOT OVERCONFIDENCE

The right criteria, the right data, and the right priorities all help decisions flow naturally, but pulling the trigger on those decisions still remains a psychological challenge. Without confidence, self-questioning can delay a necessary action. Overconfidence, though, can result in underanalysis and an equally faulty outcome. Albert Einstein had the right idea when he talked about the challenge of physics: "Things should be made as simple as possible, but not any simpler." Secure, yes; foolhardy, no.

Jack Welch, the longtime chief executive of General Electric, might be the gold standard of self-confidence. In his autobiography, written after a forty-year career at GE, Welch reported that he seldom regretted pulling the trigger: "I could scarcely remember a time when I said, 'I wish I'd taken six more months to study something before making a decision.' . . . When I asked myself, How many times should I have held off on a decision? versus How many times do I wish I'd made that move faster? I inevitably found that the latter won almost every time."

Self-assurance breeds momentum, as Welch's GE proved time and again, but excess confidence can take you over the edge. This is precisely what happened at the investment bank Salomon, where a can-do culture nearly led the company to ruin. A Salomon bond trader, Paul Mozer, made an illegal $3.2 billion bid for U.S. Treasury securities on February 21, 1991. Mozer confessed his act to his boss, John Meriwether, more than two months later, and Meriwether immediately reported it to top management on April 28. The company's chief executive, John Gutfreund, however, failed to report it to government authorities for three more months.

Salomon's culture had stressed taking financial risks to the limit, placing big bets as near the edge as possible, and its aggressive attitude had helped it become one of Wall Street's biggest and most successful players of the era. Yet that very same mind-set also encouraged Paul Mozer to cross the line and top management to look the other way. John Meriwether and Chief Executive Gutfreund were so discredited by the delay in reporting the malfeasance that they were forced out within days of its public disclosure.

The Salomon board called upon one of its own members—legendary investor Warren Buffett—to resurrect the company and its shattered credibility. With a dexterous combination of personal humility and executive resolve, Buffett forced out the entire management team and completely revamped the company culture. For instance, Buffett told all Salomon officers, "You are each expected to report, instantaneously and directly to me, any legal violation or moral failure on behalf of any employee." He provided his home telephone number and added that parking tickets were among the few exceptions to his reporting requirements.

Though Salomon paid dearly for the hubris of its prior management—customers fled, shares dropped, fines topped $290 million—the firm survived and prospered under a new team that emphasized calculated bets instead of reckless risk taking. A company that had nearly gone bankrupt in 1991 when overconfidence prevailed was sold to Citibank in 1997 for $9 billion once self-confidence was restored.

Finding the right balance of self-assurance and overassurance is as important in mountaineering as in management. With too little drive, you'll never reach your high point; with too much, you'll risk losing all. In 2002, I co-led a group of mountain trekkers to the shadow of Kanchenjunga, the world's third-highest summit, astride the border of Nepal and India. For us, it was the perfect place to study the fine line between motivating optimism and destructive overoptimism. We would need plenty of the former to reach our ultimate destination: a high mountain pass at 17,000 feet that looked onto Kanchenjunga's great unclimbed Southeast Face. But when did enough become too much?

We had arrived at a campsite on a barren ridge at 13,200 feet during a torrential downpour. The rain morphed into a snowstorm, capped with lightning and thunder roaring continuously for the next thirty-six hours. We would later learn that a cyclone in the Bay of Bengal had brought one of the region's most severe disturbances in recent memory. Lynne Dant, a chemical company manager, asked if such conditions were typical of most hiking and camping. She had never engaged in either before but had decided that the Himalayas were as good a place as any to start.

With our breakfast tent shaking in the gale, we knew that we faced a critical choice on this, our third day in the storm. If we were to have any chance of reaching the high pass, known by the lovely name of Go-Cha La, we would have to recommence our ascent today. Yet moving up in the snowstorm entailed significant hazards: The steep, boulder-strewn trail ahead carried a foot or more of fresh snow in places, and if the storm did not soon abate, a timely exit from the entire Himalayan range could be treacherous even if we did reach the high pass.

We remained confident in our basic capacity to continue upward, but we didn't want to overestimate our reserves for safely coming down. While many of our team were eager to reach the pass, others had become ambivalent about the rising risks if the snowstorm continued. To ensure that everybody was heard, we asked each trekker to candidly voice his or her own anxieties and recommendations about whether the team should proceed up or down. One of the last to speak, Lindsay Patrick, an M.B.A. student from Canada, captured the team's emergent judgment: "My gut feeling is that it's best for our mental health to keep going. The team has shown extraordinary strength, and it has the strength to go forward." We decided to push upward despite the weather.

Two days later we reached our highest campsite, a glacier-fed lake tucked at 14,200 feet among subsidiary peaks stretching up to Kanchenjunga's 28,208-foot summit. Our dinner-time discussion dwelled on the next day's plans for reaching Go-Cha La. We would rise at 3 A.M. and move up a faint trail that required no ropes but plenty of willpower. The thin air and fresh snowfall would be daunting, and our conversation dwelled on what it would take to reach the high pass—or to wisely back away if conditions suggested.

Several days earlier, we had talked trailside about the decisions Arlene Blum had made as she led an all-woman expedition to climb Annapurna, considered one of the most dangerous peaks in the Himalayas. Blum recruited well: Each of the ten climbers was a world-class mountaineer with a fierce resolve to reach the summit. On October 15, 1978, after a grueling and bitterly cold climb from a high camp, two of Blum's team reached the 26,504-foot summit. It was a crowning moment for the expedition, for women, and for mountaineering: The whole world had been waiting to see if Blum's expedition could equal the accomplishment of the all-man French team that had been the first to ascend Annapurna in 1950.

A day later, though, two other members of Blum's expedition announced that they wanted to touch an unclimbed subsidiary summit themselves—a case of personal interest trumping collective objective. At first Blum resisted. Her team had already achieved its goal of placing at least one member on top, and the expedition would gain little if others repeated that feat. Mindful of the great dangers, one of the Sherpas pressed for an immediate retreat: "Let's go to Kathmandu and have a party," he pleaded. But the two climbers insisted they be given a chance, and finally Blum relented. Two days later their bodies were found not far below the secondary summit, the victims of what appeared to be a fatal fall on its icy approach.

Without a driving urge to succeed, Blum's team would have lacked the will to move supplies up the mountain, much less send the first two climbers to the top. But the team also required an equally keen aware-ness of risk, and the second two climbers pushed that envelope too far, tarring with catastrophe what otherwise would have been a brilliant accomplishment. The headline of a *New York Times* article on a disas-trous 1996 Everest storm that left eight mountaineers dead captured the essence of this decision-making dilemma: "Scaling Corporate Heights Without Going Over a Cliff." Too little confidence, and Arlene Blum's climbers would have never reached the summit; too much confidence, and two others will never come back from it.

All of this was on our mind as we prepared for our own attempt on Go-Cha La. We were never going to summit a 28,000-foot mountain, but climbing to the highest possible point on our trek would nonetheless re-quire all the mental and physical reserves we could summon. Without an objective appraisal of our own limitations and of the potential perils of the hike, we ran the risk that our "summit fever" could overwhelm good judg-ment, endangering ourselves and others. Even at our lesser height, the thin air could easily bring on altitude sickness, or the snow trail a serious fall.

We began our climb at 4 A.M. on icy rocks around the lake's edge, and within several hours we had reached a spectacular sunrise vista. Some of our trekkers wisely decided to turn around at that point, mindful of the prior evening's discussion, but others strove upward. By noon, a dozen of us had reached Go-Cha La, and four subsequently pushed for an even higher pass another hour beyond. Bathed in sunlight, Kanchenjunga towered overhead.

All of our trekkers returned safely to a lower camp at 13,300 feet, and that evening we reflected on how so many of our team members had been able to achieve their own high point. For some it was the sunrise point at 15,000 feet; for others, the high pass at 17,000 feet. For most it would be the greatest altitude at which they were ever likely to stand. Bolstered by the camaraderie on the trail, their confidence had helped them reach the right decision to push as high as they could go. As Adrian Bland, a managing partner of a British law firm and one of the four trekkers who reached the highest pass, put it: "There was no way I could have gotten up there without the team."

Trekkers at Go-Cha La with the Southeast Face of Kanchenjunga overhead

But the team discussion the night before had also helped persuade others not to go higher than they should have gone. "There were two or three places that were very treacherous," offered Gopi Kallayil, an entrepreneur from Silicon Valley, "but I learned to be comfortable" in crossing them. Having done so, however, he concluded that he had reached his personal high and wisely turned to descend.

Self-confidence moved us up the mountain, individually and as a team. Avoiding overconfidence brought us all back down safely. Not all of us reached 17,000 feet, but in Adrian Bland's words: "Everyone got to their own Go-Cha La."

BACK TO THE LAB

Leadership decisions are what management is all about. Building a service or hiring a staff, launching a start-up or redirecting a firm, all involve myriad calls and plenty of chances to go wrong. That has always been true, but the turbulent business environments of recent years have placed a special premium on right decisions even as they've made them harder to formulate. Fast-moving markets, driven by changing technologies and nimble competitors, have added the necessity of speed, while a shaky economy and an often threatening world have interjected stress and uncertainty into the mix.

If you were going to build a lab to reproduce and intensify all those conditions, you could do little better than to model it after a soaring mountain range, or so my own experience has been. It's on those ridges, far from the daily battles of commerce, that I've formulated and tested the principles that most powerfully guide me in my teaching, consulting, and writing when I'm back home.

1. It is useful to see the world through the eyes of the chief executive or the professional guide. They are best positioned to judge the future and most obligated to look at the entire enterprise and enunciate a direction for it.
2. It is important to acquire fine-honed, real-time information about that world. Yes, undigested data can paralyze the best of us, but as the *Challenger* launch tragically shows, the absence of good, up-to-date information is far worse.
3. It is vital to subordinate personal calculus to enterprise objective. No one said it's easy, but ignoring private advantage when it conflicts with a broader purpose is an essential obligation of anybody in a leadership role.
4. Finally, it is essential to embrace self-confidence but eschew overconfidence. Insecurity impedes timely action, but as the great Greek playwrights knew and senior Salomon managers discovered, hubris lies at the heart of tragedy.

For those who risk the demanding world of rock walls and mountain slopes—or those who manage the equally taxing world of new ventures and established enterprises—the leadership calling is to reach decisions that are simultaneously right and swift. Without them, the best-laid plans are almost certain to go astray. With them, the toughest ridges can be traversed, the highest summits reached.

On Becoming an Expert Beginner

―――――

JIM COLLINS

AFTER CLIMBING FOR TWENTY-FIVE YEARS, I DECIDED TO get a climbing coach. I noticed that my climbing had reached a plateau, and I was curious to see if I could continue to grow as a climber well beyond my fortieth birthday.

My friends thought it weird. What could a climbing coach teach me, after all these years and thousands of hard routes?

It turned out to be the wrong question. Not the wrong question forever, but the wrong question to start. The most important lessons from my climbing coaches—Nick and Heather Sagar—lay not in what I needed to learn, but in what I first needed to *un*learn.

In the late 1970s, the challenging routes differed considerably from today's sport routes in that they tended to be sharply angled or nearly vertical. If you rappelled off, you would usually be able to touch the rock all the way down. Modern sport routes, in contrast, frequently jut ten, thirty, even fifty or more degrees past vertical, forming steep overhangs. On such a route, you might climb forty feet of horizontal (upside down) for every hundred feet of vertical. When you fall off, you usually just fly through the air, with nothing to hit and a big fat bolt to catch you when the rope comes tight. It's a lot like bungee jumping—scary but safe. Contrast that to the old-style routes, in which you usually slide and bang down the face, smashing limbs and losing chunks of skin—and that's if the gear holds in the first place. (Old-style routes often have insecure protection that could rip out of the rock much more easily than the big, solid protection bolts that became commonplace in late 1980s.) On bolted modern routes, the consequences of falling are minimal—you can fall as much as you want—whereas on many traditional old-style routes, you should do everything you can to *not fall.*

When Nick and Heather first began working with me, my years of experience on scary, vertical climbing taught me to fear falling and ingrained in me a careful, deliberate style that ensured survival. This conservative manner impeded my ability to ascend harder modern climbs, which require big dynamic moves constantly on the edge of fallure. To climb a modern route at your absolute limit *requires* dozens of falls before you succeed—otherwise, well, it's not at your limit.

So, as if I were a raw beginner, Nick and Heather taught me how to fall. One of Heather's assignments: "Over the next year, I want you to take a thousand leader falls."

Dutifully, I began jumping off routes. At first, I took little bitty baby falls. But after a hundred small falls, I began leaping off the rock, striving for much larger falls. I almost came to enjoy them.

"Now comes the hard part," counseled Nick. "We need to make you a worse climber for a while, so you can become a better climber. All your old tricks and techniques for getting up vertical routes hinder you on steep, powerful routes. When you get into difficulty on a hard route, you resort to your strengths, and *that's* why you fail."

"But I've always believed that you should play to your strengths," I responded.

"Yes, so long as your strengths are helpful to the task at hand. But in your case, all the old strengths that used to serve you so well are now harmful habits—at least in the realm of harder routes. You need to build a new set of strengths from scratch and, most important, not rely on your old strengths to get up routes. This means you will have to drop down a few grades while you learn anew."

Nick and Heather put me on a steep problem to demonstrate, and I made five or six foot movements to get my body position stable (staying in control, as I had always learned to do). But in my deliberate style, I ran out of strength. "No!" Heather scolded. "Do it like Nick." Nick grabbed the same holds, cut loose with his feet, threw one leg up the wall in a big arcing motion, and catapulted his body upward in a huge dynamic heave. *Ka-whap!* In a second, he was up the same ten feet I'd diddled around on. He climbed more like a gymnast swinging around on a high bar, whereas I climbed like a dowdy workman clambering up a ladder.

My climbing did indeed worsen for awhile. But then the new techniques started to click, and I felt the excitement of progress, of becoming expert again—only with a whole new style and mind-set. I was in my mid-forties, feeling a passion for climbing that I hadn't felt since my teenage years. Rather than being depressed by "stepping backward in order to step forward," I feel renewed energy. Like getting a big flywheel turning in a new direction, I had to do a lot of work to even get the thing moving at all. But as the flywheel began to build more and more momentum, I felt the excitement of seeing it break through, from 1 turn to 2, from 2 to 4, from 4 to 8, from 8 to 32, to 64, to 128, to a thousand rpms. The sense of progress acted like an internal engine of motivation, which then led to better training, which then led to more turns on the flywheel, which then motivated even more, which produced better climbing, and more motivation, and so on and so forth. The very process of improvement and growth became the very point of it all.

I noticed that many of my climbing buddies didn't really take to the Nick-and-Heather program. I kept encouraging them to try it, to become better climbers. Then it dawned on me: After years of climbing and thinking of themselves as already super-expert, they felt uncomfortable with the idea of becoming a beginner again and were reluctant to try a new technique. So they stayed with their strengths, and continued to climb at a high level—but much lower than they could potentially climb if they became beginners again.

In his classic book *The Discoverers,* Daniel Boorstin argues that the primary barrier to human progress is not ignorance, but the illusion of knowledge and the dedication to "expertise." The best discoverers, according to Boorstin, are not the smartest or the most talented, but those who either are—or have the discipline to remain—expert beginners in their field. They see more clearly the way the world really works because they are less burdened with "knowledge" of what they are supposed to see. The same holds for any creative or entrepreneurial endeavor, which requires the precision of a scientist and the wonder of a child.

I see this same pattern in the greatest corporate leaders I've studied in my research, from David Packard to Sam Walton. Walton, founder of Wal-Mart, viewed himself not as a definitive expert on retailing but as a lifelong student of his craft, always asking questions and taking every opportunity to learn. A Brazilian businessman once told me that of the ten U.S. retailing CEOs he asked for an appointment with after he'd purchased a discount retailing chain in South America, only Walton said yes. "We didn't know much about retailing, so we wanted to talk to executives who knew the business," he explained. "Most didn't bother to reply. Sam said, 'Sure, come on up.' " Only later did the Brazilian realize that Walton saw himself as the student, and the Brazilian contingent as the teachers. "It finally dawned on me that Sam was primarily interested in learning from *us*; he pummeled us with questions about Brazil for two days before I finally got a chance to ask a single question of substance. If you hadn't known that this was *Sam Walton*, you would have thought that he was a complete novice."

The late John Gardner, founder of Common Cause and author of *Self-Renewal*, believed that people stagnate in their lives and careers because they accumulate barnacles. "You'll find that your best work usually comes earlier in your career, not later," he once told me. "So the best way I know to do your best work over a lifetime is to have multiple new starts along the way." Perhaps this is why I felt such a strong instinct to set up my research laboratory in my old first-grade classroom, as a reminder that no matter how expert I become, the only way to attain higher levels of mastery is to let go of my expertise and learn as a beginner all over again.

This, of course, is hard for most of us, as we like our position in the expertise pecking order. But if comparison is the primary sin of modern life, and I believe it is, then we need to focus less on the pecking order and more on our own potential. When it comes to climbing as a classroom, I've learned perhaps this lesson above all: It is not how well you do your work relative to others that matters, but how well you do your work relative to yourself, and your own potential. And if that means becoming a beginner again, so be it.

PERMISSIONS AND PHOTO CREDITS

Pages 17, 20, and 22: Nick Sagar. Pages 49 and 54: Scott Fischer. Page 63: Charlie Shertz. Page 69: Stacy Allison. Page 78: Dick McCracken. Page 86: Tom Frost. Page 88: Glen Denny. Page 98: Chris Warner. Page 95: Chris Warner. Page 102: Dawa Sherpa. Page 123: Susi Kriemler. Page 128: Jerry Useem. Page 145: Susi Kriemler. Page 160: Cristián García-Huidobro. Page 162: Miguel Purcell. Page 164: Misael Alvial. Pages 173, 175, and 178: Edwin Bernbaum. Page 191: Evan Winslow Smith. Page 192: Al Read. Page 200: Pertemba Sherpa. Page 208: Michael Useem. Page 217: unknown. Page 222: Michael Useem.

Page 231: Stacy Allison's photo courtesy of David Hambly. Page 231: Paul Asel's photo courtesy of Michael Useem. Page 232: Edwin Bernbaum's photo courtesy of Michael Useem. Page 232: Jim Collins's photo courtesy of Nick Sagar. Page 233: Rodrigo Jordan's photo courtesy of Christian Buracchio. Page 234: Al Read's photo courtesy of Al Read. Page 234: Royal Robbins's photo courtesy of Glen Denny. Page 235: Arthur Sulzberger Jr.'s photo courtesy of Robert Pittman. Page 235: Jerry Useem's photo courtesy of Michael Useem. Page 236: Michael Useem's photo courtesy of Michael Useem. Page 236: Chris Warner's photo courtesy of Rod Richardson.

ABOUT THE AUTHORS

Stacy Allison is an extensively experienced mountaineer, the owner of a general contracting company, and a motivational business speaker. Early in her climbing career, Stacy climbed Mount McKinley (Denali) in Alaska and Ama Dablam in the Himalayas. Later she became the first American woman to top Communism Peak (at 24,590 feet, the tallest peak in the Russian Pamir Range) and to reach the summit of Mount Everest. She has also led a successful expedition to K2, the world's second-highest mountain. Stacy is the author of *Beyond the Limits: A Woman's Triumph on Everest* and *Many Mountains to Climb: Reflections on Competence, Courage, and Commitment.* She owns and operates Stacy Allison General Contracting, a residential building company that specializes in the renovation and remodeling of older homes. Stacy speaks globally on leadership, motivation, teamwork, and communication. Stacy can be reached at stacy@beyondthelimits.com, and her website is at http://www.beyondthelimits.com.

Paul Asel brings fifteen years of experience investing in and working with emerging growth companies. As a general partner with Telos Venture Partners and senior vice president at Delta Capital, he advised more than a hundred startups. Paul has served as an adviser in restructuring the banking and financial systems in the former Soviet Union, and his advisory work has brought him to more than twenty countries in Europe, Asia, and South America. He began his career in investment banking with Merrill Lynch. Paul received an M.B.A. from the Stanford Graduate School of Business and a B.A. from Dartmouth College. In his free time, Paul enjoys triathlons and mountaineering. Paul has climbed extensively in the Alps, the Himalayas, the Andes, Africa, Asia, and the American Northwest. Paul prefers glaciers and ice to rock. The summits he has reached include Mount McKinley, Kilimanjaro, Elbrus, and Mont Blanc. Paul can be reached at Paul_Asel@hotmail.com.

Edwin Bernbaum holds a doctoral degree in Asian studies from the University of California, Berkeley, and is presently a research associate at the university. He is director of the Sacred Mountains Program at the Mountain Institute, working on developing ways of taking the cultural and spiritual significance of mountains into account in environmental programs. Ed is the author of *The Way to Shambhala,* a study of Tibetan myths and legends of hidden valleys resembling the fictional Shangri-la of *Lost Horizon,* and of the award-winning *Sacred Mountains of the World,* which was the basis for an exhibit of his photographs at the Smithsonian Institution. He consults and lectures widely on mountains, leadership, and teamwork; he has conducted extensive research on the role of mountain metaphors in leadership; and he has climbed, trekked, and led groups on mountains around the world. Ed can be contacted at bernbaum@socrates.berkeley.edu.

Jim Collins is a student and teacher of enduring great companies—how they grow, how they attain superior performance, and how good companies can become great companies. Having invested more than a decade of research into the topic, Jim has authored or coauthored four books, including the classic *Built*

to Last, a fixture on the *BusinessWeek* bestseller list for more than five years, and *Good to Great,* a *New York Times* general nonfiction bestseller with more than 1 million hardcover copies sold and translations into twenty-one languages. Previously, he taught at Stanford University's Graduate School of Business, where he received the Distinguished Teaching Award in 1992. Much earlier in his life, Jim was one of the top rock climbers in the United States. Today, Jim climbs mainly for recreation and camaraderie, although he still on-sights at the 5.12 grade and redpoints at the 5.13 grade. Jim can be reached at jimcollins@aol.com.

Rodrigo Jordan is founding director of Vertical S.A. in Chile, an organization devoted to using mountains as a classroom for groups ranging from company managers to schoolchildren. He holds a doctorate in organizational administration from Oxford University, and he teaches innovation management in the M.B.A. program of the Universidad Católica de Chile. Rodrigo has climbed throughout the Andes, summited Mount Everest by the difficult East Face in 1992, and led a Chilean team in 1996 in a successful ascent of K2. Rodrigo is the author of *Everest: The Challenge of a Dream* and *K2: The Ultimate Challenge,* and his ascent of K2 was featured in 2001 in the National Geographic television series *Quest for K2.* In 2002, he led a four-person team in an unsupported 250-mile traverse, much of it unexplored, of the Ellsworth Mountains in Antarctica. *Time* magazine identified him in 1995 as one of the leaders of the "new millennium." Rodrigo can be contacted at jordan@vertical.cl, and information on Vertical is available at http://www.vertical.cl.

Al Read is president of Exum Mountain Guides in Grand Teton National Park and executive vice-chairman of Geographic Expeditions in San Francisco. After graduating from Georgetown University, he worked in Nepal for twelve years, first as an American diplomat and then as managing director of the largest trekking and mountaineering oufitter in Asia. He pioneered river rafting in Nepal and founded its first rafting company, creating a new industry in that country. His mountaineering expeditions include Dhaulagiri, Minya Konka (or Gongga Shan; the highest peak in China), and Mount Everest. He led first-ascent expeditions to Gaurishankar and Cholatse, and made the first ascent of the East Buttress of Mount McKinley. He also co-guided a successful crossing in 2000 of South Georgia Island, retracing Ernest Shackleton's historic route. Al is a former director of the American Alpine Club, a founding director of the American Mountain Guides Association, a former professional ski instructor, and a licensed pilot. Information on Geographic Expeditions can be found at http://www.geoex.com and on Exum Mountain Guides at http://www.exumguides.com.

Royal Robbins is an acclaimed mountaineer, adventure kayaker, and founder of Royal Robbins, Inc., a distributor of outdoor and travel clothing. His climbs include many first ascents in North America and the Alps. In 1957, he made the first ascent of the Northwest Face of Half Dome in Yosemite Valley; he went on to make first ascents of the three great faces of El Capitan, and he was the first to solo climb that wall as well. Royal pioneered many other routes, including one that was then considered the hardest rock climb in the Alps. In 1975, he became involved in kayaking and went on to make more than thirty first descents in California and Chile. He also started a rock-climbing school. He is the author of *Basic Rockcraft* and *Advanced Rockcraft* (which together have sold nearly half a million copies), and he is an honorary member of the American Alpine Club. Royal can be contacted at royalrobbins@earthlink.net.

Arthur Sulzberger Jr. is chairman of The New York Times Company, and, as the company's senior executive, he is responsible for its long-term business strategy. The New York Times Company publishes *The New York Times,* the *Boston Globe,* and sixteen other newspapers; owns eight television stations and two radio stations; and maintains more than forty websites. Arthur is also publisher of *The New York Times,* which he runs on a day-to-day basis. He was named Publisher of the Year in 2001 by *Editor & Publisher* magazine. In 2002, *The New York Times* won an unprecedented seven Pulitzer Prizes, and the company ranked first in the publishing industry in *Fortune's* 2003 list of America's Most Admired Companies. Arthur is a founding board member and former chair of the New York City Outward Bound Center, and he is an avid rock climber who is frequently to be found on weekends climbing in the Shawangunks (in New York State). Arthur can be reached at asulz@nytimes.com; information on The New York Times Company can be found at http://www.nytco.com and *The New York Times* at http://www.nytimes.com.

Jerry Useem is a senior writer at *Fortune* magazine, where he writes about general management and corporate enterprise. His articles have focused on subjects including crisis leadership, the history of the CEO, why companies fail, New York Yankees manager Joe Torre, and such Fortune 500 standards as General Electric, Wal-Mart Stores, and Boeing. A graduate of Williams College, Jerry was previously a senior writer at *Inc.* magazine and a casewriter and researcher at Harvard Business School. His writing has also appeared in such publications as the *Boston Globe, Wired,* the *American*

Prospect, and *Business 2.0,* while his commentaries have been heard on National Public Radio. Though he grew up hiking the White Mountains of New Hampshire, it was on such peaks as Mount Rainier, Mont Blanc, the Grand Teton, and those in the Mount Everest region that he established his reputation for mediocrity in the mountains.

Michael Useem is professor of management and director of the Center for Leadership and Change Management at the Wharton School of the University of Pennsylvania. He is author of *Leading Up: How to Lead Your Boss So You Both Win, The Leadership Moment: Nine True Stories of Triumph and Disaster and Their Lessons for Us All,* and *Investor Capitalism: How Money Managers Are Changing the Face of Corporate America.* He has consulted on organizational development with companies, the U.S. Agency for International Development, U.N. organizations, and other agencies in Latin America, Asia, and Africa. His university teaching includes M.B.A. and executive-M.B.A. courses on leadership and management. He offers programs for managers in the United States, Asia, Europe, and Latin America, and he has climbed in the United States, Africa, Europe, and Asia. Mike can be contacted at useem@wharton.upenn.edu, and information on Wharton Leadership Ventures may be viewed at http://leadership. wharton.upenn.edu/1_change/trips/index.shtml.

Chris Warner is the founder and president of the Earth Treks' Climbing Centers, based in Maryland. Earth Treks is one of the largest indoor climbing gym chains and climbing schools in the United States. Chris has guided more than seventy-five international mountaineering expeditions, including three trips on the North Ridge of Mount Everest, and he has pioneered some of the harder Himalayan routes on peaks such as Ama Dablam and Shivling.

Chris was the first American to completely solo climb an 8,000-meter peak with his thirty-four-hour nonstop ascent and descent of the deadly South Face of Shishapangma (26,399 feet). Chris founded the Shared Summits Program, a Web-based educational partnership among Earth Treks expeditions, schoolteachers, and more than 20,000 schoolchildren. Chris's adventures have been featured in hundreds of newspaper and magazine articles, and he has appeared on dozens of television and radio programs, including CNBC, Outdoor Life Network, and ABC. Chris can be reached at cw@earthtreksclimbing.com, and information on Earth Treks may be found at http://www.earthtreksclimbing.com.

INDEX

acclimatization, 138–40, 195
action, 104
adventure-travel industry, 187,
   197–204
adversity, as lesson, 74
Agilent, 179
Alger, Horatio, 6
Allison, Stacy, 47–73, 231
alpine-style climbs, 99, 170–71, 172
Altair computer, 129
Alvial, Misael, 161, 162, 165, 166
ambiguity, 19, 21
ambition, 6
Andersen, Arthur, 58
Annapurna, 5, 10–11, 131, 220
Annapurna (Herzog), 5
Annapurna: A Woman's Place (Blum),
   10
Apple Computer, 129, 171
ascents, first, 78, 81–83, 85, 119,
   131, 172, 188–89, 199
Asel, Paul, 116–47, 231–32
attitude, 77–78, 81–83, 91, 155, 184
authority, 72
autonomy, 56

Bailey, Phil, 76
Ballmer, Steve, 125
barriers, mental, 25
Belk, Q, 48, 49, 55, 56, 57
Bernbaum, Edwin, 3, 168–85, 232
Black, Dave, 48

blame, 64
Bland, Adrian, 221, 222
Blum, Arlene, 10–11, 220–21
Boitano, Aldo, 161, 167
Bonington, Chris, 97, 123, 124, 145
Boorstin, Daniel, 226–27
Bragg, John, 23, 24
Breashears, David, 28–30
Built to Last (Collins, Porras), 2, 28,
   146
bull market of 1990s, 45
Buracchio, Christian, 157
Burgelman, Robert, 45
Burke, James, 9–10
business, climbing as metaphor for,
   3, 168–70, 183–84

Canion, Ron, 135–36
Carnegie, Andrew, 1, 6
centeredness, 184
Challenger shuttle disaster, 209
challenges of business, 88–91, 101
Chambers, John, 11
change, 70, 119
Charles Schwab & Co., 146–47
Cho Oyu, 93–95
Chouinard, Yvon, 6–7, 85
Cisco Systems, 11
clear vision, 117, 126–30, 152–53
climbing
   alpine, 99
   expedition-style, 48–50, 51, 99

Hillary, Sir Edmund, 9, 60, 65, 68
Himalaya mountains, 7, 56–57, 194.
 See also Everest, Mount;
 Shivling Peak
Himalayan River Exploration, 187,
 198–99
Hissong, Scott, 126
Hoey, Marty, 134
HP Way, The (Packard), 139
Hua Shan, 175–77
humility, 37, 38, 44–46
Hunt, John, 9

IBM, 26, 65, 128
ideas, core, 177–79
identity, corporate, 179–80
IDEO, 120
individuality, 51, 56
inflection points, 131–32
information, 209–12, 223
InnerAsia, 201
innovation, 118, 136–38
Intel Corporation, 31, 125, 131–32,
 133
Into Thin Air (Krakauer), 118

Jenkins, Dan, 97–103, 107, 110–12
Jobs, Steve, 26, 171
Johnson & Johnson, 9–10
Jordan, Rodrigo, 7, 148–67, 233
judgment, 45
Jules Verne climb, 38

Kailas, Mount, 177–79
Kallayil, Gopi, 222
Kami (Sherpa), 63–64
Kanchenjunga, 219–22
Karstens, Henry, 126
Kelley, David, 120
Khumbu Icefall, 60–63
Kimberly-Clark, 21
Kleenex, 21

Kozlowski, Dennis, 213–14
Krakauer, Jon, 118
Krauss, Wes, 48, 50, 51, 56
Kriemler, Susi, 122, 126
K2
 Allison on, 66–73
 Jordan on, 148–49, 151–52,
  160–68
 1978 American Expedition,
  123–24, 125
 Warner on, 92–93

Lao-tzu, 176
Lay, Kenneth, 58, 207, 213
leaders
 characteristics of, 10
 decision making and, 66, 156–58,
  205–23
 new, 72
 responsibilities of, 55, 66, 71
leadership
 absence of, 51, 52, 53–56, 58–59
 dilemma of, 10
 effective, 71–73, 156–58
 goals and, 212–13
 by example, 65
 for long term, 181–82
 service and, 73, 173–74
Lees, Evelyn, 48, 51, 56
Left for Dead (Weathers), 7
Lethbridge, Peter, 126
letting go, 19, 20
limits
 finding, 22, 57, 83
 ignoring, 140
 pushing, 12, 24–25, 81, 86, 96,
  115, 118, 121
Logan, Jim, 33–35, 37
Longs Peak, Colorado, 30–31
long term, 181–82
Lucero, Claudio, 156–57
luck, 11, 38, 44–46